The Nation without Art

Frontispiece. Mordecai Ardon, *Mount of Olives,* Oil on Canvas, 38 x 51 ins., 1938. Collection Alex Marx. Reproduced with the permission of Professor Michael Ardon. Photograph © Ismael Ramirez.

The Nation without Art

Examining Modern Discourses on Jewish Art

Margaret Olin

University of Nebraska Press

Lincoln and London

Publication of this volume was assisted by grants from the Lucius N. Littauer Foundation and The School of the Art Institute of Chicago. Publication was also supported by a generous grant from the Cleveland Foundation to the Department of Religion at Case Western Reserve University as part of a project on Jewish-Christian relations directed by Professors Susannah Heschel and Eldon Jay Epp.

Acknowledgments for the use of previously published material appear on page xxvi.

Library of Congress Cataloging-in-Publication Data
Olin, Margaret Rose, 1948–
The nation without art : examining modern discourses on Jewish art / Margaret Olin.
p. cm. – (Texts and contexts) Includes bibliographical references and index.
ISBN 0-8032-3564-X (cloth: alkaline paper)
1. Art, Jewish. 2. Judaism in art. 3. Art–Historiography. 4. Jews–Identity. I. Title. II. Texts and contexts (unnumbered)
N7415 .O45 2001 704.03'924 dc21 2001027555

For Rob, Ben, and Sheba,
Different people,
living in the same place.

Contents

Illustrations

PREFACE

Reflections from Vienna

This book began in Vienna. It began against my will, in the margins of the notes for my dissertation on the Austrian art historian Alois Riegl, whom I researched in Vienna during the years 1979–80. Reminders of anti-Semitism sporadically intruded into my work on turn-of-the century art historical theory. In the archives I read scholarly correspondence that interrupted theoretical discussions to complain about anti-Semitic incidents and newspapers that juxtaposed art reviews with notices of pogroms or announcements of excursions for anti-Semites to the International Exposition in Paris in 1900.[1] Among writings about historical monuments, I was struck by a letter that an unknown correspondent named Richard sent in 1902 to the art historian Franz Wickhoff. He sought Wickhoff's support in an effort to prevent the construction of a museum by the architect Otto Wagner on Vienna's Karlsplatz, home to Johann Fischer von Erlach's eighteenth-century Church of St. Charles Borromeus. Fearing that Wagner's opulent structure would clash with Fischer's masterpiece, he urged the professor to take immediate action.

> Say that in front of your window a dear, helpless merchant, who is harmlessly going about his business and living modestly without bothering anyone else – let's call him David Cohn – is set upon and strangled by a couple of punks. You'd see that. And, Herr Hofrat, since, to speak in Viennese terms, you're a good, lovable chap – you'd – well you wouldn't exactly go charging down there immediately and place yourself at his service, but you would make an earnest attempt to call out for help – with all your strength. Now, David Cohn is a good man, but there are many, many of that sort around; for the purposes of cultural history he can easily be replaced. Even Herr Süss must admit that!
>
> But I will tell you, and prove it, that presently in Vienna artistic punks, a pair of brutal architects, want to attack and murder not an innocent Jew, but the great Church of St. Charles by Karl Fischer von Erlach! Cry out and protest![2]

Wagner's design was not built, and Fischer's church remains in all its grandeur unfettered by the bland modernist museum built next to it after World War II (see figures 1 and 2).[3] But the correspondent was wrong about the David Cohns. Their supply was not unlimited. They were killed or they fled, and the good, lovable chaps of Vienna closed their windows and did not call out for help. In 1979, when I read the letter, the Jewish presence in Vienna was little more than a memory.

The interdisciplinary dissertation that I was engaged in writing concerned an art historian known for his work in formal theory, historical preservation, and the reevaluation of the neglected art of the Late Roman Empire.[4] I studied his theories in relation to Viennese cultural contributions in music, psychoanalysis, philosophy, and architecture. To do so, I deployed historical, psychological, literary critical, and philosophical methods. Broad though it was, however, my method could not encompass the documents of anti-Semitism that surrounded it. The connection between the aesthetic disruption of Karlsplatz and the violence against David Cohn was poetic, but to pursue it seemed unscholarly.[5] I treated any commotion that might have occurred outside a Viennese professor's window as at worst a momentary distraction like the anti-Semitic tract that appeared in my room when my landlady discovered I was Jewish. It distracted me briefly from my research but did not affect the way I wrote the research up.

A colleague studying a logical disputation of the late fourteenth century encountered on a building in central Vienna a fifteenth-century inscription celebrating a pogrom. When further research revealed a connection between the commemorated pogrom and the logical disputation that preceded it, he concluded that abstract positions of theologians can "help shape decisions and justify actions that left an indelible imprint on the lives of their peers, the leaders of the Hussite movement, and the Viennese Jews."[6] My letter, too, suggested a context that intellectual history alone did not: it indicated that formal art history was not conceived and hotly debated in the serene and rarefied atmosphere of the ivory tower. Yet I reacted to my archival material as if it were completely independent. One of Wickhoff's correspondents, a young assistant in the Berlin print cabinet in the 1880s named Friedrich Portheim, kept up a vivid, sometimes irritable correspondence with Wickhoff until Portheim died, at the age of twenty-eight, leaving a slim but highly regarded volume on the dissemination of Hellenistic art. In at least one letter he complained about anti-Semitism in Berlin. But when he characterized the scholar Hubert Janitschek as "uncouth" because he had assigned an orthodox Jew the topic of the Baptism of

1. Otto Wagner, View of Central Pavilion, Historisches Museum der Stadt Wien, preliminary competition project, 1902. From *Der Architekt* 8 (1902), 6. Courtesy of the Art Institute of Chicago.

2. Johann Fischer von Erlach, Karlskirche. Vienna, 1716. Photograph: Margaret Olin.

Christ, and even compared the scholar's intolerance with a newspaper report he had read about a Jew being battered to death with a ham, I found myself feeling he had gone too far.[7] Jewish medievalists, I reasoned, cannot expect to avoid Christian iconography. My response assumed a realm of pure scholarship above religious or ethnic divisions.

Friedrich Portheim assumed no such thing. Perhaps his distress was unjustified.[8] Even if it was, however, it remains a historical fact worthy of analysis. Yet instead of placing his complaint in a historical context, I argued against a young man who died in 1888 as though he stood before me in 1980. My misperception of his environment may have been due to a willful misperception of my own: to admit the possibility that seemingly disinterested scholarly research can be used as a weapon to exploit an ethnic group meant to relinquish for myself as well as others the possibility of retreat into a pure realm of ideas.

The retreat ended, my attempts to discover the context in which Portheim's objections to the Baptism of Christ made sense led me to write this small book tracing concepts of Jewish art through a variety of discourses. For reasons that this book, I hope, will make clear, I do not attempt to define the field of Jewish art, either as it is or as it should be. Many of the most important discoveries and issues shall go unexamined.[9] I will not address the ontological status of Jewish art or appeal to art history departments who have not done so already to add a specialization in "Jewish art," whether this means art associated with Jewish ritual or art made by Jewish artists. Indeed, the meaning of the word "Jewish" will depend entirely on the context of any given chapter. Instead, the book will examine the way notions of Jewish art have appeared in various key discourses since the early nineteenth century, investigating institutions and alternative venues in which Jewish art has been discussed or avoided or in which discursive space has been cleared where the discussion of "Jewish art" can take place. Rather than the closed discourse of traditional intellectual history, which the magnitude of the subject prohibits, I hope to offer insight into the variety of ways in which thinkers have tried to extract themselves from the same quagmire or to argue that the quagmire is the best place to live after all.

Portheim never attempted a solution to the anti-Semitic structure of art history. Most probably a convert to Christianity, he studied predominantly Christian art and did not try to make a place for the art of Jews within artistic studies.[10] He did have time in his brief life span, however, to resist in at least one modest way: he used his scholarship on the dissemination of Hellenistic art to reject the most strident claims of German nationalism. His Austrian colleagues appreciated these efforts; the efforts themselves, however, speak as much to his Jewish, as to his Austrian, allegiance.[11]

In trying now to make amends for my inattention to Portheim's complaint, I do so in part to validate the attempt that he and others made to breach the constraints of their discipline in order to use it as a weapon against the ethnic hatred of their time.

The organization of this book is thematic rather than strictly chronological. Each part, however, strives for a coherence of its own, and a network of shared themes, reassessed personalities and ideas, and reconsidered works of art structures the book as a whole. It is not necessary to notice all of these connections to understand the present book, but the reader who notices them may be struck by the ways in which competing discourses can overlap, and the same concerns carry over into such seemingly very different contexts of Zionism, scholarship, and the criticism of contemporary art.

Part 1, "Defining Jewish Art," introduces the nationalist discourse of the Jewish "nation without art," traces its insinuation into the art historical paradigm, and assesses the difficulties that it entails for the discussion of Jewish art. Turning to Zionist discourse immediately thereafter seemed important to dispose of the possibility that the coming into existence of a Jewish homeland could presume to offer a solution to the problems that arise from nationalist paradigms. My limitation to just one, among many, Zionist institutions, the Bezalel School of Arts and Crafts, while it only hints at the diversity and complication of views regarding nationhood and art, does suggest their lack of resolution. One institution gave rise to three others, whose visions of nationhood differed from one another and from their common parent. The example is also suited to attack what is left of the myth of Zionist (and nationalist) homogeneity.[12]

Part 2, "Reclaiming Jewish Art," presents three studies showing how practitioners of art history – Jewish and others – tried to subvert or overturn the paradigm of the nation without art, primarily in Germany and Austria between the world wars. A clear focus necessitates omissions. David Kaufmann is important here less for his wide-ranging scholarship than for his contribution to the first important art historical study of a Jewish monument, the Haggadah of Sarajevo. Martin Buber is included not for the Zionist context of his views of Jewish art, but because these views developed out of his art historical training. My study of the reaction to the synagogue at Dura-Europos omits some of the important research on the monument and addresses some major thinkers, such as E. R. Goodenough, only briefly. Instead my study uses the reaction of a group of German and Austrian scholars to the synagogue's discovery to understand how an espousal of Jewish art could be considered an academic reaction to the experience of the Nazi regime.

Part 3, "Abstaining from Jewish Art," moves to another field, that of avant-garde art and criticism, and another time, the period since the Holocaust. There are better contexts than the present one to discuss the issues pertinent to the representation of the Holocaust, but the period itself has, in part through reaction to the genocide, seen changes in tone in the discourse of Jewish art. Both critics such as Clement Greenberg, who discussed Jewish art very little, and artists such as Chantal Akerman, who grapples directly with the import of being a Jewish artist, represent ways of exploring Jewish artistic identity that depart from, while still being rooted in, earlier models.

The years spent on this project have had an effect. I have found myself influenced both by the thinkers I have studied and by the ones who have offered me advice and encouragement. Growing familiarity and historical understanding have given me empathy for life choices quite unlike my own: for example, for Zionism, for orthodox and conservative Judaism, and for conversion. Some of this empathy inevitably colors my text. My target, however, is not any particular position regarding Judaism, its practice, or its theory. My target is nationalism. I intend my study to be a contribution to a growing number of critiques of the nationalist, ethnocentric paradigms of current disciplines. Assumptions about the unity of national consciousness have been challenged by recent postcolonial critiques, by research into non-Western models of national identity, and by such discourses of identity as feminism and queer theory, fueled primarily by the recognition, by Michel Foucault and others, of the connection between power and the organization of knowledge.[13] Art history has begun to absorb the effect of these critiques.[14] This study is a partner to these still ongoing critiques because concepts of Jewish art pose a challenge to the national unity implied in concepts of discrete national arts.

If nationalist paradigms of art history had not begun to break down, this book would not have been written. Yet, as demonstrated by the efforts made by thinkers chronicled in this book to overturn the paradigm of Jewish art, the effects and power of discourse do not simply vanish because discourse is challenged. Discourse is tenacious, as the continued organization based on nations and nationalism in departments of art history makes clear. It takes repeated, joint efforts to effect change. These efforts are made possible both by the opening up of art history to questions of visual culture and by the current interest among art historians in interrogating the history and the foundational assumptions of the discipline.[15]

The present study, as a book in an interdisciplinary series, falls outside these discussions organized by art history; it does, however, take part in another discourse. My work joins that of several scholars who have been interrogating traditional assumptions about the relation of Jews to the image. Most of this work is relatively recent, but conferences have begun to take place, and important studies have been made.[16] Some of the studies that deal directly with art have produced astonishing results, and the present study is deeply indebted to them.[17] The historian Richard I. Cohen, in *Jewish Icons,* has challenged head-on preconceptions, accepted even by Jews, about the Jewish relation, or lack thereof, to images.[18] *Jewish Icons* explores the remarkably long-standing and prolific use of images in the ongoing dialogue between Jews and non-Jews throughout the modern period conceived broadly, showing definitively ways in which Jews have trafficked in images, which historians and theologians have simply overlooked. In religious studies, Kalman Bland, in his book *The Artless Jew,* offers a new understanding of Jewish thought about images during the medieval period, the ways in which this paradigm changed in Jewish thought in the modern period, and how this change gave rise to misunderstandings about medieval

Jewish thought.[19] *The Artless Jew* makes it unnecessary for those who come after to assume that premodern Jews held anything like the aniconic views commonly attributed to them. Because it begins with the modern aniconic consensus, *The Artless Jew* is an excellent companion to the present book. New work is promised. We can expect Steven Fine, who has already begun to challenge assumptions about Jewish art in late antiquity, to do in his forthcoming book for that period what Kalman Bland has done for the Middle Ages.[20] Catherine Soussloff's ongoing work on Jewish subjectivity, beginning with sections of her *Absolute Artist* and including the important volume *Jewish Identity in Modern Art History*, will soon be followed by a searching investigation of identity and subjectivity in portraits of Jews at the turn of the twentieth century.[21]

I have been privileged to receive encouragement and advice from these latter four scholars, each of whom has read and criticized several chapters of this book, and all of whom have given valuable advice and support whenever called upon. The anonymous reader for the University of Nebraska Press, whose swift and incisive readings improved the text, was also clearly a specialist in the subject and generous with both time and expertise.

It was not my idea to write a book on this subject. Norman L. Kleeblatt of the Jewish Museum in New York commissioned an initial article, on Clement Greenberg, and Sander L. Gilman asked me to expand it into a book for his series Texts and Contexts. Without these two people, and their continued interest in and support of the project they instigated, the book would have remained unwritten.

Along the way, many others read parts of the manuscript and helped me with their expertise, particularly Ulrike Wendland and Joan Hart, from whose expertise on Panofsky and other German art historical figures we can expect important results soon, and my colleagues at the Work in Progress Seminar in the Getty Research Institute in Los Angeles, in particular Heinrich Dilly, Lydia Goehr, Thomas DaCosta Kaufmann, Robert Nelson, and Anna Wessely, each of whom read more than the required portion. Audiences in Boston, Chicago, Dallas, Los Angeles, New York, and Santa Cruz helped me hone my ideas. I thank the organizers of these occasions for invitations to speak, in particular Janice Bergman-Carton, who organized the stimulating conference "Prophets and Losses: Jewish Experience and Visual Culture," at Southern Methodist University, and Catherine Soussloff, who extended two of these invitations.

Material, advice, bibliography, and other useful interchanges were provided by more people than I can name, among them Al Boime, Paula Buber-Agassi, David Carrier, Jay Clarke, Tom Cummings, James Elkins, Ernst Gombrich, Joseph Gutmann, Géza Hajós, Irmgard Hutter, Norman Kleeblatt, Ruth Kluger, Donata Levi, Suzanne L. Marchand, Pier Marton, Ruth Mellinkoff, Paul Mendes-Flohr, Bezalel Narkiss, Ernst Osterkamp, Gideon Ofrat, Kym Pinder, Griselda Pollock, Michael Roth, Erika Rummel, Ursula and Kurt Schubert, and Arnold Jacob Wolf. Judith Zeitlin and Amy Stanley provided invaluable help at crucial moments.

The staffs of many libraries and archives proved expert and helpful, including, in Vienna, the Nationalbibliotek, the Library of the Jüdischer Gemeinde, the archives of the University of Vienna, and especially the archives of the Institut für Kunstgeschichte, where Dr. Hans H. Aurenhammer gave me access and generous assistance; in Jerusalem, the Manuscript Division of the Jewish National and University Library, the Central Zionist Archives, and the Archives of the City of Jerusalem; in New York, the Leo Baeck Institute; in Los Angeles, the library and special collections of the Getty Research Institute; and in Chicago, the Departments of Special Collections and Interlibrary Loan of the University of Chicago, and the Asher Library of the Spertus Institute of Jewish Studies, where Dan Sharon, as usual, proved himself a reference librarian beyond compare.

I was privileged to have the help of highly skilled translators for languages in which I am not proficient. Martha Marton translated for me from Hungarian, Mark Wegner and Dan Sharon from Hebrew, Alex Lauterbach from Polish, and Georgi Radomirov Parpulov from Bulgarian. Georgi and Charles David Forster Jr. were extraordinary research assistants.

I received assistance in acquiring illustrations and other material from Michael Ardon, Irmgard Hutter, Alex Marx, and Michele Vishny; from Vivian Mann, Kathryn Potts, and Sarah E. Lawrence of the Jewish Museum, New York; from the Visual Services Department of the Getty Research Institute; from Bruce Jenkins, of the Walker Art Center, Minneapolis; from Mark Akgulian, Betsy Gomberg, Rhoda Rosen, and Olga Weiss, of the Spertus Institute of Jewish Studies, Chicago; and from Diana Aaronson and the staff of the Sherwin Miller Museum of Jewish Art (formerly the Fenster Museum), Tulsa, Oklahoma.

Permission to reproduce my own work was generously given by the editors of those publications where earlier versions or parts of chapters first appeared: chapter 1, "From Bezal'el to Max Liebermann: Jewish Art in Nineteenth-Century Art Historical Texts," in *Jewish Identity in Modern Art History*, ed. Catherine M. Soussloff, pp. 19–40 (Berkeley: University of California Press, 1999), © 1999 the Regents of the University of California, reprinted by permission of the University of California Press; chapter 2, "The Search for a Jewish Art in Palestine: Bezalel, 1906–1948," *Das jüdische Echo* 48 (October 1999): 375–89; chapter 5, "'Early Christian Synagogues' and 'Jewish Art Historians': The Discovery of the Synagogue of Dura-Europos," *Marburger Jahrbuch für Kunstwissenschaft* 27 (2000): 7–28; chapter 6, "C[lement] Hardesh [Greenberg] and Company: Formal Criticism and Jewish Identity," copyright © 1996 by The Jewish Museum, New York, under the auspices of The Jewish Theological Seminary and Rutgers University Press, New Brunswick, New Jersey, previously published in the exhibition catalog *Too Jewish? Challenging Traditional Identities*; and chapter 7, "Graven Images on Video? The Second Commandment and Jewish Identity," *Discourse: Journal for Theoretical Studies in Media and Culture* 22, no. 1 (2000): 7–30. Parts of the preface appeared in "Nationalism, the Jews, and Art History," *Judaism* 45 (1996): 461–82.

Financial help was provided by the Lucius N. Littauer Foundation, which came through at two crucial stages, and the National Endowment for the Humanities. The Getty Research Institute invited me to complete the manuscript there during a year as a visiting scholar, where the excellent staff supported me in style. My always sympathetic Department of Art History, Theory and Criticism at the School of the Art Institute of Chicago, and especially my chair, Stanley Murashige, and my dean, Carol Becker, generously allowed me to take these grants and provided me with Faculty Enrichment Grants to lessen the financial strain even more. The editors and staff at the University of Nebraska

Press have seen me through the long process thoughtfully and patiently.

My greatest debt, however, is to my fellow citizens of the boisterous multicultural realm that a colleague once called "the Hapsburg Empire in miniature": my children, Benjamin and Sheba, and my husband, Rob.

PART ONE

Defining Jewish Art

– But do you know what a nation means? says John Wyse.

– Yes, says Bloom.

– What is it? says John Wyse.

– A nation? says Bloom. A nation is the same people living in the same place.

– By God, then, says Ned, laughing, if that's so I'm a nation for I'm living in the same place for the past five years.

– So of course everyone had a laugh at Bloom and says he, trying to muck out of it:

– Or also living in different places.

– That covers my case, says Joe.

James Joyce, *Ulysses*

CHAPTER ONE

Jewish Art Defined

From Bezalel to Max Liebermann

The conception of Jewish Art may appear to some a contradiction in terms. **Cecil Roth** in *Jewish Art: An Illustrated History*

Jewish art: is there any such thing? **Franz Landsberger** in *Einführung in die Jüdische Kunst*

Treatments of Jewish art invariably feel constrained to begin by discussing whether there even is such a thing as "Jewish art." **Steven Schwarzschild** in *The Pursuit of the Ideal*

Such a command as that of the Decalogue (Ex. xx. 4; Deut. v.8) would have been impossible to a nation possessed of such artistic gifts as the Greeks, and was carried to its ultimate consequences . . . only because the people lacked artistic inclination, with its creative power and formative imagination.
"Art Among the Ancient Hebrews," in *The Jewish Encyclopedia*

The Absence of Jews in the Survey

"Jewish art" is the name of a concept, but few scholars profess to believe it corresponds to anything that actually exists. As a category it is not very precise. A multitude of disparate objects could fall under the heading, such as the secular work of Jewish artists, sacred manuscripts, and the murals and mosaics that adorn early synagogues. A few of these objects – the murals of the synagogue at Dura-Europos, the Sarajevo Haggadah – have attracted the attention of art historians.[1] Yet for the general public, including the Jewish public and much of the art historical world, the term "Jewish art" remains something of an oxymoron. Jews may have made images, but that does not make the images, themselves, Jewish for every onlooker, for the images may not reflect the Jewish experience and might better be described as American, for example, or Socialist. Almost by definition, or rather by commandment, Jewish art does not exist: the Second Commandment prohibits Jews from making likenesses of "anything that is in heaven above, or is in the earth beneath, or that is in the waters beneath the earth."[2]

Whether or not the Torah really proscribes the practice of the visual arts (a growing consensus holds that it does not) can be disputed.[3] But the widespread assumption that it does colors all treatments of Jewish art, from the recommendations and interpretations of rabbis and scholars of Judaica, to the scholarship of the professional art historian and the reviews of the professional art critic. In the latter, secular context that is the primary focus of this book, the proscription might seem to make self-evident the neglect of the study of Jewish art. But that would be comprehensible only if Jewish art were perceived in isolation, as a matter concerning Jews alone. For professional art historians and critics, the concept of Jewish art functions within art historical discourse and thereby affects the interpretation of art beyond the immediate problem of whether Jews who make images offend their religion by doing so.

These wider consequences of the concept of Jewish art suggest the way in which art history structures an understanding of its material, emphasizing certain categories of material and marginalizing others. Therefore, keeping in mind that a concept of a nonexistent art has made its way into the discourse of art, I begin this book by delineating the place of the discourse about Jewish art, or rather about the lack thereof, within the structure of discourses about art history as they took shape along with the growth of the art historical discipline during the nineteenth century. A set of related concepts of Jewish art formed in the nineteenth century, partaking of imagery borrowed from several ethnic stereotypes, often contradictory. The analysis of this discourse therefore demands the use of a group of problematic distinctions, including such terms as "Orientalism," "anti-Semitism," "anti-Judaism," and "racism." In the context of Jewish art, such stereotypes do not, in accord with the "transparency phenomenon," oppose an unmarked category, or norm, as blackness does whiteness (a norm, however, visible only to whites).[4] The opposing categories were positively formulated just as assiduously as the concept of Jewish art, in the endeavor of nations to understand themselves in their own cultural particularity.

The difficulty of defining the notion of Jewish art, then, and the variety of the distinctions used to isolate it throw into confusion the nationalist assumptions upon which art history was founded and which still govern the discipline as traditionally practiced. But in the attempt to understand the stake of nationalism in art history it is important not to overvalue the racist paradigms it utilizes. To distinguish the role of anti-Semitism in the paradigm of Jewish art from that of Orientalism, for example, on the basis of what peoples or things they discriminate against, at least with any rigor, risks validating the very distinctions that the tendencies labeled by them promote, because it risks reifying such stereotypes as Oriental and Jew. Therefore the argument of this chapter, while it aims at a conceptual link between nationalism and the concept of Jewish art, strives to do so in a way that lessens the risk of reinforcing the nationalistic structure I am trying to critique, defended by the powerful weapons of racism.

In the nineteenth century, the particular nature of art history's entailment with nationalism imbued it with a pattern of aims and categories it would eventually share with modern anti-Semitism. Cultural phenomena such as art were already among the diverse, conflicting criteria by which early-nineteenth-century scholars began the task of classifying people into races or nations.[5] Anti-Judaism, an antagonism to the religion that did not necessarily extend to its practitioners, entered early into nationalist discourse, in accord with the emphasis of early nationalism on shared beliefs and culture rather than blood. But modern, or racial, anti-Semitism would eventually take on a character of racism that helped give nationhood a basis in biology.[6] By the 1840s, when art historical surveys began to solidify into a genre, such narratives could be used to chronicle a people's emerging awareness of nationhood, showing its reflection in cultural forms.[7] Anti-Semitism, as a category of racism, was therefore positioned to define the nature a people's self-awareness could be expected to take.

As we shall see, the anti-Semitic stereotype of the inartistic Jew borrowed the construction of the exotic Oriental from Orientalist paradigms beginning with the first art historical surveys, so that by century's end, anti-Semitic art historians such as Josef Strzygowski often used the terms "Oriental" and "Jewish" interchangeably.[8] Like Orientalism, anti-Semitism took a unique shape when it entered into such academic pursuits as art history, acquiring a vocabulary and a scientific basis. Racism, Orientalism, anti-Judaism, and anti-Semitism: all of these concepts simmered together as the science of race became an increasingly important pursuit during the nineteenth century, inflecting (and infecting) the humanistic disciplines.[9] In what follows, we shall see how the concepts settled into art historical language as rhetorical distinctions and organizational forms that took on their own life. Tailored specifically to the needs of an artistic discourse, they became very difficult to dislodge, components of a disciplinary unconscious.

In German-speaking countries, where art historical scholarship initially took shape, art history was intertwined with nationalism throughout the century. When Johann Gottfried Herder used language as a criterion to identify a shared cultural heritage that makes up a people in the sense of modern nationhood, Johann Joachim Winckelmann had already inaugurated modern art historical scholarship by tying Greek art to Greek climate, culture, and form of government.[10] The visual was thoroughly bound up in the national by the time German Romanticism promoted Gothic as a German national style, and certain media, such as wood, were cultivated as part of a German heritage.[11] Institutional art history grew up amid such phenomena. By 1871 art history was established in several German and Austrian universities, and scholars of art history, like other German professors, were civil servants, appointed directly by their governments to posts in museums and universities.[12] Art historical surveys, too, were often written or underwritten by government officials or dedicated to royalty. In 1942, Franz Kugler dedicated his *Handbuch der Kunstgeschichte* to King Friedrich IV of Prussia.[13]

Art history was absorbed intimately into the activities that related to the pursuit and achievement of German unity in 1871. While some of the resulting scholarship responded critically or sought to guide nationalistic ideas in one or another direction, much of it uncritically supported national claims.[14] A nation can be viewed as a contingent phenomenon, but the project of nationalism was to reveal it as the unchanging element that made history cohere. This function made the investigation of origins central to nationalistic narratives. Scholars argued that a national art must be grounded in primal traits identifiable in their pure form in early handicraft and ornament.[15] They sought to define German nationhood through the works of tribes that later became German. Hubert Janitschek searched "back to the darkness of the tribal past" for "the soft and gradually perceptible stirrings of the artistic spirit of the Germanic tribes."[16] He traced official German nationhood to the Treaty of Verdun in 843 and German national feeling to a much earlier date as evidenced in art (see figure 3). A Swedish scholar attributed the growth of his own discipline, prehistoric archaeology, to the good powers that supported "the urge of the people for self-knowledge."[17]

Linguistics teaches, however, that a language does not consist in just one word but needs a system of words to delineate meaning.[18] Similarly, the language of nationalism could not consist in the name of just one nation. Nationalists had to compare or contrast their own nationality to a network of alternative ones. To define Gothic as German was to deny that it was French. To define the German spirit as like the Hellenic required a definition of both peoples. Industrious, practical Romans and beauty-loving Greeks were crucial to the construction of Germanic spiritual depth. The immutable character of Indian imagination and Chinese materialism, and of the so-called "primitive" peoples, conceived as stagnating on a low level for centuries, provided a thorough

3. Silver brooch from the graves at Dürfheim. From Hubert Janitschek, *Geschichte der deutschen Malerei* (Berlin: G. Grote, 1890).

bass beneath the melody of rapidly developing and highly evolved Western art. One popular handbook, for example, wrote that the art of the East "could neither reach a high degree of development nor any positive progress. . . . In this respect, this art, though the growth of ages, ever remained a child, obliged to have recourse to outward symbols, instead of employing intellectual means of expression."[19] The project of detecting the essence of each people corresponded to attempts to identify pure languages and explore their unsullied roots.[20] The importance of ethnic Others to the shaping of German identity meant that a German scholar could form a consciousness of German identity in studies of the art of ancient Rome, baroque Italy, the Levant, or India. Jews were one element in this vast complex.

The details of academic art history as we now know it are less fully elaborated in the naming of professorships, in which a few scholars in a limited number of fields represent the entire discipline, than in surveys and handbooks that attempt to cover a wide range of artistic phenomena globally and comprehensively. While drawing distinctions between the worthwhile and the less worthwhile, these books sought to include both. Thus an academic art history department, in which nationalists set the terms of the discourse, where works were placed in a unified evolutionary scheme and the contributions of countries, peoples, and races headed the scholarly agenda, might have little room for scholars specializing in obscure, undervalued works made by artists not identified with a particular country. Since handbooks or surveys might well cover such phenomena, they make a useful starting point for an investigation into the treatment of a marginalized art historical concept.

In fact, nineteenth-century art historical surveys uniformly carried a section explicitly devoted to ancient Jewish art. Coverage of Jewish art attests not only to the continued authority of the Bible but to an intimate relationship between early art history and religious studies, which recalls the ties that secular hermeneutics had to religious, along with Humanist, hermeneutics.[21] The important art historian Karl Schnaase actively sought to relate art to Christianity and edited the *Christliches Kunstblatt*, one of several art historical journals identified explicitly as Christian.[22] Schnaase, inspired by Georg Wilhelm Friedrich Hegel, was convinced of both the significance of religion as the barometer of a people and the position of Christianity in a developmental process.[23] If religion was the barometer of a people, art was the people's primary activity. Schnaase explained art's significance as follows: "Art is the central activity of peoples. In art, all aspirations and feelings, spiritual, moral and material, come into the most intimate contact and define themselves. Therefore, art provides the means to measure and determine the direction and strength of these individual potentials."[24]

Given the religious associations of art historical scholarship, a concept at least of ancient Jewish art appears to have been indispensable. Since the biblical monuments do not survive, and some scholars admitted ignorance of their appearance, the discussions of Jewish art were brief and confined to what could be culled, selectively, from the Hebrew Bible. Yet scholars expended great efforts to describe the monuments meticulously by conjecture and to draw from them wide-ranging conclusions about the Jewish artistic character. These conjectural portrayals of Jewish art created patterns that later scholars found ready-made for them. These patterns formed a bridge between anti-Semitic or Orientalist tropes and modern art historical scholarship.

The notion of Jews as fantastic Orientals appears in the earliest significant survey, *Handbuch der Kunstgeschicte,* published in 1842 by Franz Kugler. Kugler's book self-consciously proclaimed its own innovation, and its pioneering status was accepted by later writers.[25] Certainly Karl Schnaase acknowledged Kugler's priority in his own survey published the following year. He dedicated his study to Kugler, whom he had never met, "in recognition of his successful effort in the field of art history," and included a preface defending his right to publish on the same subject.[26] Albeit with modifications, the structure of Kugler's handbook prevails even today.[27] Its continued importance may be due in part to Kugler's influential student, the art historian Jakob Burckhardt, whose help Kugler enlisted in completing the second edition.[28] Between them, Kugler and Burckhardt helped shape the discipline of art history in its earliest stages.

Kugler was genuinely interested in appreciating the great wealth of artistic material available to him. Yet he reached, in true nineteenth-century fashion, for a nonchronological, developmental structure to give form to his chaotic mass of facts. Although he recognized the arbitrariness of his starting point, the Prussian Kugler in effect gave art history a Germanic cast by beginning and ending the volume with German art, making it appear to be both the source and the goal of art history.[29] He entailed art history in nationalism, even imperialism, beginning with the preface: "Our whole science is still quite young. It is an empire, with whose conquest we have just begun to concern ourselves, whose valleys and forests we still have to clear, whose barren Steppes we have yet to make arable" (x).

The inclusion of Jewish art in Kugler's map of territories to be conquered illuminates the significance of the concept of Jewish art to early conceptions of art history. In Kugler's narrative, the Jews, even before their entrance into the Promised Land, assume an exotic role. Although lack of evidence inhibits his descriptive zeal, Kugler can say with assurance that the people were Syrian or Semitic. The attribution alone enables him to impute to ancient Jews the love of external luxury associated with Orientalism: "And so we know, that in their artworks, in greater or lesser degree, their main consideration was splendor and luxury, that namely they loved bright metallic decorations, and to cover their architectural interiors and also sculpture with expensive metallic materials; [and] that ornament of splendidly colored, cleverly woven fabrics was continually found necessary to fit out these works" (70). The reference to the splendid color of the fabrics may not have been complimentary. Some nineteenth-century authors found few distinctions between colors in the Bible and on that basis imputed to them the lack of a refined sense, or even a defective sense, of color.[30] Well into the twentieth century, Jews were still trying to refute the charge of congenital color blindness, a trait that could lead to the use of garish colors.[31]

Another trait Orientalists attributed to the people of the Near East was fantasy. Thus the cherubim on the ark of the tabernacle became "fantastic figures, characteristic of Asiatic visuality. The human figure was predominant in them; it was combined with wings and other animal parts."[32] Kugler did not use such terms to describe the boy angels at the feet of Raphael's Sistine Madonna, the painting he later called the "freest outpouring of Raphael's spirit" (727).[33]

Both the tendency to begin with the Bible and the tendency to describe Jewish art as composed of fantastic composite forms tenaciously held on. In 1895, the pioneering study of Roman art, Franz Wickhoff's introduction to the *Wiener Genesis*, observes the Bible carefully for signs of the demise of Jewish art. At its height, however, Jewish art produced "giant watchmen, composed fourfold of the head of a man, the body of a lion, the wings of an eagle, and the hooves of an ox."[34]

Some art historians, with the Hebrew bible in mind, were puzzled by the gulf between the greatness of Jewish poetry and the frailty of Jewish art. Elie Faure, in 1909, would condemn Solomon's temple artistically as the "house of a terrible and solitary god," their sole artistic effort, unworthy of "that Jewish genius, so grandly synthetical, but closed and jealous . . . whose voice of iron has traversed the ages."[35] Karl Schnaase, however, offered a thoughtful and, for the postmodern reader, potentially subversive reading of the relationship between poetry and painting in Judaism. He differentiated his survey of art history from that of Kugler on the basis of Kugler's metaphor of geographical conquest. While Kugler creates a map of art, he, Schnaase, uses art to penetrate the soul of the peoples who create it. Although his methods may be different, his judgment of Jewish art is similar to that of Kugler. Like Kugler, he is aghast at the cherubim for their combination of human and animal forms, criticizing them for the "unnatural affixing of wings."[36] Like Kugler, he attributes to the Jews a love of luxury and condemns them on that basis. In accordance with the strictures of the Arts and Crafts movement, which was taking shape at that time, he contrasted a true architectural sense, which likes to see construction itself, to the Jewish sensibility that, like the costume of Barbarians, hides the body with heavy clothes.[37] In accordance with his Hegelian ideas, Schnaase tied his judgment to "internal national character," relating it primarily to religion.[38]

The passage draws heavily on ideas associated with Gotthold Ephraim Lessing's *Laocoön*, about the distinction between painting as an art of space and poetry as an art of motion.[39] It finds the ancient Jews incapable of artistic sensibility in the visual arts, compared to the "richness" of their poetry. Schnaase attributed the discrepancy to their concern for constant motion, a strength of their poetry, which, however, kept them from achieving distinction in the visual arts.

Their fantasy is too much in motion, the movement is too vigorous, too strong, too bold, to permit it to be carried out quietly in the visual arts. Every pictorial image that is introduced in the soul immediately evokes a new one, which drives out the first. Either this does not suffice for the metaphoric aim, and the second is called forth to supplement it, or it evokes, through the many faceted nature of its appearance, a memory of something else that relates to the object, and therefore also emerges and obscures the first image.[40]

Tracing links between religion and art, however, Schnaase argued that the Jews' religion kept them in constant motion because it was based on fear, and for this reason he found the Jewish religion ill-suited to visual arts. Schnaase tied these terms to the language of form. Jewish art, he argued, turns on cause and effect rather than on the "soul" of the individual object: "No single thing holds its own and stands out in its complete physicality and independence. Everything blends into a large image, into a unity, in which only the opposition between the Lord and the transitory earth can be repeatedly felt, but also repeatedly suspended. Because of this lack of autonomy, of the individual thing, of man, of peoples, observation also pertains less to the inner qualities, the soul of things, than to their relation to others, their relative significance" (1:238–39).

He backed up this assertion by means of the analysis of metaphors in Hebrew poetry: "How the eyes wander, illuminating with a lightning stroke now this object, now that, heaven and earth, land and sea, the mountains with game in their forests, the plains with their fruit trees, the person and the flower. Each single thing emerges suddenly sharply and individually out of the dark, but slips back into it just as quickly, because now another is illuminated" (1:238). While today we might regard the sensibility he accorded the Jews as cinematic, thus recuperating it for art, Schnaase probably intended it to bear out his opening justification for the study of periods of "lesser artistic production," which depended on an analogy with the study of the human organism in "a diseased condition" (1:51).

The ornate prescription for the tabernacle in the book of Exodus lent itself to visions, like Kugler's and Schnaase's, of Jews as purveyors of fantasy.[41] But in art historical writings, it was generally overshadowed by the Temple of Solomon, which evoked a variety of different, although related, tropes. These stereotypes concerned the Jews' lack of artistic character and their chameleon imitative propensities, considered characteristic of Jews in most fields of endeavor and a threatening quality, making them more difficult to detect.[42] The lively interest in biblical history and archaeology saw to it that the site of the temple was studied, and speculations about its original appearance abounded, a development noted by Schnaase in the second edition of his book.[43] The result was a variety of reconstructions of the temple and its progeny.[44] The archaeologists Georges Perrot and Charles Chipiez meticulously reconstructed not the Temple of Solomon, "an edifice of modest size," but the Temple of Ezekiel, "a unique and curious mixture of reality and fiction . . . the last word of sacerdotal ambition . . . also the most powerful effort in which the Hebraic genius asserted itself to translate its ideas into sensible forms . . . its most beautiful work of art, one could even say that it is the only one that it produced."[45] On paper, the authors reconstructed the temple in fanciful detail down to the details of the representational and ornamental program in the sanctuary (see figures 4 and 5). They regarded the edifice that they spent so much effort reconstructing, however, as diminutive compared to the monuments of Karnak and Luxor and, more importantly, as unoriginal. Most of its motifs were borrowed from the valleys of the Nile and the Euphrates.[46] They marveled that of the entire ancient world, the greatest description of architecture passed down to us was the temple of this people, whom they regarded as the "least artistic of the great peoples of antiquity" (5:475).[47]

They could as well have marveled that the temple had continued to attract a great deal of literary attention in the nineteenth century, including their own time, for they felt the need to justify the attention they lavished on it. "The disproportionate role that the little Jewish people has played in the history of humanity" justified the interest in everything they touched.[48] Their interest was ostensibly based in religion, on the heritage of Christianity, "born in the shadow of their temple," but the authors introduced the Jews initially in relation not to religion but to capital and finance: "Today it is not without a kind of consternation that modern society seeks to estimate the enormous mass of capital that has accumulated in their hands" (5:125, 122). In contrast to Schnaase, Perrot and Chipiez discounted the difference between Jewish poetry and the visual arts. They found the same deficiencies in both.[49]

Other art historians also disseminated the view of Jews as shameless imitators. Wilhelm Lübke wrote in his survey in 1888 that "Jews, having no art-ideas of their own, borrowed architectural forms which they

4. Interior of the sanctuary, the Temple of Ezekiel. Reconstruction by Charles Chipiez. From Georges Perrot and Charles Chipiez, *Le Temple de Jérusalem* (Paris: Hachette, 1889). Courtesy of the Getty Research Library.

5. Priests' forecourt, Temple of Ezekiel. Reconstruction by Charles Chipiez. From Georges Perrot and Charles Chipiez, *Le Temple de Jérusalem* (Paris: Hachette, 1889). Courtesy of the Getty Research Library.

employed on an eclectic principle from the nations dwelling around them."[50] Various authors had different conjectures about the source of Jewish art. The cherubim, for example, were said by the author of a French survey to be "identical with the winged bulls of Assyria," while Lübke perceived in them "undoubtedly Persian ideas," reminiscent of the relief of Cyrus, and his English editor corrected him as to the form, without suggesting an alternative source.[51] While from a postmodern standpoint, there is a certain appeal to the proposition that Jews appropriated their art, a nineteenth-century writer who asserts that Jews borrowed from others the art they could not create on their own only lent a historical basis to the anti-Semitic stereotype of Jews as chameleon-like parasites. All such conjectures about sources are accompanied by dismissive judgments of Jewish art.

The two views we have discerned so far, the view of the Jews as a people without art and the view of the Jews as exotic purveyors of fantasy, were not always incompatible. Schnaase, for example, although he advanced the notion of excessive Jewish fantasy, cited the participation in the construction of the Temple of Solomon by the Phoenician Hiram as proof that Jews did not have an indigenous architecture.[52] Excessive fantasy, apparently, did not express itself in the creation of art.

Neither of these two views, however, is as insidious as a third, which evoked the Second Commandment, forbidding graven images, to portray Jews as a people against art. Hegel discharged a barrage of metaphors in his early essay "The Spirit of Christianity and Its Fate," to portray Jews as representations of pure isolating negativity. The spiritual emptiness of the Jews reflected emptiness in all their creations: their sanctuary was an "empty room," their day dedicated to God an "empty time," their God invisible.[53] "They despise the image because it does not manage them, and they have no inkling of its deification in the enjoyment of beauty or in a lover's intuition" (192). Years later, under the influence of a founder of the Wissenschaft des Judentums (see chapter 3), Hegel would welcome Jewish spirituality into his system as the devotion to truth.[54] This constructive reinterpretation of an unappealing stereotype, however, continued to regard Jews as alienated from the visual arts, which were still defined by beauty, and did nothing to prevent assumptions about the intolerant and domineering Hebrew God, jealous of the reverence for images, from making their way from anti-

Semitic tracts to mainstream art historical explanations. The absence of Jewish art in one Hegelian interpretation turned into the rejection of art by Jews in another, and eventually active Jewish hostility toward art became an art historical trope.[55] In the antiartistic mode, Jews grew into a threatening antinationality and could reenter art history as the villain, evoking Jewish "cosmopolitanism," a lack of national identity some critics found menacing.[56] Just as Richard Wagner feared Jews as a threat to Western music and visual art, so art historians could portray Semitic antiart as a diabolical force, giving anti-Semitism a voice in art history.[57]

An Anti-Semitic Art History: Josef Strzygowski's Orient

At least one serious scholar incorporated anti-Semitism directly into his art historical research. Born in 1862, Josef Strzygowski lived and worked in Austria at the turn of the twentieth century, during the last decades of the Austro-Hungarian Empire. In accordance with the historical training then accorded people whose studies focused on art, he studied art history as inseparable from other cultural manifestations, governmental forms, and human propensities of different social groups. His work would seem to reflect similarly the openness to distant cultures of the multinational empire in which he lived. Like his compatriot Alois Riegl, he opened the field of art history to unimagined vistas. Specialists in Late Roman art owe their livelihood to Riegl, who first reevaluated that period, heretofore thought to exemplify decline. Scholars in a variety of fields found support for their relativistic studies of undervalued cultures through his groundbreaking concept of the *Kunstwollen* that paralleled the cultural "*Wollen*" of an age or a people.[58]

If anything, however, later scholars owe an even greater debt to Strzygowski, for he did more than reevaluate an underappreciated art – he discovered and appreciated arts that had been ignored almost completely. Initially given a tradesman's education, he rose to become professor first in Graz, then in Vienna. He launched expeditions to Persia, India, Syria, and Egypt, discovering there evidence of achievements he thought led from the Greek-influenced Hellenistic Orient to classic Roman, Romanesque, and even Gothic art and architecture. Strzygowski put these outlying sites on the art historical map and turned them into respectable fields of Western art historical scholarship that challenged the right of Rome to its central position.[59]

There is some irony in his efforts on behalf of these marginalized areas, however; they were directly inspired by his own origin in a marginalized area. His upbringing in a German-speaking area of Polish Silesia, where he was born in 1864, left him an ardent German nationalist.[60] His mode of argumentation reveals this nationalistic purpose. In *Orient oder Rom*, he traced Hellenistic influence in a variety of social groups but routinely ascribed motifs and monuments on the basis of national character.[61] The ornament on the Church of the Holy Sepulcher in Jerusalem, for example, is Greek because it was made by "an artist devoted with love to his work, a spirit aimed at the painterly-attractive, not the Roman, academically trained engineer, who wants to create an imposing effect."[62] The Ashburnham Pentateuch, with its "incomprehensively crude" composition, cannot have been painted by Germanic artists, whose works are "full of the finest rhythm and an unusual ideal unity of spatial order." This artistic evidence of national character, in addition to iconographic evidence, suggests that the model for the miniatures must be by "Jewish Christians" (37–39) (see figure 6). Not artistic cultures were in question, Strzygowski stressed: "It is the contrast of two races, that to which the Greeks and Romans belong and the Semitic" (39). The book ends as the Orient, crippled by Semites, is about to succumb to "the great Germanic artistic flowering in the North" (150). A few years later, in another work, he made clear the significance for present days of his critique of the Ashburnham Pentateuch: "In the miniatures of the Ashburnham-Pentateuch, anything that remains of Hellenistic art is strangled by Jewish imitation of reality. Modern Jewish art, with Liebermann at the head, is in fact absolutely national in its vigorous development of this racial characteristic, and the Zionist movement would do well to bring this fact self-consciously to evidence [*zur Geltung zu bringen*.]"[63]

The passage makes modern realism, represented by the Berlin painter Max Liebermann (1847–1935), the racial heritage of the Jews. Strzygowski softened the inherent racism of his judgments in works such as these, written for scholars, but he unleashed it in full in essays for general readers. Evoking Eugène Delacroix's *Massacre at Chios* in his essay

6. *The Childhood of Moses.* Ashburnham Pentateuch. Paris, B.N.F. nouv. acq. lat 2334. From Josef Strzygowski, *Orient oder Rom: Beiträge zur Geschichte der spätantiken und frühchristlichen Kunst* (Leipzig: J. C. Hinrichs, 1901). Reprinted from Anton Springer, *Die Genesisbilder in der Kunst der frühen Mittelalters, mit besonderer Rücksicht auf den Ashburnham-Pentateuch* (Leipzig: S. Hirzel, 1884).

"Hellas in des Orients Umarmung," he compared the spotless maiden of Greek independence, abducted by a ruthless Turk in the painting, to the beautiful maiden of Hellenic art who sells herself to an "old Semite."[64] The Semite keeps her as the jewel of his harem, surrounded by the "Semitic pack" teeming with silk, gold, and jewels. She becomes a whore, who "persecutes the viewer with her look" and strives for effects through the "seductive luxury of clothing" (326). This hedonistic art culminated in the proliferation of flat patterns that "celebrated their orgies in the Arabesque" (326). To capture the tenacity of the race that created it, Strzygowski uses the phrase *der ewige Jude* (eternal Jew), thus uniting Jew and "ruthless Turk" in a narrative that had little to do with either (315).

The very terms suggest fear of miscegenation, and indeed, in the same essay, Strzygowski not only mourned the disintegration of the race of Hellas, he compared it to the German race, worried that it would similarly lose its purity. Germany, apparently a masculine version of Greece, would not be raped but would succumb to Italy, a "prostitute from whose magic even the sunny, Greek-like barbarians of the North cannot tear themselves away during the Middle Ages" (326). Italy's allure threatened to turn the "powerful Germanic breed" to mannerism (314).

Strzygowski celebrated the "blood relationship" that bound Germans. In a passage that alludes to the immensely popular German nationalist volume *Rembrandt als Erzieher,* by "ein Deutscher" ("a German"), he attributed to Albrecht Dürer and Rembrandt a "German depth of feeling," "acquired . . . along the way as their ancestral inheritance."[65] German Jewish artists, however, did not have depth of feeling by birthright, as we infer from a 1907 critique of Liebermann in Strzygowski's *Die bildende Kunst der Gegenwart* (see figure 7). "In order to salvage the title of art for painting that lacks ideas of its own, he called the search after new variations in artistic qualities 'fantasy.' Naturally fantasy takes place completely in the artist: it emerges from purely sensory presuppositions. At the basis of this concept is race."[66] In the early twentieth century, the term "race" was as likely to signify culture as blood. But Strzygowski makes his meaning clear in a footnote: "Notice also that Orientals in general have considerable fantasy, but this is only seldom purified into what is at issue in art: the need for a simple and clear expression of impulses of the soul, over and above sensuality" (270 n.). Liebermann, who was born and raised in Berlin, must have had the "Oriental" in his blood, since it was certainly not in his culture.

Strzygowski waited impatiently for the great savior of German art. His writings of the turn of the century are full of allusions to this hoped-for hero: "Will it be a single master, like Leonardo, Bramante, Michelangelo? If not, certainly a unifying social idea, that will then affect the masses?" (272). "Not with the human figure and measure can we Germans hope to reach the peak of art, but with landscape and space. Hans von Marées sensed the problem. When will the hero come that will solve it? When the time that will bring him forth?" (275).

When the savior appeared, not only of German art but of all German culture, Strzygowski was ready. Before he died in 1941 he vowed to continue to serve his Führer through his work and filled his last years with verbose ranting about émigré Jewish art historians who led international conspiracies from New York.[67] Because his early, often quoted works were not yet Nazi, some scholars disassociate these valuable contributions to the field from his late tirades. Yet as a result of them, although he opened to serious art historical study the art of the entire Near East and India and contributed to many art historical disciplines and controversies, discussions of his genuine scholarly significance are often burdened by embarrassment or excused by reference to physical or emotional illness, and sometimes his work is discredited altogether.[68]

Whatever good came out of even his earliest trips to the Middle East and the scholarship derived from them, however, they, too, were conditioned by pan-Germanic ideological concerns just as were his later speculative works. Strzygowski's ethnic ideas were not peripheral to but at the heart of his art history, for he used formal analysis, in itself a neutral tool, to identify not merely similarities but blood relationships and pathways not of influence but of migration, conquest, and miscegenation. Consistently, he directed his research to the identification of national spirits and sought out adversarial relationships in which he saw them reciprocally asserting their identities. Many of these struggles pitted blood relationships, identified with the people, against institutions of power, generally imperial power. Within blood relationships, more or less insidious strains battled pure strains. From the beginning, Strzygowski's agonistic art history was a battle cry of the racist and a

7. Max Liebermann, *The Studio of the Artist at the Brandenburg Gate in Berlin*, 1902, oil on canvas. Saint Gall, Kunstmuseum.

warning against cultural influence. Art history, he wrote, showed us "how two currents fight with one another and one finally achieves victory."[69] Real blood could flow from such arguments.

Marginalized in the Mainstream: The Haggadah of Sarajevo, 1898

The remarks of art historical scholars about the art of the ancient Jews, like their discussions of primitive Germanic tribes, employ a myth of origins to assess the distinctive artistic character of Jewish artists, both ritual and secular, beginning with Bezalel, the maker of the tabernacle in the desert, and encompassing even the Berlin-born Impressionist Max Liebermann. Jewish artists could be described as possessing a strange and Oriental sensibility, as devoid of artistic sensibility or as antagonistic toward art altogether. Jews were written out of art history either as marginal to it or as a people defined by their deficiencies: a lack of history, a lack of land, and a lack of art.[70] We have seen, for example, how Josef Strzygowski wrote Max Liebermann out of contemporary art history by transforming him into a fantastic Oriental personage, even though his thoroughly acculturated family had lived in Prussia for generations and Berlin's most fashionable society frequented his studio (see figure 8).[71]

Sometimes, however, Liebermann was considered a maker of French art, since his most powerful artistic influence was French Impressionism.[72] This characterization was not more benign. Liebermann could well have made Jewish art *because* he was a German making French art, and many art critics recognized the anti-Semitism underlying an identification of Liebermann as French.[73] A true German, after all, can only have made German art. When in the course of an attack on French Impressionism, in his book *Böcklin und Thoma,* the German nationalist Henry Thode identified Liebermann's main influence as the Dutch painter Josef Israels, another Jewish artist, the effect was to locate the origin of Liebermann's internationalism in his cosmopolitan Jewishness. Thode proceeded to deny the Berliner any German character: "Liebermann could just as well work in Holland or in France and be just as much at home; nothing explicitly German is present in him."[74] He contrasts Liebermann in this respect with another, non-Jewish, German painter influenced by French Impressionism and, incidentally, a friend

Einzelheft 20 Pf.
0,35 Schilling

Die Lesestunde

Zeitschrift der Deutschen Buch-Gemeinschaft

Berlin / Wien / Breslau / Danzig / Frankfurt a. M. / Hamburg / Köln a. Rh. / Königsberg i. Pr. / München

4. Jahrgang / Nummer 14 • Berlin am 15. Juli 1927

Der 80jährige Führer der Kunst Professor Max Liebermann malt den 80jährigen Führer des deutschen Volkes Reichspräsidenten v. Hindenburg

8. Cover, *Die Lesestunde,* 15 July 1927, showing the painter Max Liebermann with his portrait of President von Hindenburg. Courtesy of the Department of Special Collections, the University of Chicago Library.

of Max Liebermann, Fritz von Uhde: "In him, the German essence manifests itself very effectively in the treatment of related problems" (101). Even recourse to his German pedigree could not save Liebermann from charges of Jewish cosmopolitanism. As late as 1950, a critic looking back recalled that "Germany . . . came to recognize Liebermann . . . as her most characteristic contemporary painter." The key word was "most." That proved, said the critic, that "the achievements of assimilated Jews involved excesses." Liebermann's excess was an "excess of German rectitude."[75]

A similar means of stripping Jews of their citizenship characterizes some of the more xenophobic contributions in the volume *Ein Protest deutscher Künstler.* The protest was a collaborative lament against modernism, conflated, as it often was in Germany, with anxiety about the cultural supremacy of France. The intrusion of French paintings and styles into German art was its subject. Its editor, Carl Vinnen, fueled it with stock phrases equating blood and nation. "*A people,*" he wrote, "*can only be elevated by artists of its own flesh and blood.*"[76] Vinnen criticized the amount of money and gallery space spent on French art, the importation of French styles, and the consequent rejection of iconography in favor of formal values. Yet the protesters did not blame the French for cultural imperialism. They instead accused international conspiracies based on the accumulation of capital, rhetoric that anyone familiar with anti-Semitic discourse will recognize. Furthermore, their targets are not French but German, and most of those mentioned by name are Jewish or of Jewish descent: the painter Max Liebermann, the art critic Julius Meier-Graefe, and the gallery owner Paul Cassirer.[77] Max Liebermann could well have been the mercenary "leading Berlin artist" (38), who, according to a contributor who signs himself Professor Keller of the Düsseldorf Academy (probably Ludwig Paul Wilhelm Keller, 1865–1925), said that dealers make a city into an artistic capital, not good painters. One of the most explicit arguments against the protest identified the anti-Semitism behind this maneuver. The critic Wilhelm Hausenstein classified the protesters succinctly among the those who "improve the world with the logic of anti-Semitism. . . . They are among those who allow themselves to be represented by . . . the henchmen of Mayor Lueger."[78] The Hapsburg Emperor himself sought to protect the Jews from the likes of the anti-Semitic mayor of Vienna,

Karl Lueger, preventing him for two years after his election (from 1895 to 1897) from assuming his post. He remained, however, a popular mayor until his death in 1920, and a role model for Adolf Hitler.

Hausenstein was right: explicit anti-Semites were as frequent in art history as anywhere else. But the worry about miscegenation that was explicit in an openly racist scholar such as Strzygowski was implicit everywhere in art history written on national lines. Characterizations of Jewish art in effect distinguished it from the art of cultures in which Jewish artists participated, leaving these cultures unproblematically German, French, or Spanish. Thus the voice of anti-Semitism was built into the language along with nationalism and became part of the structure of art history even where anti-Semitism was not the object. Indeed, once the structure of the discipline was set, it was difficult either to fit into it a work that engages Judaism directly within that structure or to account for such a work without falling into anti-Semitic language.

The first scholarly study of a work acknowledged as "Jewish," the 1898 Vienna publication of the newly discovered fourteenth-century Haggadah of Sarajevo, could not avoid these problems (see figure 9). It was a major scholarly collaborative work of the art historian Julius von Schlosser and the paleographer David Heinrich Müller, with an appendix by the rabbi and scholar of Jewish art David Kaufmann. Such collaborative projects were frequent by then in manuscript studies, having been inaugurated in 1889 by the publication of *Die Trierer Ada-Handschrift,* edited by Karl Lamprecht, and continued by joint projects such as Franz Wickhoff's study of the manuscript of the Vienna *Genesis* with the paleographer Wilhelm Ritter von Hartel.

Lamprecht's study took the Ada manuscript as a signifier of the development of the German nation.[79] Wickhoff's work centered on a definition of Roman art.[80] With national character in the foreground of such models, Schlosser's interpretive essay "Die Bilderschmuck der Haggadah" inevitably dealt with its subject in national terms. Schlosser grappled repeatedly with the tropes of Jewish art. His essay begins with racial characterizations, speculations about the racial mixture of Jews with surrounding peoples, primarily Ashkenazim and Sephardim, and allusions to phylogenetic theory. Involvement in racial theory was not in itself racist. Schlosser was antagonistic to racism in its uglier aspects and regarded himself as an Italian-German crossbreed.[81] He may have

9. *The Parting of the Red Sea*, Sarajevo Haggadah, Spanish, 14th century. From David Heinrich Müller and Julius v. Schlosser, eds., *Die Haggadah von Sarajevo* (Vienna: A. Holder, 1898).

meant his discussion of Jewish racial identity to confound the simplistic assumptions of his contemporaries, for his essay suggests that the Jews took on the characteristics of the peoples around them and thus were not an alien race. The "bolder, prouder physiognomy" of Spanish Jews (Schlosser's characterization makes them seem stereotypically Latin) comes from mixtures with Moorish residents of Spain, while German Jews have different physical characteristics that cannot be attributed only to the northern climate and differing social conditions.[82] Yet his remarks, and the literature he cites in his discussion, reveal that he found racial determinations – the racial character of the artist – indispensable for art historical analysis: "There appear also to be racial differences [between Sephardim and Ashkenazim]. This is particularly important just now, when the development of modern natural sciences forces us to inquire into the question of phylogeny, into the role of ethnicity in the work of art" (216–17).

In his discussion of the Haggadah, Schlosser draws on literary sources and histories by both Jews and Christians. For the great preponderance of specifically Jewish subjects he chooses from among established Jewish scholars, and his credentials as a scholar with a friendly interest in Jewish issues were respectable.[83] He was, for example, a member of the Gesellschaft zur Sammlung und Erhaltung von Kunst- und historischen Denkmälern des Judentums in Wien (Society for the Collection and Conservation of Artistic and Historical Monuments of Jewry in Vienna).[84] Yet he also used a number of subtly anti-Semitic sources and from them availed himself of a storehouse of often contradictory stereotypes at different stages of the argument. Thus Jews are Oriental makers of "exaggerated and monstrous art" (248). But when working in the styles of the surrounding society they become drab borrowers as described by the likes of Lübke: they never "progressed beyond clever imitation" (241). Their imitations fall short of the originals.[85] Unlike Islam, which created for itself an original decorative style, "Jews do without any artistic manner of their own" (242). Furthermore, when they deviate from surrounding styles, rather than imitate them exactly, Schlosser characterizes the deviations as distortions rather than calling them, as he could have, creative embellishments (248). He attributes some of the contradictions in his argument to his subjects. Like Schnaase, he identifies the Jewish character with motion. But he marvels twice over the amazing way in which Jewish "flexibility and agility" coexist with "an inertia beyond compare" (248).[86]

As evidence for the meager artistic gifts of Semitic peoples, he draws on his own time, citing Josef Israels as the sole living Jewish artist of any note, thus omitting from the canon a number of well-known Jewish artists with whose work Schlosser would have been familiar, such as Camille Pissarro and Max Liebermann.[87] Liebermann's name, if not Liebermann himself, is referenced a few pages later, in a passage referring to the "gezierte [decorated]" (245) names of Frankish Jews.[88] The designation "gezierte" gives a disparaging tone to a passage intended ostensibly simply to bolster the argument for the Jewish ethnicity of the medieval poet Süsskind von Trimberg. Schlosser took the reference from a Viennese journal, *Germania*, which later engaged in anti-Semitic activities.[89]

Significantly, Schlosser posits a Jewish role in art history in two brief passages. One role is social-historical. Jews' imitative capacities, he suggests, disseminated Western artistic ideas throughout the world, a "mission of cosmopolitans" that their "exceptional historical fate" vested in them in other cultural areas as well.[90] The other role is pedagogical. Schlosser describes as telling and interesting for the study of medieval art the Jewish treatment of forms developed by Christians, an assertion he supported with a quotation from a Jewish scholar, Moritz Steinschneider, who seems to make modest claims for Jewish studies: "We do not mean to point to a Jewish mine full of unsuspected treasures. The Jewish lights are reflections, but often very accurate [ones]. Their sketches [*aufzeichnungen*] often have minute features to offer that are lacking elsewhere and complete our historical picture" (251–52).[91] These remarks, which Schlosser cites in closing, marginalize Jews by suggesting that if Jewish art is telling for the study of medieval art, it is because it was not part of, but rather a reflection of, that art. By assigning to Jewish art the role of an emissary, Schlosser makes the Jewish contribution essential rather than peripheral but in so doing perpetuates the myth of Jewish internationalism and outsider status, in effect attributing any art that Jews produce to the cultures surrounding them. Jewish artists become messengers.

Steinschneider's remarks appear all the more damning in that they referred not to art but to literature, generally regarded as a field in which Jews excelled and to which they made original contributions. Moreover, the essay appeared in a journal edited by the son of Abraham Geiger, the champion of the Jewish Reform movement. Yet he probably intended, in accord with his larger project, not to denigrate Jewish literature but to discourage the ghettoization of Jewish studies. Schlosser's citation, then, exemplifies a way in which the words of Jewish scholars could be used against them.[92]

Schlosser's lightly disparaging remarks about Jewish art, and his misuse of Jewish scholarship, are perhaps less revealing, however, than the laconic reaction to them of a young scholar who would soon be the first Jewish professor of art history, Adolph Goldschmidt (1863–1944). Reviewing Schlosser's edition of the Haggadah, Goldschmidt concluded that he found no indication that the manuscript took part in an "artistic development of its own."[93] Goldschmidt's training and propensity as an art historian made him a specialist in careful stylistic analysis.[94] To lay claim to an independent artistic development, a group of artifacts would have to show a unified style. Schlosser's analysis of Jewish art as imitations or distortions of mainstream styles meant, therefore, that Jewish art could not be accommodated within mainstream art history as Goldschmidt understood it. Schlosser's characterizations were not mere anti-Semitic tropes, however, but themselves outcomes of the structure of art history. By articulating the acceptable subject matter for art historical study into distinct styles defined nationally, this structure marginalized the Haggadah.

CHAPTER TWO

The Nation with Art?

Bezalel in Palestine

A perfected Jewish art, like a perfected Jewish culture in general, will be possible only in a Jewish land. **Martin Buber** in *Die jüdische Bewegung: Gesammelte Aufsätze und Ansprachen*

On top of the stone was the figure of Bezalel, the son of Uri, leaning up against his divine work, the holy arc [*sic*], the shrine which he made for the tablets; with eyes full of love he looked as though he was waiting for [the people]. . . . No names of any particular artists there were. It was a collective work, created by the genius of the Jewish people. **Boris Schatz** in Di *geboyte Yrusholem*

One art school is more important than a hundred settlements. **Ahad Ha-am** in "Tehyat Ha-Ru'ah"

The Artificer

Not long after Hubert Janitschek sought to naturalize the recent unification of Germany by tracing its primeval origin in art "back to the darkness of the tribal past," Zionists began building a national consciousness based on the return to Eretz Israel (the land of Israel).[1] They were not a unified group, but many of them, including some political Zionists substantiating their claims to statehood, cultural Zionists seeking to inspire the creation of a national character in the Diaspora, and practical Zionists rising to the challenge of a self-supporting Jewish settlement in Palestine, accepted the premise that a people must have its own art to prove its right to statehood and its own art history to prove itself a nation. Against the repeated denials of Jewish art not only from institutional art history but, as we shall see in later chapters, from some sectors of the Jewish intelligentsia, Zionists used art to extricate a positive definition of a nation from a negative definition of a non- or even anti-nationality.[2]

Like anti-Semites, some Zionists looked to biblical history for Jewish art. They found their model, however, not in the Commandments but in the first Jewish artist associated with them. In the desert, during the biblical flight from Egypt, Bezalel, son of Uri son of Hur, of the tribe of Judah, crafted the ark of the tabernacle out of acacia wood. The Lord Himself commissioned Bezalel, saying, "I have endowed him with a divine spirit of skill, ability, and knowledge in every kind of craft."[3] One could point to Bezalel's appearance, at the very moment of the Golden Calf and the giving of the Ten Commandments, to prove God's blessing on art.[4] It also showed that Jews did not need to depend on foreigners such as Hiram, builder of the Temple of Solomon; they could draw upon their own artistic genius.

More importantly, Bezalel's feat situated art at a moment crucial to nation building, the flight from slavery in Egypt, and in the heart of Jewish religiosity, the tabernacle. The glorification of the craftsman Bezalel did for Jewish art what the return to Eretz Israel did for Jewish nationalism: it made possible a positive conception of Jewish art as the art of ancient Israel. Zionist leaders well understood the connection. "For generations upon generations," wrote Henrietta Szold (1860–1945), founder of Hadassah, "either because the world shut [the Jew] out, or because he shut himself out, from living influences, he forgot that in one of the niches of his nation's history there stood one Bezalel, the artificer."[5]

Szold made her remarks in reference to a school of arts and crafts in Jerusalem named after the great artificer, Bezalel. Theodor Herzl is also said to have grasped the magic of the name "Bezalel." The Russian-born sculptor Boris Schatz (1867–1932), founder of the school, never tired of reprising the moment in 1903 when, playing Bezalel to Herzl's Moses, he presented to the Zionist leader his idea:

> "Good, we shall do that," he said, quietly and resolutely, and after a brief pause, he asked: "What name will you give to your school?"
>
> "Bezalel," I answered, "after the name of the first Jewish artist who once built us a temple in the wilderness."
>
> "A temple in the wilderness," he repeated slowly, and the beautiful sad eyes seemed to look into an endless vista, as though he felt that he would never see it himself.[6]

The Bezalel school is routinely cited as the founding institution of Israeli art, but in its original form it did not last until the creation of the Israeli state.[7] Established in 1906 as the Bezalel School of Arts and Crafts, it had already closed for lack of funds and support by the time Szold praised it in 1929. It reopened in 1935 as Bezalel HaChadash (New Bezalel), with new leadership and a new philosophy. In 1965, it became the Bezalel Academy of Arts and Design. Similarly, its museum reopened as a separate institution in 1935 and, in 1965, merged with other collections to form the Israel Museum.

Bezalel was no more coherent than Zionism itself. Competing conceptualizations of Jewish, and later Israeli, nationality and different models of nationhood itself helped adapt successive incarnations of Bezalel and its museum to Palestinian conditions, with correspondingly different political and cultural allegiances and new supporters. These interconnected institutions saw major battles in the struggle to define Jewish art in Palestine, and each definition had to grapple with competing discourses on Jewish nationalism. These several institutions by no means comprise the whole of Israeli art, if there is such a whole, or even a representative cross-section of it.[8] Their story, however, shaped by and revealing of the dissonance between notions of what constitutes nationhood, offers a vantage point on the relationship between art and national identity in a chain of events that turned out to be the formative stages of a nation-state.[9]

Boris Schatz and the Bezalel School of Arts and Crafts

"Mr. Shatz [*sic*], although a Russian by birth, has cast his lot with the small group of art pioneers who are . . . courageously braving the hardships and difficulties inherent to the development of a national art in a new country, where the material needs of man overshadow his cravings for the beautiful."[10] This description of the founder of the Bezalel School of Arts and Crafts refers not to his work in Palestine but to his activities in another new country, Bulgaria, where he gained practical experience in constructing national identity through art. Although he recounted with pride his achievements in Bulgaria, Boris Schatz did not probe the effect of Bulgarian nationalism on his Jewish nationalism in his often retold autobiographical parable, in which the anguish of assimilation gives way to the euphoria of liberation. His devotion to the school named after Bezalel the artificer obscured his earlier willingness to make another country's struggles for self-identification his own.

In Schatz's account, his early vision of Jewish art gave way to a universally religious one. He wished initially to paint "the tomb of our Mother Rachel and the Wailing Wall." Instead, however, "strangers, non-Jews, taught me art and gave me their ideal, . . . I looked upon art as a temple and upon artists as its priests. . . . Art was the language of my soul which every man of feeling can understand, no matter to what nation he belongs or what language he speaks. I wished to put my art to the service of all mankind and to bring joy to all."[11] Schatz developed these ideas in Paris, where he won medals for his achievements in a realist style indebted to his teacher, the Jewish sculptor Mark Antokolski (see figure 10). Schatz's subjects included a portrait plaster of Karl Marx.

The Yiddish author Leo Koenig, who studied at Bezalel, reports that Antokolski gave Schatz the idea for the school.[12] If so, however, Bulgaria benefited from it first. According to Schatz, his work brought him to

10. Boris Schatz, *Mattathaias, der Vater der Makkabäer*, 1894. From *Ost und West* 3 (1903): 293–4. Courtesy of the Asher Library, Spertus Institute of Jewish Studies.

the attention of the Bulgarian monarch Prince Ferdinand I, who invited him to Sofia and made him official royal sculptor.[13] Presumably it was after this time that he abandoned the idea of universal art and began to strive for an art purely Jewish. His Jewish themes, however, predate his years in Bulgaria; he had impressed the Bulgarian ruler with his 1894 sculpture of Mattathiaus the Hasmonean, an anti-assimilationist hero of the Jewish holiday of Chanukah. If Ferdinand admired this piece, Mattathiaus's significance for the fight for national liberation may have struck a chord in him, just as Herzl had when he met the prince in 1896.[14]

Schatz's employment was part of Bulgarian nation building. The founding of the nation-state in 1878, a result of Russia's military victory over Turkey, was the culmination of a lengthy movement for political independence from the Ottomans and cultural independence from the Greek Patriarchate of Constantinople. Only after 1894, however, when Prince Ferdinand I gained full power, did the movement for cultural independence include efforts to found an academy of fine arts. The Society for the Promotion of Art in Bulgaria, founded in 1893, drafted a resolution, and the minister of public education, Konstantine Velichkov (1855–1907), convinced the National Assembly to adopt it. The resolution ran into difficulties, but ultimately Velichkov's assurances of the benefits accruing to industry from education in visual arts persuaded the delegates to accept the school.[15] With two other professors, Schatz founded the academy of art in Sofia in 1896.

The intertwining of nationalism, industry, and art links Bulgarian artistic activities to the Arts and Crafts movement that began decades earlier in England and Europe with the founding of museums and schools of applied arts. Like William Morris and his followers, the Bulgarian government officials accepted as an axiom that artistic regeneration should begin with the handicrafts. In Bulgaria, arts and crafts took a pronounced nationalist form. Ivan Shishmanov, president of the Society for the Promotion of Art and later minister of public education, encouraged the study of Bulgarian folk art and the history of Bulgarian icon painting and ornament in order to determine what was authentically national in it.[16] The poet Ivan Vazov, another founder of the Society for the Promotion of Art, accentuated nationalist aims by asserting that only native themes, not cosmopolitanism, would build a national art.[17]

Schatz absorbed these lessons on how to form a national art. In 1900, he exhibited a "box in an old Bulgarian style." [18] A Bulgarian journalist observed in his work "a thorough knowledge of our [national] types. His Bagpipe Player portrays a folk singer singing ancient Bulgarian folk songs with his head dreamily bent down and his eyes half-closed" (see figure 11).[19] In an 1895 letter to Shishmanov, Schatz offered strategies to encourage a feeling for art in the broad mass of the populace. He suggested securing the participation of the intelligentsia, offering free admission to the society's permanent exhibition, organizing traveling exhibitions, and opening a school that would offer "evening classes accessible to the average civil servant, craftsman, university student and other kind of person occupied during the day." [20] He claimed a role in the revival of carpet making by hand, a quintessential activity of the Arts and Crafts movement, which, he said, helped the carpet industry make a substantial contribution to the Bulgarian economy.[21]

In 1901 or 1902, inspired by Zionism, embroiled in marital difficulties, and, as Bulgarian artists increasingly joined modernist artistic currents, perhaps disappointed by diminishing prospects for his own academic style, Schatz proposed to Herzl the founding of a school of art in Palestine.[22] Forces brewing in Zionism were favorable; Martin Buber called for a Jewish art on Jewish soil at the Zionist Congress in 1901. In 1906, Schatz traveled to Jerusalem to found the Bezalel School of Arts and Crafts, accompanied by the *Jugendstil* painter and Cultural Zionist, E. M. (Ephraim Moses) Lilien. The director of the Academy in Sofia, Jan Mrkvička, helped select Bezalel's faculty.[23]

Schatz instituted in Jerusalem the nation-building skills he had learned in Sofia. The Zionist board, like the Bulgarian National Assembly, accepted the argument that the revival of handicrafts would strengthen Palestine's commercial position and provide employment.[24] In Bezalel, the students were to become proficient in the crafts as well as the fine arts and sell their goods to tourists and art aficionados. New industries, carpet making included, were to be founded (see figure 12). Bezalel would give farmers employment during the off-season, training them and their wives to combine crafts with agriculture and providing them with designs. Evening classes were established, like those recommended by Schatz to the Bulgarian authorities.

Schatz's plans for Bezalel's economic contribution to Zionism were

11. Boris Schatz, *Bagpipe Player*. From *Ost und West* 3 (1903). Courtesy of the Asher Library, Spertus Institute of Jewish Studies.

12. Boris Schatz among Bezalel rugs, c. 1912.
Collection Israel Museum, Jerusalem.

visionary. The school had been open only five months when he predicted that "the time will come when the artisans who bear the title 'workers of the Bezalel,' will join into a mighty union with school of the Bezalel, its bureaus, and the firms associated with it, so that, as soon as the natural colonizing of Palestine begins, the inhabitants will be better enabled to bring over their relatives, their friends, and their acquaintances, and place them upon a firm footing."[25] The school would become the center of a large complex, housing artists and their workshops and spawning outposts throughout the rural areas. The school's one outpost, a Yeminite community at Ben Shemen, existed only briefly, between 1911 and 1914, but by 1910, Bezalel was the largest employer in Jerusalem.[26]

Schatz's vision for Bezalel in Zion was not only economic but stylistic. His school would "prove to the world that there is such a thing as Jewish art and that it may lay an example for Jewish artists, and prompt them to create in the Jewish spirit."[27] Bezalel had to prove the existence not merely of Jewish artistic ability but of the primordial Jewish character, a demand he thought meant to transcend the European Diaspora and reflect its Oriental setting and its biblical heritage. Not only the detractors of Jewish art, as we have seen, but its champions as well often conceived Jewish art along Oriental lines. A critic, contrasting the Prussian-born Jewish painter Lesser Ury to the Saxony-born non-Jewish painter Fritz von Uhde, wrote: "There lived in Ury the old flame of the Orient, the hot breath that sweeps over the raw earth, the giant figures of elementary creation before the grandiose background of an immeasurable expanse."[28]

Schatz mixed sources from biblical history and the present to create Jewish art. The image of the artificer decorated key products (see figure 13). The reconstructions of the Temple of Ezekiel by Perrot and Chipiez, reprinted in a Jewish journal without their deprecating text, supplied the motif of the cherubim flanking the ark (see figures 4 and 14).[29] Bezalel also looked to the natural endowments of its chosen homeland. In order to lend "a peculiarly Jewish, Palestinian character, . . . we employ as models, various Palestinian animals, bird collections and insect collections."[30] Israel Aharoni, a biblical zoologist who emigrated to Palestine in 1904, became curator of the "natural historical Bezalel Museum."[31] By 1908, when Bezalel acquired permanent premises, the museum possessed samples of stuffed birds and preserved reptiles, and Aharoni began planning a zoo (see figure 15).[32] Among the native species were Palestine's human inhabitants, who served as colorfully clad models for drawing classes, while local plants were stylized to create ornaments.[33] Schatz encouraged the use of native woods, such as olive wood, walnut, and fig.

The Hebrew language figured in the creation of a national identity and in Bezalel's curriculum. Eliezer Ben-Yehuda, to whose tireless efforts the revival of modern Hebrew as a spoken language is often credited, lived near the school's first quarters. His wife, Hemdah, worked briefly as Bezalel's secretary in 1906.[34] The family's relations with Schatz and his students continued after the school moved.[35] In the 1920s, Schatz published in *Do'ar Hayom* (Daily Mail), a conservative newspaper founded by Ben-Yehuda's son.[36] Schatz stipulated that the students learn Hebrew and engaged Aharoni, the naturalist, to teach them.[37] The development of Hebrew calligraphy for the graphic arts was high on Bezalel's agenda (see figure 16). Hebrew letters appeared on Oriental-inspired, European-designed carpets (see figure 12).

European artistic currents made their way into Bezalel as well. E. M. Lilien remained only briefly in Palestine in 1906, but he supplied Bezalel with its seal and a *Jugendstil* look that it maintained well into the 1920s in the work, for example, of Ze'ev Raban (see figures 14, 17, 18, and 32). Along with Arab-inspired designs by native craftsmen and references to Assyrian art, Bezalel artists appropriated indigenous techniques through studies of filigree in Damascus and enamel in Cairo.[38] Orientalism and art nouveau mingled with the academic naturalism of Boris Schatz.

The association of old and new reflects Schatz's adaptation of William Morris's socialist medievalism, itself indicative of a tendency to adorn social ideologies of the moment in historical raiment.[39] Schatz's writing moves quickly from evocations of free laborers reclaiming the soil – "The erst barren hills are covered again with plantations" . . . the "new and healthy life . . . again awakening" there – to descriptions of an exotic "Jewish Palestinian style" that "reflects the beauty of the Biblical age and the fantasy of the Orient."[40] His utopian novel, *Jerusalem Rebuilt,* similarly combines Herzl-inspired modernist fantasies, such as the use of solar energy and a socialist vision of children raised

13. Bezalel School of Arts and Crafts (Ze'ev Raban), cabinet, c. 1920. Detail, Bezalel and the Ark of the Tabernacle. The Sherwin Miller Museum of Jewish Art (formerly The Fenster Museum), Tulsa, Oklahoma.

14. Title page, *Bezalel Archives* 1, Tischri, 5688 (1927). Illustration by Ze'ev Raban. Courtesy of the Asher Library, Spertus Institute of Jewish Studies.

15. Photograph of a turtle in the animal corner at Bezalel, 1908. Collection Israel Museum, Jerusalem.

16. A student [Ya'akov Stark] making designs consisting of decorative Jewish characters. From *New York Zionist Annual* (Zionist Council of Greater New York), 16 December 1906.

17. Binding for a Bezalel photograph album including the Seal of Bezalel, India ink and watercolor on cloth. Collection Israel Museum, Jerusalem.

18. Students and faculty at Bezalel Institute, under the direction of Ze'ev Raban, Aron Hakodesh (Holy Ark), 1913–23. Detail, Carrying the Ark. Collection Spertus Museum, Spertus Institute of Jewish Studies, Chicago. Photograph: Margaret Olin

in cooperatives, with references to biblical garb and submission to the Sanhedrin.[41] In a 1914 catalog, Schatz wrote of creating a new art on the foundation of Hebrew tradition: "The great idea is not to copy Arab or European models, but to derive new inspiration from Hebrew ideals, from the flora and fauna of the land, to create an art neuveau [*sic*], with a Hebrew background, to utilize incidents of Palestinian life – old and new – to mould the Hebrew alphabet into artistic forms for decorative purposes, in short, to create a Palestinian renaissance."[42]

Schatz sought to remake himself in the new "Hebrew Style" of the East.[43] His costume, Bedouin robes worn with a pith helmet, gave him a colonialist appearance, strengthened by the fitting setting he gave the school by acquiring two nineteenth-century buildings belonging to one Abu Shakir (see figure 19). He Judaized this "Turkish Harem," as it was sometimes called, with added sculptural reliefs on biblical themes and a seven-branched menorah on the roof that gave it the appearance of a temple.[44] An album sent to members of the Bezalel Committee shows the menorah astride the museum and the Zionist flag flying above the school (see figure 17).

The two symbols reflected the double motive of Bezalel. In Schatz's estimation, Bezalel was to be nothing less than the foundation for the Third Temple. Several Zionist artists shared the dream of reconstructing the temple, and there was no agreement about its style or the use to which it would be put. The architect Oskar Marmorek speculated on a modern style, probably the Secessionist style of his teacher, Otto Wagner. In it, Judaism would be practiced in accord with the modern denomination.[45] Herzl rejected Marmorek's design for a Congress building in Basel in 1898, however, as inexpressive (*nichtssagend*). Herzl must have realized that, to be seen, ethnicity must be "staged" with a recognizably Jewish look.[46] He wanted the Congress building to employ a "neo-Jewish [*neu-jüdischer*] style."[47] He tried to inspire Marmorek with his own rough sketch, but the neo-Renaissance loggia it portrays recalls the late-nineteenth-century historicist buildings on Vienna's stately Ringstrasse, hardly a Jewish source (see figure 20). Similarly, in his utopian novel, *Altneuland* (first published in 1902), Herzl describes the rebuilt temple as a "powerful and sumptuous building that gleamed white and gold. Its roof rested on marble columns. Yes, it was a whole forest of columns with gilt capitals." The vision, more

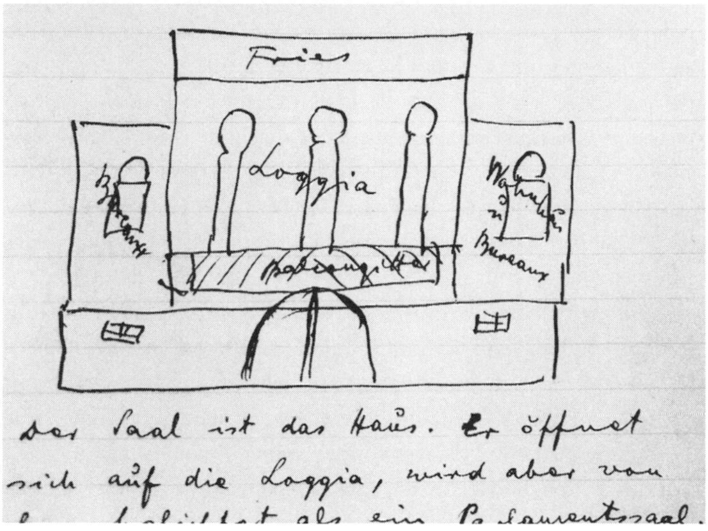

19. Photograph of Boris Schatz and Arnold Lachovsky in front of the Bezalel buildings, 1909. Collection Israel Museum, Jerusalem.

20. Theodor Herzl, design for "Judenhaus in Basel" (drawing), 1898. Central Zionist Archives, Jerusalem. Photograph: Reuven Milon.

neoclassical than neo-Jewish, recalls Perrot's and Chipiez's reconstruction of the ancient temple from *Ost und West* (see figure 5).[48] Schatz's own efforts to construct a temple of art in Jerusalem were more than a metaphor. When he imagined the temple in *Jerusalem Rebuilt,* he secularized it: a museum like that of Bezalel formed the tabernacle at its heart.[49] The school could then be devoted to the economic and cultural regeneration of the secular nation – hence the flag and menorah on the Turkish Harem.

With some success, Bezalel catered to the Zionist desire to make Jerusalem a worthy center of Jewish life.[50] Its exhibits generated interest, its concerts and balls became major social events, and it forged ties with important literati.[51] Its most important achievement, however, was its look. This eclectic mixture of Eastern influences and Western fantasies created a visual image of Palestine as the Jewish homeland.[52] Bezalel gave an artistic identity if not to the Jew, then at least to the Zionist movement. Yemenite craftsmen from Bezalel manned arts and crafts booths at Zionist and British Imperial exhibitions.[53] Many a Western Jewish museum and synagogue display examples of "prizes" (menorahs, decorated albums, decorated Megillot) received yearly by dues-paying members of the Friends of Bezalel.[54] The visual style of official Zionism abounded in Bezalel's incongruous, but telling, juxtapositions: photographs of the new pioneer tilling the soil nestled incongruously in decorative frames (see figure 21). After Bezalel's 1926 tour of New York, Philadelphia, and Chicago, Schatz triumphantly reported that "Bazalel [*sic*] convinced that we are a nation, we can create things national . . . through Bezalel it was recognized that there is a national Jewish art, which means that we are a people."[55]

At this exhibit, Bezalel displayed the school's crowning achievement, the "Aron Hakodesh" [Holy Ark], designed in 1913 by Raban (see figures 18 and 22). One hundred students worked on it intermittently for ten years. The creation of an ark reflects on the namesake of the school, Bezalel, creator of the first ark. Its iconography celebrates the relationship between the law, the ark, and the land, in its equation of the carrying of the ark of the covenant and the carrying of the grapevine from Canaan, by spies, back to the camp of the Israelites.[56] It celebrates Palestine in its materials, gathered from the Dead Sea and Galilee, in its use of enamel techniques that appeared Oriental (repoussé, and cloisonné,

21. *In the Galilee,* from a series of postcards published by Y. Ben-Dov. Photograph, pen, India ink, and brown wash on paper. Collection Israel Museum, Jerusalem.

22. Students and faculty at Bezalel Institute, under the direction of Ze'ev Raban, Aron HaKodesh (Holy Ark), 1913–23. Image courtesy of the Spertus Museum, Spertus Institute of Jewish Studies, Chicago.

however, rather than filigree), and in the flora and fauna that frolic on the surface. Above, cherubim guard the tablets of the Commandments with their wings, and above them are written the old Hebrew names of the planets, an inscribed dome of heaven.[57]

The ark, with its riot of images and writing, probably served a purpose beyond that of nation building. It could put to rest the notion that the Second Commandment forbids Jews to create art. Given the unabashed appropriation of the nationalist paradigm of artistic identity and led by a figural sculptor, Bezalel had few reasons to accept the myth of Jewish aniconism. Although Bezalel's relationship with religious Jews was occasionally strained, these difficulties appeared to turn on fear of competition and the cultural prejudice with which Schatz, for example, claimed that in his first months he "rescued" eight Orthodox pupils "from the doze and lethargy of their Yeschiba [*sic*] life."[58] The Jewish inhabitants of Jerusalem, who seem to be at issue here, were disdained by European visitors as dirty and lazy. Much of the Bezalel literature focused on redeeming them by giving them productive work and exposure to art.[59] Herman Struck, one of Bezalel's earliest European supporters, was Orthodox.

In 1907, the Orthodox Zionist leader Rabbi A. Y. Kook welcomed the new school with a letter that praised its mission to promote Jewish art. In apparent answer to some Jewish thinkers who might distrust visual beauty as a sign of paganism, Kook argued that ancient Israel had rescued the "delicate flower" of beauty from the "dirty and blood-soaked hands" of paganism.[60] In accord with rabbinical exegesis, rather than the modern discourse of Jewish art, he distinguished pagan beauty from the work of the biblical Bezalel, as the carving of idols is distinguished from the creation of art.[61] The Second Commandment, he wrote, serves to remind Jews of paganism and their triumph against it. Almost any kind of representation was possible in obedience to this commandment. Only a complete human visage is forbidden, and there are ways of circumventing even this stricture, "such as through the help of a gentile assistant in the final stage of a prohibited sculpture," that is, one depicting the human face.[62] The only "small point of the whole long line" of prohibition that remains are "pictures specifically characteristic of idolatry, whether of the pagan world of past or present or of the Christian world."[63] Perhaps in an effort at obedience to Rabbi

Kook's warning, Schatz accepted similar strictures. Thus an awkward situation developed when Leopold Pilichowski, the painter of a famous portrait of Herzl, offered Bezalel a Pietà.[64]

Jewish nationalism in Israel can only appear natural if it be shown that the Second Commandment does not prohibit art. Rabbi Kook certainly recognized this when he granted Jewish artists permission to hire a Shabbas Goy to ensure that the commandment cannot prevent Jews from participating even in the most realist artistic styles.[65] The mission of the "Aron Hakodesh," saturated in an iconophoric orgy of representation, can be understood in this light: it constitutes a reproach to those who would deny to Judaism the enjoyment of images. Moreover, it does so in the center of the Jewish cult itself, where the Torah scrolls are preserved and revered. Yet its symbolic nature is assured by the quotation marks around the designation on its base, "Aron Hakodesh," showing that, although fully functional, it is an ark by title only: a fictional ark. Indeed, it is not known ever to have held Torah scrolls. It remained unsold for years after the death of Boris Schatz, presumably until Maurice Spertus bought it for his collection, sometime after 1938.[66]

International Art, Israeli Art

The glory of the ark, and the support of intellectuals and artists abroad (from Max Liebermann and Josef Israels to Albert Einstein), did not enable Bezalel to achieve the primary goal of its exhibition in New York: to rescue the faltering school from financial ruin.[67] At its height in 1912, the school comprised 450 students. During World War I, however, it was often closed, its students and faculty stranded abroad, its director in exile in Damascus.[68] After the war, Schatz complained of everything from the diminishing support of Zionist authorities to "anti-Semitic" tourist bureaus who kept tourists away.[69] A tense relationship between the school and official Zionism left most of Schatz's utopian ideas without funds; his own lack of organization doomed the rest. The rural centers failed to attract and hold their Yemenite members. The similarities between the ills of Bezalel and those to which similar ventures in the European Arts and Crafts movement had succumbed were not lost on C. R. Ashbee, whose Guild of Handicraft may have been the model for Bezalel's plans for rural cooperatives. While he recommended modernizing the school during his time as civic advisor in Jerusalem (1919–22), Ashbee was exasperated by the refusal of the participants in this "brilliant failure" to learn from the experiences of the European Arts and Crafts movement.[70]

Although Schatz sought economic independence for the school through product sales, Bezalel depended on support, at first from its skeptical European board and later from the Palestine Jewish Board of Education.[71] Fund-raising, always a priority, consumed Schatz entirely in Bezalel's last years. He spent more time abroad, increasingly in the United States, where he created support organizations, accompanied exhibits, lectured in Hebrew and Yiddish, and begged in vain for funds from organizations for which Bezalel remained the visual expression of Jewish identity (see figure 23).[72] After the school closed in 1929, Schatz continued his fund-raising in hopes of reopening it. He died on such a mission in Colorado in 1932.

Lack of funds was the effect, however, not the cause, of the school's demise. Zionism's success insured that other conceptions of Jewish life in Palestine could compete with Bezalel's view of the Jewish nation growing out of Oriental and biblical roots on the soil of its homeland. Beginning in 1919, the third and fourth Aliyot (waves of immigration) ensured a larger and more diverse Jewish population.[73] The cultural community that developed increasingly accepted art as part of a Zionist society, which allowed conflicting artistic ideas to flourish. In the 1920s a group of Bezalel students abandoned a style that began to look *retardaire.* Some left to study in Paris. New studios and exhibition societies in Tel Aviv wooed Francophile artists from Jerusalem. Zionist authorities, too, began to focus their hopes, and their attention, on the modern city of Tel Aviv. The year Schatz died saw the opening of the Tel Aviv Museum of Art in Dizengoff House, where, in 1948, David Ben Gurion announced the State of Israel.[74]

In 1935, Bezalel reopened under the auspices of émigrés from Hitler's Germany. These new immigrants often sought refuge in Jerusalem, not only from the Nazis but from Tel Aviv's Parisian pretensions. Jerusalem appealed to them not because of its ties to biblical Jewry but because of the thriving German Jewish intelligentsia that awaited them there. Artists Anna Ticho, who had been in Jerusalem in 1912, and Leopold and Grete Krakauer, who arrived in 1925, were at the center of a lively culture that would include Martin Buber and the poet Else Lasker-Schuler.

23. A Social moment at the Boris Schatz Exhibit, September 1932. From Philip L. Seman, *Community Culture in an Era of Depression* (Chicago: Jewish People's Institute, 1932).

The Bezalel HaChadash (New Bezalel) took over the premises of Schatz's school. Its name conveyed the atmosphere of continuity and rupture in which it took shape.[75] Its director, Joseph Budko, was a Polish-born artist who had studied with Hermann Struck in Berlin. After Budko's death in 1940, the directorship passed to Mordecai Ardon, also Polish-born. Ardon, under his birth name of Max Bronstein, had studied at the Bauhaus in Weimar with Johannes Itten, Wassily Kandinsky, and Paul Klee in the early 1920s. Both Budko and Ardon emigrated to Palestine in 1933. Ardon, involved in revolutionary worker's politics, would initially have preferred to emigrate to Paris.[76] His interest in Zionism, therefore, however sincere and genuine it may eventually have become, was nurtured as much by the external necessity to emigrate to Palestine as by ideological conviction.

Budko and Ardon could not pursue the quest for a quintessentially Jewish art out of biblical Judaism and the Orient. The refugees that came to Palestine on the heels of the Nazi takeover of Germany were interested instead in transplanting to Palestine the ideas and institutions of modernism threatened by the Nazis. If anything, blood and soil nationalism too closely resembled the German ideal they had left behind: connection to the soil of the homeland had been a slogan of the enemies of modernism.

The directors' conceptions of nationality differed widely from that of Schatz. The directorship of New Bezalel was sought to impart the ideals of the international style to the students. Inspired at least as much by the Bauhaus as by the Bible, Budko and Ardon measured nationhood in terms of the ability to stand as equals on the same modernist footing as other nations. They spoke German, not Hebrew, in the hallways and ordered equipment from Germany. Instruction emphasized graphic arts and metalwork intended for modern, commercial purposes, rather than calligraphy and filigree intended as souvenirs. Artists of New Bezalel designed modernist advertising posters, not ornamental designs to frame photographs (see figure 24). Unsurprisingly, the attitude of the new director toward the artists of Schatz's Bezalel, some of whom still maintained studios on the premises, was less than charitable. Budko evicted Raban and another teacher, Meir Gur-Aryeh, telling them that if they were to be engaged to teach at Bezalel (they were not), "I could only give them the teaching of a purely technical part of the work,

24. Rudi Deutsch, "Buy Local Products." Advertisement, 1940s. From Gideon Ofrat, *Bezalel Hachadash* (Jerusalem: Bezalel Academy of Art and Design, 1987).

as the manner in which they had taught was not in accordance with my artistic ideas."[77] Under Budko and Ardon, New Bezalel acquired an international outlook.

Tensions between international modernism and nationalism came to a head over New Bezalel. The Jewish National Fund had stipulated that the name "Bezalel" must be part of the name of the new school.[78] However, a writer in *Do'ar Hayom* objected to the final choice: " 'Bezalel,' but not the 'New,' Mr. Budko, 'Bezalel,' but not the 'New.' "[79] The eviction of Raban and Gur-Aryeh elicited angry responses pitting acculturated German immigrants against Hebrew-speaking old-timers. "The Jewish heart was broad and happy at seeing the creations of Bezalel, full of beauty and the grace of tradition, imprinted with the stamp of the renewed and revived land of the Hebrews," the same journalist continued, complaining that New Bezalel tries "to erase all memory of the past." The author mourned the advent of New Bezalel in the same words that signaled the rise of the evil pharaoh of Egypt in the book of Exodus: " 'And a new king arose' . . ."[80]

Two groups were opposed not only culturally but politically. Josef Klausner (1874–1958), honorary secretary of the Bezalel Company, an organization founded in 1925 to support and expand the school, was a Hebraist and cultural critic who had accompanied Schatz when he presented to Herzl the proposal for a Jewish art school in Jerusalem.[81] His defense of Bezalel and Schatz continued long after the former's closure and the latter's death.[82] Klausner also actively supported Vladimir Jabotinsky's right-wing World Union of Zionist Revisionists, founded in 1925, which aimed at establishing a Jewish majority in Palestine by means of massive and immediate Jewish immigration.[83] From 1933, he edited the revisionist newspaper *Beitar,* with B. Z. Netanyahu.[84] Bezalel had reciprocal relations to Jabotinsky. Its students painted his portrait, along with that of other heroes.[85] Jabotinsky's Jewish Legion ordered medals from Bezalel and donated the majority of items for the museum's permanent exhibit commemorating the liberation from the Turks. In contrast, Arthur Ruppin, founder of the Gesellschaft Bezalel HaChadash in 1935, far from promoting revisionism, supported the organization Brit Shalom, which promoted peace with the Arab population.

To the acculturated population that supported New Bezalel, the appeal to the nostalgia for a primeval Judaism rooted in the Orient seemed an attitude more appropriate to the makers of souvenir kitsch than to a serious art school. Schatz himself became a symbol of the sentimentality of early Zionism, a target of animosity toward Eastern European Jewry, and an object of contempt. The German art scholar Rachel Wischnitzer recalled her refusal to publish his work in the Hebrew journal *Rimon*, which she edited in the 1920s.[86] Karl Schwarz, the founder of the Tel Aviv Museum, called Schatz's "Maccabi Statue" a "pathetic knickknack that displays an over-constructed pose but is neither great nor impressive."[87] As late as 1971, Alfred Werner, while ostensibly crediting Schatz as the "father of an Israeli art," ridiculed his work mercilessly, dismissing Schatz's numerous medals with the (justifiable but gratuitous) remark that "prices [*sic*] and commissions often fell to innocuous mediocrities."[88]

Politics entered into critical assessments of Schatz. Klausner's support of Schatz related to Jewish migration: he honored Boris Schatz as the poet of the "broken soul in the Diaspora" and the "longing for our redemption," or release into Zion.[89] Schwarz and Werner, however, saw Schatz as hopelessly enmeshed in the ghetto mentality of the Galut (exile), a term Schwarz used dismissively. In the opposition of the Diaspora and the Galut, opposing lines of Zionist discourse were etched into Schatz's artwork.[90]

The reopening of the school initiated a sharp break of another kind: the school and the museum separated. The union of the two followed an established precedent of the Arts and Crafts movement.[91] The museum acquired some independence in 1925, when Mordecai Narkiss took over its management and it opened to the public as the "Jewish National Museum Bezalel in Jerusalem."[92] Narkiss, born Mordecai Potash in Austrian Galicia, had studied with Schatz at Bezalel and became his loyal assistant and ardent supporter. Like Schatz and many other artists at the school, he named his own son Bezalel, perhaps at Schatz's insistence.[93] Narkiss successfully separated the museum's fate from that of the school after its closure. He founded the Friends of the Bezalel National Museum in 1932 and reopened the museum in 1935.

Yet the differences between the museum and the school cannot be exaggerated. Supporters of both museum and school had to struggle for an equilibrium between the rhetoric of the old and new institutions. Once established, the romance of Boris Schatz's Bezalel was too powerful to be ignored; both institutions claimed the honor of being its successor, especially when fund-raising was in question.[94] Further, Joseph Budko often chose Jewish subjects in his own art (see figure 25). His teacher, Hermann Struck, remained as staunch a supporter of the New Bezalel as he had been of the old. Members of the Gesellschaft Bezalel HaChadash were promised yearly prizes, as the members of Bezalel had been in Schatz's day. While the design proposed for the first year's prize by a former teacher in the old Bezalel, Jacov Eisenberg, was rejected, an original engraving by Struck maintained a sense of continuity, even though it was printed in Germany.[95] A few former students of Bezalel, such as Ze'ev Ben-Zvi, taught at New Bezalel, establishing further continuities.

Even secular artists of New Bezalel, once in Palestine, began to explore Jewish identity. After his arrival, Ardon continued to adhere to the abstract modernism he had learned under Klee's influence at the Bauhaus but also took up a genre, that he had previously neglected, landscape painting, in order to paint the environs of Jerusalem. The rectangular, roughly horizontal brush strokes that fill Ardon's *Mount of Olives* (1938) identify the rocky landscape with the painterly surface (see frontispiece). But the distinctive rounded shape of the Pillar (or Tomb) of Absalom at its heart is more precisely delineated than the rocky slope. Its architectural details, articulated in orange and white borders, distinguish it from the expressionist green cross-hatching that dominates the painting, thereby giving the nearly abstract landscape its focal point. This focal point was distinctly Jewish, for this much-reproduced monument had distinctly inspired early Zionist artists of the Holy Land, including those of Bezalel (see figures 26 and 27). His landscapes of Kidron, Ardon wrote, represented the extent to which "the Jewish artist" changes in confrontation with the Kidron Valley: "For a change has occurred in the painter. . . . he himself, the detached, has changed and become earth, out of a first touch with the real earth of his people."[96] Later, even more explicitly, he incorporated symbols from the Kabbalah into paintings still structured on visual grammars of the international avant-garde. By then Max Bronstein had become Mordechai Ardon-Bronstein, and finally, simply Mordechai Ardon. The seal of New Bezalel, designed in the same year as Ardon's painting, expresses

וְאֶת־עֲמָלֵנוּ אֵלּוּ הַבָּנִים.
כְּמָה שֶׁנֶּאֱמַר

כָּל־הַבֵּן הַיִּלּוֹד הַיְאֹרָה תַּשְׁלִיכֻהוּ
וְכָל־הַבַּת תְּחַיּוּן׃

יב

25. Josef Budko, illustration to *Haggadah Shel Pesach* (Hebrew) (Berlin: Levitt, 1921).

26. Hermann Struck, *Tomb of Absalom*. From Adolf Friedemann, *Reisebilder aus Palästina* (Berlin: Bruno Cassirer, 1904).

27. Etrog container in the shape of Absalom's Tomb, Jerusalem, early 20th century, olive wood, carved with painted inscription, 10 x $4\frac{1}{8}$ x $4\frac{1}{8}$ in. Gift of Harry G. Friedman, F 1485. Photograph: Richard Goodbody. Courtesy of the Jewish Museum NY/Art Resource NY.

28. Eleazar Preis, seal of Bezalel HaChadash (New Bezalel), 1938. From Gideon Ofrat, *Bezalel Hachadash* (Jerusalem: Bezalel Academy of Art and Design, 1987).

a similar union of Middle Eastern tradition and Western modernity. It simplified Bezalel's Turkish Harem, making it look almost modern (see figure 28). But its shape referenced the ḥamsa, a motif in the shape of a hand frequently employed as a symbol in, and of, the Mideast.

Schatz handed over to Mordecai Narkiss a museum founded as a repository for Jewish history, for the artifacts of the Jewish Orient, and for Jewish works worldwide that could prove the existence of Jewish art. In 1930, Narkiss continued to conceive of the museum exclusively in Jewish terms as the central museum of the Jewish people.[97] He focused his early efforts on Judaica, mounting exhibits of artists like Ben-Zvi, who "grew completely from Palestinian soil."[98] A work did not have to have a Jewish subject to be Jewish. He accepted Uriel Birnbaum's illustrated *Alice in Wonderland* because he thought it "Jewish in spirit" and thus "indispensible for a library, especially when it has set itself the goal of considering Judaica in particular."[99] During World War II, Narkiss inaugurated a fund, named after Schatz, dedicated to saving threatened works of art from European countries and bringing them to Palestine. Without a school to provide artwork, however, the 266 members of the Society of the Friends of the Jewish National Museum Bezalel (the name of the association of friends of Bezalel in that year's newsletter) received, in 1941, not a decorated menorah, but Narkiss's monograph "The Artcraft of the Yeminite Jews."[100]

Other changes had to do with developments in Narkiss's understanding of nationhood. Narkiss came to conceive a national museum not as the repository of national traits, part of the quest for uniquely Jewish art, but as the treasure house of a great nation, where precious items worldwide are deposited. Not only Jewish art but great art of all peoples belonged in the central museum of the Jewish people. He reiterated this theme frequently: "Although we originally wanted to have a unique collection of Jewish art, we never had the intention to establish an exclusively Jewish Museum. Jerusalem is a city to which the whole world looks for inspiration. Jerusalem should present the art of every land."[101] He compared Bezalel to the Louvre or the National Gallery, and "just as the Washington National Gallery does not collect exclusively works of American artists, . . . so the Jewish National Museum Bezalel . . . is to gather together the artistic work of all generations and peoples, while at the same time paying special attention and stressing the creative works of its own people. . . . Only by exhibiting Jewish art of all ages, with particular reference to its continuity, will the world be enabled to recognize our contribution to universal art and our essential qualities."[102] Narkiss and his staff struck similar themes in letters requesting donations of funds or of works of art. A curator informed a prominent rabbi that "we are not only interested in works by Jewish artists. Our task is not only that of a national education but also that of opening a broader mind generally. Art in Israel is not a luxury, but part of spiritual development."[103] The rhetorical approach presupposed a Jewish national identity no longer seen in terms of its own internal cohesion and development but by virtue of its equality with and contribution to an art regarded as universal. Presumably, separation from the museum also affected the school's fund-raising. This, however, was on a smaller scale than the museum's. Furthermore, its dependence, in the 1930s, on the Department for the Settlement of German Jews makes New Bezalel look more like a Jewish rescue organization than a school, especially after 1939, when the school encountered significant obstacles in obtaining visas for its students.[104]

Personal ties, as well, bound the institutions, who were friendly neighbors for much of their history. Mordecai Ardon found in Mordecai Narkiss a friendly supporter immediately upon his emigration, and the two became close friends.[105] Under Ardon's directorship Narkiss taught a weekly course in the history of Hebrew script at New Bezalel.[106] Both Mordecais had already transformed their heritage in response to new visions of nationhood.

The successors of these institutions only intensified the changes begun in 1935. What was first the Bezalel School of Arts and Crafts and then Bezalel HaChadash (New Bezalel) is now the Bezalel Academy. While the Academy shares with its earliest forebear its renown for silversmithing and has reclaimed Lilien's design as its seal, its international reputation rests not on its ability to supply souvenirs of Jewish art to Zionists but on its ability to compete in an international marketplace (see figures 17 and 29). Having grappled with the move from the "international style" to "multinational capitalism," only a few aspects of the instruction, such as its Rosenthal Competition on the subject of Judaica, distinguish it from other art academies. Since the mid-1980s, it has been located in new buildings near the Mount Scopus Campus of

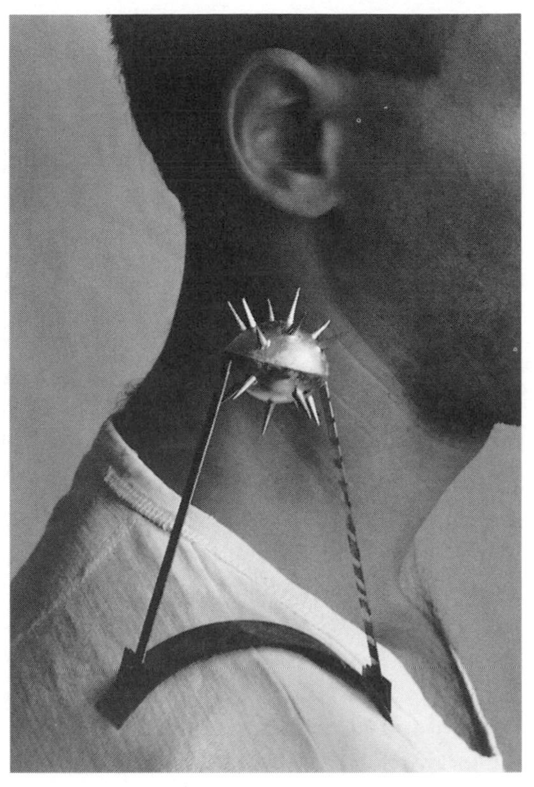

29. Student work, Gold and Silversmithing Department, Bezalel Academy, 1985. From *Bezalel Academy of Art and Design Jerusalem* (Jerusalem: Bezalel, Department of Public Relations, 1982).

Hebrew University, leaving the Turkish Harem to adult education and an adjoining art gallery.[107] It remains a rite of passage for many Israeli artists.

The successor to the Bezalel Museum has departed even more sharply from the ideals of Bezalel. The Israel Museum unites the former Bezalel collection with an archaeological museum, a youth wing, a shrine for the Dead Sea Scrolls, and a sculpture garden. Far from fostering exclusively Jewish art, the Bezalel Wing initially paid little attention to either Israeli or Jewish art, only opening a pavilion for Israeli art in 1985.[108] It barely acknowledges its past as the Bezalel Museum or the contribution of Mordechai Narkiss.[109] Instead, the Israel Museum seeks to serve as a center for the collections of a nation, Israel, whose diversity and divisiveness it must confront or reject. This is not the place for a complex exposition of contemporary Israeli art, but exhibitions of the Israel Museum interrogate both Jewish and Israeli identities.[110] An exhibition in honor of the fiftieth anniversary of the founding of the Israeli state, *To the East: Orientalism in the Arts in Israel,* has been cited as an example of Edward Said's influence on Israeli discourse.[111] The exhibit illustrates the way in which Israeli diversity transcends the homogeneity envisioned even by such titles as *One Nation out of Many Peoples,* an exhibit mounted at the Bezalel Museum in 1953, after five years of statehood. While the Bezalel School of Arts and Crafts, in its Orientalist trappings, makes an appearance in *To the East* as part of Israel's prehistory, most recent work in the exhibition grapples with Israel's relations with its Arab population. Wall copy announced with regret the refusal of Arab Israelis to participate in the exhibition.[112] Of course, many of the artists in the show studied at the Bezalel Academy. Yet one could almost say that the exhibit *To the East* is about the struggle, and the failure, to overcome a notion of Jewish art beholden to the ethnic definition of nationhood that brought Bezalel, and Israel, into being.

Nation without Boundaries: Jerusalem, Capital of Jewish Art

The Bezalel Academy and the Israel Museum are focused on their mission to the nation of Israel. Israeli identity, however, has the added strain of having to serve Jews elsewhere, who focus their dreams on the Jewish state without having to live there. A third institution that "descended" from the original Bezalel takes its point of departure from this fact. After Mordecai Narkiss's death in 1957, Bezalel Narkiss decided to follow his father's career path and become an art historian. The management of the Bezalel Museum sent him to study art history in London, in hopes of having him take over the museum. Returning to Israel in 1963 to find his father's museum disbanded, he lectured at Hebrew University in Jerusalem and, in 1974, founded the *Journal of Jewish Art*. Published initially in Chicago by the Spertus College of Judaica, the journal moved to Jerusalem in 1978, when Narkiss founded the Center for Jewish Art at the Hebrew University.

One of its projects is the *Index of Jewish Art*, which emulates the *Index of Christian Art* at Princeton University, founded in 1917 by Charles Rufus Morey.[113] Bezalel Narkiss cited his father's exhibit *One Nation Out of Many Peoples* as initiating "the first attempts to document the visual art of the different Jewish ethnic groups."[114] A comparison between the *Index* and this exhibition, which took place five years after the establishment of the State of Israel, however, shows the differences between the younger and the older Narkiss's concept of Jewish peoplehood conceived internationally. *One Nation* celebrated the diverse ethnic origins of the people comprising the New State of Israel, "the arts and crafts expression of the various 'peoples' or 'communities' which through historic compulsion lived in the Diaspora and now that they are becoming rooted in Israel, might evolve into One Nation."[115] The Zionist goal of nation building centrally involved this effort to link the art of disparate peoples in a common Jewish experience, and the catalog even warned of the "possible dangers of unintegrated groups to national unity."[116] To identify a visual unity in Hebrew, as Richard I. Cohen has pointed out, meant to expend great effort to provide exact art historical descriptions in a language with no precedent for such work.[117] The "nation" addressed by Bezalel Narkiss's project, however, was the diverse international community of Jews, few of them resident in Israel, but for whom Jerusalem is the center of Jewish life internationally conceived.

As tireless a proselytizer as Mordecai Narkiss and nearly as indefatigable a traveler as Boris Schatz, Bezalel Narkiss has proved cognizant of the significance for Jewish identity of the various projects of his Center for Jewish Art. The center operates with several heuristic concepts of Jewish artistic identity. Its publication *Journal of Jewish Art* has preferred not to define its topic but broadens its boundaries to include articles about artists who rejected or ignored their Jewish origins, and Jewish stereotypes in the work of artists who were not Jewish at all.[118] The *Index of Jewish Art,* however, calls for a narrower definition. It postulates religion as the determining characteristic of the community. Thanking Israel's chief rabbi for his support, Narkiss affirms that "Jewish Art in this context refers to objects made for the use and appreciation of people living according to the Jewish tradition, in their ritual and everyday life, including artifacts created by non-Jewish artists."[119] Identity and religion are intertwined in the mission statement: "The survey was motivated by the assumption that the knowledge of Jewish visual culture, eastern and western alike, will develop Jewish identity and will contribute to the growth of a sense of beauty, in order to interpret and create beautiful artifacts in the constant tradition of 'This is my God and I will beautify Him.' "[120] The most controversial aspect of Narkiss's definition of Jewish art, its declaration that Jews can deepen their identity by studying works that were not made by Jews, meant that Narkiss (unlike scholars of Judaica on the model of those discussed in the following chapter) did not need to prove that Jewish manuscripts were illuminated by Jews.

The Center for Jewish Art engages a wider view of Jewish identity than can be encompassed by the nation of Israel. Therefore, in revisiting the attempt to define Jewish art, Narkiss has produced notions of Jewish art capable of slicing through borders in different ways, creating overlapping nonidentical "identities" that connect and articulate diverse, cosmopolitan populations. The unity of "Jewish art" conceived this way depends on the position of Jerusalem not as its origin or its goal but as its center. It seeks to serve, for art, the same role that Israel seeks to serve for the "Jewish community" as a whole, conceptually creating the population that it maintains. The center's recent book *Ingathering of the Nations: Treasures of Jewish Art: Documenting an Endangered Legacy* produced, like the Israel Museum's exhibit *To the East,* in honor of the fiftieth anniversary of the State of Israel, brought the far-flung Jewish community together. The book "gathers" images from nine countries into a space between ancient Israel, which begins the book, and modern Israel, which ends it. In *Ingathering,* unlike in *To the East,* the Orientalist trappings of Bezalel disproportionately represent Israel. Of the five Israeli illustrations, two are by Ze'ev Raban (one is on the cover).[121] Bezalel still stands for Israeli art in this most loyal of its offspring.

Bezalel and its heirs all affirm the right of Jews to possess art, even in the service of religion, a tenet central to Zionist practice. Israeli books on modern and contemporary Jewish art seldom dwell on the Second Commandment.[122] When Israeli scholars write about the Second Commandment in the context of the history of Jewish art, the reference often introduces a discussion of religious architecture and its role as a visual symbol of Judaism.[123] Israeli art historians were among the first to claim the paintings in the synagogue at Dura-Europos, discovered in 1932, as definitive examples of Jewish art. Concepts of Jewish art conformed to different conceptions of Israeli nationhood that they helped to build, whether this was seen as grounded in the biblical land of Israel or as a modern nation among nations. The vision that Schatz founded, that of a symbolist art inspired by the Bible and one with the soil of the ancestral Jewish homeland, developed into an art school where art now helps a nation to compete in an era of international capital, a museum where a national Israeli art has begun to gesture toward a postcolonial, multiethnic concept of nationhood, and a Center for Jewish Art, which encourages the Diaspora to view Jerusalem as the center where its heritage is preserved, studied, and created.

All of these manifestations of nationhood need art because they assume that art constitutes the nation. But how does art constitute the nation? Certainly ideas about what a nation is affect the notion of who can contribute to the formation of its art. If a nation is thought to be created through institutions and education, the possibility that anyone can contribute to its art is open, because the art and the people are constructed together through their own efforts; the nation is created by those who want it to come into being. If the nation is thought to grow organically from the blood of its people and the soil of its homeland, then anyone already a foreigner must remain so and must be conceptually excluded from its art. These ideas are not pure, and in some places, such as Palestine, both positions were in play at the same moment.[124] Just as the art of the people of ancient Israel was Jewish art because it could be cited to create the typology known as Jewish art, so the art of modern Israel was Jewish art only insofar as Israel is seen as a homogeneously Jewish nation.

But even where art does play a role in constituting the nation, how can art be said to represent the nation? If a nation is understood as having a soul, must art express it, recognizably describing the nation to an onlooker? Or is a corporate understanding of a nation possible, where the nation simply possesses enough art, an artistic gross national product that is sufficiently high, or of a sufficiently high quality, to win respect from other, similar nations with similar standards? In other words, must Israeli art look Israeli, or must it look like art?

Under its different guises and names, Bezalel has grappled with each of these possibilities. The history of Bezalel, then, can illustrate the role of art in building a nation-state. But I did not choose Israel to begin my explorations of responses to the paradigm of Jewish art in order to end it there. Caught in competing nationalist paradigms of art, Bezalel raises more questions than it can answer. The founding of a nation did not provide an authoritative concept of Jewish art. Therefore, unlike a certain strain of modern Jewish narrative, which ends redemptively in Palestine or Israel, the present narrative will carry on and investigate other answers.[125]

PART TWO

Reclaiming Jewish Art

Wo immer auf der Welt Juden sind, oder wo sie zu gewissen Zeiten waren, wird ihrer künstlerischen Thätigkeit nachzuspüren, diese im Bild zu sammeln sein.
[Wherever there are Jews in the world, or wherever they were at certain times, there their artistic activity should be traced and an image of it assembled.] **Heinrich Frauberger**

CHAPTER THREE

David Kaufmann's Studies in Jewish Art

Die (Kunst)Wissenschaft des Judentums

Industriousness and great learning were always at home in Judaism. Not so artistic discernment, which in the pressure of the centuries more often had to give way to the opposite tendency toward a corruption of taste. Only through [his] dominant artistic sense did Kaufmann become that which he was often described as being: a Jew at heart, a Hellene in form. Theology and philosophy he could learn from the Jews. His love of art could only have been inborn. In order to develop his aesthetic discernment, however, he had to learn from the Hellenes. **Samuel Krauß** in *David Kaufmann: Eine Biographie*

The Second Commandment Revisited: Die Wissenschaft des Judentums

Zionists in Palestine may have ignored or defied the established discourse on the absence of Jewish art, but in Europe, the discourse of the absence of Jewish art extended far beyond the confines of academia proper to affect art critics, museum officials, and gallery owners. Avowed anti-Semites were not the only scholars to pursue it. Jews themselves posited the absence of Jewish art centrally within the structure of art history. A critic wishing to defend a contemporary Jewish artist such as Max Liebermann would have had to cope with his own misgivings about the art of the ancient Israelites. Georg Hermann, celebrating Liebermann in a book on Jewish artists, found it appropriate to bring the foreign builders of Solomon's temple into the discussion: "Let us consider that there is no Jewish art. Indeed, perhaps there never was a Jewish art. Solomon, after all, obtained Sidonian carpenters to build the Temple."[1] Jews, then, internalized the discourse of Jewish art and, perhaps most significantly, embraced the iconophobic interpretation of the Second Commandment.

The growing discipline of Jewish studies in the nineteenth century could have been expected to sweep aside such prejudices, as it did so many others, at least among Jews. Jews themselves had not been the first to pursue studies of their own past. Italian Humanists such as Pico della Mirandola had begun to advocate the study of Hebrew by the middle of the fifteenth century.[2] By the end of the sixteenth century, knowledge of Hebrew had spread to theologians north of the Alps, pioneered by Johannes Reuchlin, and Hebrew was well-established in Christian theology departments. The rise of comparative linguistics and critical philology in the nineteenth century gave it a new impetus, beginning with Wilhelm Gesenius.[3] Christian theologians and historians, however, interpreted the Jewish past from their own, often unsympathetic points of view. Some scholarship was directed at the conversion of Jews, as in Franz Delitzsch's Institutum Judaicum in Leipzig, founded in 1886, while other, such as that of Paul Anton de Lagarde (1827–91), of the University of Göttingen, was openly anti-Semitic.

As a result of emancipation in the late eighteenth century, Jewish history began to capture the interest of academically minded Jews as well.[4] Emancipation also encouraged religious Jews to seek a rapprochement between traditional Judaism and modernity, and between Jewish and secular culture, giving birth to the Reform, Conservative, and Neo-Orthodox movements. Beginning in Germany and spreading elsewhere, Jews studied their own history and remade their religious practices and beliefs to adjust to their own changing circumstances and in response to Christian objections to Jewish practices.[5]

National ideas figured in both these endeavors. The Reform movement in Judaism grew up simultaneously with the development of art history as discussed above and was in part conditioned by the same need to come to grips with nationalism. When the first art historical surveys implanted the image of the antiartistic Jew into the scholarship of art history during the early decades of the nineteenth century, Jews were not numerous in cultural life. Over the course of the following decades, however, Jewish participation in the cultural and social life of European countries increased.[6] Jews experienced conflicts as their concept of their own national affiliation accordingly changed. The desire for, and later experience of, emancipation demanded allegiance to the national entities in which Jews found themselves. Many of them began to repeat with less than wholehearted enthusiasm the desire, whose recitation prayer books demanded daily, to return to the biblical land of Israel (it was omitted from the German translation of some prayer books beginning in 1815).[7] These conflicting national allegiances provided Reform Judaism with an early focus.

Nationalism worsened the already difficult dilemma of reconciling conflicts between demanding Jewish practice and the customs of surrounding contemporary Christian societies. Jewish modernizers, even when they began to drop references to the return to Israel from new liturgies, still had to face the resistance of contemporary societies to Jewish expressions of European patriotism. Many Christians thought Judaism a "nation within a nation," irreconcilable with loyalty to the state.[8] Jews and Christians alike sometimes used a term, "host state," which treats Jews as guests in their native lands.[9] Reformists grappled with competing views among European Jewry as well, with denotations such as "spiritual nationality," "denomination" (Confession), or "religious community," each carrying different consequences.[10] Early Zionism, too, perpetrated a sharp divide, threatening the progress of acculturation. "We are first and foremost Germans, Frenchmen, Englishmen, Americans - only then Jews," proclaimed a hostile reviewer of *Rom und Jerusalem*, the early Zionist manifesto published in 1862 by Moses Hess.[11]

Reformists and those allied with them sought not only to remedy the exclusion of Jews from European nationalities, understood as the right to belong in European spaces, but also to gain for Jews admittance into European time. To many of their fellow citizens, the Jewish religion represented an ahistorical entity. Some governments had a vested interest in keeping Judaism mired in an outworn past; they resisted allowing Judaism to resemble Christianity too closely. Other governments legislated mandatory change as though in an effort to make Judaism disappear.[12] The reformists had to find a way to remain Jews and yet become Europeans, to adapt to the present while retaining the Jewish religion's ties to tradition. One response to Christian hostility was to argue that Judaism was a pure source of the universality claimed by Christians. Judaism's mission, to represent monotheism in a pure form, was thus vital to Christianity.[13] Others, sensitive to the age's obsession with historical development, sought to delineate the ways in which the Jewish religion, like the Christian, had never ceased to develop and grow in response to changing circumstances.[14]

Like the Jewish Reform movement, the scholarly movement known as the *Wissenschaft des Judentums* (science of Judaism) addressed itself to a dual audience, within and outside of the Jewish community. To the Christian environment, the scholars sought to make Judaism palatable by explaining it in terms close to those of the surrounding scholarly environment. The term "Wissenschaft" (science, or scholarship) signaled their desire to conform to the latest trends in German scholarship.[15] Jews could win the support of German scholars by resembling them and refute anti-Semitic libel using methods that Christian scholars would have to accept. In an early manuscript, Leopold Zunz, the father of modern Jewish historical studies, extolled this potential of the Wissenschaft des Judentums for battling the prejudices of anti-Semitism.[16] Jewish scholars self-consciously pursued acceptance through both subject matter and form. One of them, writing at the end of the century, described the priorities this way: "First was to solidify firmly the proof of the link between the general culture and Jewish culture, hence general literature and Jewish literature. Secondly was, in form and in literary style, that is, in externals, to maintain the same level as scholarship in other areas."[17]

These efforts at combating Christian prejudices were aimed at recommending the Wissenschaft des Judentums to the increasingly acculturated and therefore historically minded Jewish intelligentsia. To Jews whose secular education had previously exposed them only to the Christian notion that the Jewish contribution to history had come to an end, it offered a positive interpretation of Judaism's place in history. If the Reform movement was called, by one of its leaders, "an alliance against apostasy," the same could be said for the historical study of Judaica.[18] Presumably, if a secular education was not to turn Jews into Christians, Jews would have to provide it.

Jewish self-justification corresponded to the historical justifications that Christians, too, sought to understand and justify their religion. Both the Wissenschaft des Judentums and the Christian historical understanding were outgrowths of historicism and, like historicism, were products of, and reactions to, the Enlightenment.[19] Because of its roots in the project of integration into European culture, however, the Wissenschaft des Judentums, unlike its mainstream European counterpart, rarely associated its aims with nationalism. Few of its proponents initially welcomed Zionism. Heinrich Graetz was among the exceptions.[20] Many remained aloof from religious considerations as well. While Abraham Geiger remained loyal to radical religious reform, some of its practitioners, such as Leopold Zunz, eventually disassociated themselves from reform; still others, such as Moritz Steinschneider, sought to disassociate the scholarship of Judaica from theological considerations altogether.[21] Both positions only added to its aura of scholarly disinterestedness.

Its distinguished scholarship, and its appropriation of German scholarly methods, however, could not win for the Wissenschaft des Judentums total acceptance in the mainstream academic community. By 1842, when Kugler wrote his survey, Jewish emancipation was well under way. The Jewish presence in cultural life had begun to make an impact. Jews attended universities in increasing numbers. None, however, at least in Kugler's Prussia, had been allowed to rise even to the rank of *Privatdozent*, the lowest academic post.[22] Even where universities welcomed individual Jews into their ranks, academia continued to exclude Jewish studies, although Christian theology and studies of Christianity were firmly established.[23] The first professorship in Jewish history "in the Western world" was established at Columbia University in New York in 1930.[24]

In the absence of opportunities to specialize in Judaic studies in universities, the scholars associated with the Wissenschaft des Judentums remained marginalized in academia. Its practitioners generally received rabbinical training as well as a university education. Since their Jewish-oriented specialties left them without hope of academic employment in a university, they found other occupations, shepherding congregations or teaching in rabbinical schools, which took part in moderate Jewish reforms. While the scholars often had an impact within these professions, the limited presence of Judaic studies in universities is significant because by the middle of the nineteenth century, scholarship had begun to require the legitimating stamp of university affiliation.[25]

Opportunities were no better in art history. By the 1870s, individual scholars of Jewish heritage, when properly baptized, could attain professorial chairs in most fields. The first unbaptized Jewish professor of art history, however, was Adolph Goldschmidt, who occupied the chair in Halle beginning only in 1904, and in Berlin from 1912.[26] Even the elevation of Jewish scholars to the rank of professor did not produce legitimization for Jewish art, however, since academia did not tend to become the site of a reconsideration of Jewish art. While other respectable outlets, such as museums or private institutes, afforded opportunities to art historical scholars, these institutes, too, ignored the subject for decades. Although the Warburg Institute, founded by Aby Warburg, would be important in saving the lives of Jewish scholars, for example, its journal published few studies of Jewish art.[27] The Villa I Tatti, founded by Bernard Berenson in Florence, played host to Jewish graduate students among others, but it, too, did not notably foster Jewish studies.[28]

The marginalization of those interested in Jewish art accorded with the marginalization of scholars of the Wissenschaft des Judentums generally. There was, however, another obstacle in the way of a reevaluation of the concept of Jewish art: the hostility to it of practitioners of the Wissenschaft des Judentums. While many of them fought diligently for the establishment of departments of Judaica, no one even suggested that art history departments fill art historical chairs with specialists in Jewish art. This is perhaps unsurprising, since chairs for art historians in universities were themselves still somewhat of a novelty until relatively late in the nineteenth century. More compelling, however, is the fact that their freedom from academic constraints could have given scholars of the Wissenschaft des Judentums the ability to address Jewish art seriously had they so desired. But they did not. Even for these scholars, the national structure of art history remained intact. To accept Jewish art, they would have had to address the same assumptions about the importance of national styles and the absence of Jewish art that kept their professional counterparts from pursuing Jewish subjects.

In the main, then, the Wissenschaft des Judentums was not more hospitable toward the idea of Jewish art than was the culture at large. Gershom Scholem suggested that, with the exception of Leopold Zunz and Moritz Steinschneider, the tendency to spiritualize Judaism, under the influence of German Romanticism and Jewish theology, kept the scholars from the study of collective expressions.[29] Scholem does not mention visual art among these expressions, but even Zunz vacillated on the subject. In 1818, reviewing the many contributions that Jews had made to culture that deserve inclusion in the curriculum of a science of Judaism, he ventured to mention art, albeit tentatively in a footnote. "An aficionado could gather some material even on painting and embroidery, at least in modern times," he ventured.[30] Yet in another early programmatic statement, he omitted painting and did so, even according to one modern commentator, "wisely."[31]

Other scholars embraced wholeheartedly the Christian claim that Jews lacked the capacity for the visual arts. Not that the Wissenschaft des Judentums ignored art altogether. Instead, as Kalman Bland has shown in detail, it used the lack of Jewish art, and the Second Commandment that seemed to forbid it, to put Jews on an equal footing with iconoclastic, Protestant Germans.[32] It also separated them from other "Orientals." Moritz Güdemann, the chief rabbi of Vienna, took an interest in art. Nevertheless he could exhibit the Jewish rejection of images as evidence of Jewish spirituality: the more exalted the idea of

God, the narrower the boundaries of art.[33] While rejecting racial theories commonly used to explain Jewish artistic failings, Güdemann also took care to distinguish Jews from other "Orientals" and bring them closer to Germans. He quoted Heinrich Heine, approvingly, as saying that "one could look upon the former Palestine as an Oriental Germany."[34]

The heart of such arguments was that the rejection of images supported a Jewish claim central to the Wissenschaft des Judentums: the claim to bear the standard of monotheism in a pure form. Transforming incompetence into virtue, Heinrich Graetz, the historian who brought the Wissenschaft des Judentums to fruition in his vast synthetic history of Judaism, ascribed the gap between the Hebrews' alleged artistic inadequacies and the Greeks' undeniable artistic ability to their differing religious outlooks. His comparison was not objective. In forceful language, his early essay "The Structure of Jewish History" attributes Greek artistic ability, focused on representing the physical charms of their anthropomorphic gods, specifically to "idolatry and immorality."[35] The philosopher Hermann Cohen cited the Second Commandment to argue similarly, although less explicitly sexually, that monotheism explained why Jews were less gifted in the visual arts than the ancient Greeks.[36] While beginning to admit the possibility of art, the prominent reform rabbi Kaufmann Kohler fleshed out these arguments in graphic detail by contrasting the "sense of chastity" of the Jews, and their desire to "lift God above the realm of the sensual and corporeal," to their lewd suspicions of the heathen, including Greeks, who were said "to go a whoring" and have "sexual intercourse with beasts."[37] The implications of these arguments are uncompromising: if Christians deride Jews for not making art, Jews could retort that if Christians were really the monotheists they claimed to be, they would not produce art either.

Jewish scholars, then, could turn the Christian disdain for Jewish art against Christians. The notion that pious Jews cannot, and should not, produce art, became a source of pride. When Güdemann urged Jews to abandon the eclectic, borrowed designs previously favored and to adopt instead a properly Jewish design for houses of worship, he proposed a dome, modeled after the heavens and allowing light to flow in. "Mystical darkness," he added, in an implied reproach to the enthusiasm for mysticism that was already beginning to flourish at the turn of the century as he spoke, "should be avoided in any case. For in the synagogue, nothing mystical happens."[38] Nothing mystical, and apparently very little artistic. Light might stream in, but not in order to illuminate art.

An Appendix on Jewish Art

The arguments developed by scholars of the Wissenschaft des Judentums discouraged serious consideration of Jewish art for decades. But by the time Moritz Güdemann spoke, the situation had already changed. He made his comments on the rational nature of the Jewish religion in a venue that fostered Jewish art: the journal of the newly founded Gesellschaft für Sammlung und Conservirung von Kunst- und historischen Denkmäler des Judenthums (Society for the Collection and Conservation of Jewish Artistic and Historical Monuments).[39] His article, which sought to find a place for art in Jewish life, appeared the same year as the first major scholarly appreciation of a Jewish work of art, Julius von Schlosser's edition of the Haggadah of Sarajevo, a work funded by the society.[40] The society and Güdemann's article were part of an effort within Judaism to make art into an arena in which Judaism could position itself within modern culture. These efforts demonstrate that despite the hostility of Jewish and Christian scholars alike, some Jewish writers did seek to remove the Second Commandment as a barrier between their culture and the Christian and to reconceive Jewish art for modern artistic circles. These efforts are paradigmatic of other attempts to insert Judaism into modernity.

For reasons that must by now be evident, the first scholars to make serious attempts to proselytize for a change in attitude toward Jewish art, in the late-nineteenth and early-twentieth centuries, necessarily had to do so from outside the academy. They were not professional art historians in university departments of art history or in museums. Rather, they came from other fields, with primary loyalty not to art but to Judaism. They aimed primarily at an audience of Jewish intellectuals, especially art collectors, and accordingly confined many of their writings to Jewish literary journals or Zionist publications. Like the scholars who originated the Wissenschaft des Judentums on the basis of modern scholarship, theorists of Jewish art remade their subject in the image of a recognizable artistic discourse. This endeavor was made all the more difficult by the fact that in encountering the established discourse, Jewish art found a subject for which, as we have seen, its own absence was foundational.

One of the first such efforts was found in Schlosser's and Müller's edition of the Sarajevo Haggadah, in its appendix on the history of Jewish manuscript illumination. It was written by David Kaufmann (1852–1899), an outstanding exponent of the Wissenschaft des Judentums. Kaufmann, an ordained rabbi, received his education at the Breslau Rabbinical School, founded by Zacharias Frankel, a reformer generally considered the founder of Conservative Judaism.[41] While he supported only moderate reforms in worship and ritual, Frankel was devoted to combining secular with religious learning. His school required its students to seek a secular education at a university as well as to complete rabbinical studies. Accordingly, Kaufmann's teachers included both Heinrich Graetz and the philosopher of hermeneutics Wilhelm Dilthey. After completion of his studies, Kaufmann befriended the elderly Leopold Zunz, to whom he dedicated sermons he gave in competition for the vacant rabbinate in Berlin. He received his doctorate in Leipzig in 1874 and completed his rabbinical training in Breslau in 1877. That same year, having been rejected by the Jewish authorities in Berlin for his conservatism in religious matters, he was appointed to the newly constituted, state-sponsored Landesrabbinerschule in Budapest, a position he retained until the end of his life.[42]

An obituary described Kaufmann's combination of secularism and conservative religiosity: "He whose spirit was drenched in the concepts of philosophy, for whom the development of human culture in all phases and branches lay open, modern through and through, a critic and prober of the past, the greatest sorrow that he felt in his sick bed was that he did not have the strength to lay tefillim in order to say his morning prayers properly."[43] This duality served him well in the Landesrabbinerschule, modeled after the seminary in Breslau, where Kaufmann continued to divide his time between the secular and the sacred. In its gymnasium, he taught classic German literature; in its seminary, Jewish philosophy.[44] His voluminous scholarly output includes works on medieval Jewish philosophy, Hebrew and Arabic philology, and the religious and secular history of the Jews, including many genealogical studies.[45] It also contains studies of secular literature. Some, although not all, pertained to Jewish issues, most notably his essay "George Eliot and Judaism" on George Eliot's novel *Daniel Deronda*.[46]

Kaufmann was the first dedicated proponent of the study of Jewish art. He embarked on his art historical scholarship without even touching on the ethnological and racial considerations that most art historians deemed necessary to the topic. He did, however, directly address the assumption, promulgated by his fellow practitioners of the Wissenschaft des Judentums, that the Second Commandment prevented Jews from making images. His refutation of this assumption, which was not theoretical but historical, appeared in the London *Jewish Quarterly Review* and, expanded, in the first report of the Vienna Society for the Collection and Conservation of Artistic and Historical Monuments of Jewry, an organization in whose founding he participated.

In these essays, Kaufmann surveyed Jewish thought from Josephus to Maimonides to show that, throughout history, Jewish thinkers who objected to images did not tend to do so on the basis of the Second Commandment. His strategy generally involved the equation of Jewish with Christian thinkers. Rabbinical exhortations to the abolition of images from the synagogue resembled outbursts concerning art in the church, for example. "Just as one does not wish to toss Tertullian and Eusebius among the Barbarians because of their deep-rooted rejection of all art, one ought not to use individual rabbinical statements about the removal of all images from places of worship as proof of this alleged Jewish abhorrence of the world of beauty."[47] Responsa and other arguments that justified images in the temple, or mandated their absence, usually did so for other than scriptural reasons. The distracting influence of such images, he argues, was the primary excuse for banning them.[48] He disarmed one such prohibition by pointing out that it applied only to new ornament and did not mandate removing previously existing ornament. But even where the hostility to images was real enough, he argued that this hostility should be considered in individual, local terms. Christian analogues existed here as well:

> In spite of the many interpretations attempted by commentators, the thirty-sixth canon of the Council of Elvira, expressly prohibiting pictures being affixed to the walls of the churches, cannot be explained away. But as in this case a local spirit of opposition to imagery, finding expression in this prohibition,

may be assumed, so the Rabbinical condemnation of art in the synagogue, pronounced in the Middle Ages, and occasionally being pronounced even at the present time, must not at once be considered as general, but should be judged of from local and individual points of view.[49]

Having shown that the Second Commandment did not ban images, Kaufmann proceeded to demonstrate the existence of likenesses in the temple. To do so, he cited rabbinical arguments that favored the placement of lions below the ark. In fact, according to Kaufmann, practical considerations weighed more heavily than theoretical ones, with the result that lions often appeared even above the ark.[50] The version of the essay published for the Society for the Collection and Conservation of Artistic and Historical Monuments of Jewry went further than this in response to the need to defend the use of the term "artistic" in the title, which echoed that of the state commission on historical preservation, the Commission for the Conservation of Artistic and Historical Monuments. Accordingly, that version of the essay concluded triumphantly by discussing the interiors of several Polish synagogues, richly decorated with representational designs.[51]

Complementing his historical proof that the Second Commandment did not prohibit art, Kaufmann sought to prove historically the existence of Jewish artists. He began this work in 1891, when he brought to light documentary corroboration of the existence of an Italian Jewish painter of the early sixteenth century, Moses Castellazzo. Kaufmann not only described Castellazzo as a portrait painter of high standing but pointed to evidence that Castellazzo had at least planned illustrations for a Pentateuch, thus showing the artist's willingness to introduce art into a religious context.[52] Later scholars in fact discovered a version of this illustrated Bible and published it in facsimile (see figure 30).[53] These efforts to document Jewish artists resulted in his collaboration on the edition of the Sarajevo Haggadah. His boyhood friend, David Heinrich Müller, a philologist at the University of Vienna who edited the Sarajevo Haggadah with the art historian Julius von Schlosser, probably arranged for Kaufmann's participation in the project. The tone of Kaufmann's appendix contrasted dramatically with Schlosser's essay. Kaufmann neither speculated about the racial makeup of Jewish communities nor impugned the creativity of the Jews. Instead, as though blithely unconscious of the reflections being made elsewhere in the

30. *The Akeda* (Sacrifice of Isaac). Picture bible of Moses dal Castellazzo, folio 26, early 16th century. Formerly in the collection of the Jewish Historical Institute, Warsaw. Courtesy of the Getty Research Library.

volume about the lack of originality in Jewish art and its possible racial basis, Kaufmann celebrated the originality and freshness of many of the manuscripts he studied: "Animal ornament as well as vegetal ornament reveal the hand of a master, and especially in their highly original combinations."[54] His rhetoric often evoked not only borrowings from but friendly rivalry with the Christian environment of the artists: "By no means satisfied anymore by the representations of such harmless models as the figures of animals and birds, soon they recognized no more limits before which one must halt, and enjoyed competing with the boldest Gothic in high-spirited dragon fights and extravagant diabolical caricatures."[55]

As the passage suggests, Kaufmann assumed that medieval manuscript painting progressed toward individuality, natural observation, and liveliness. The approach echoes the arguments of other scholars of his day, who were also interested in locating early signs of artistic naturalism in medieval art.[56] Indeed, his proof that the manuscripts were illuminated by Jews, rather than Christians working for hire, depended not only on codicological sources (the scribes claimed the illustrations, along with the text, as their own) but on artistic and religious proof as well that accords with the theory of medieval naturalism: "The illustrations of my two-volume Machzor manuscript in Octave, completed in Pesaro in 1481, exude such an intimate knowledge of the ceremonial of the synagogue, whose individual aspects they represent, that the Jewish origin of this masterwork of miniature painting seems assured for that reason alone."[57] The very accuracy of the depiction of the rites served Kaufmann as an indication of the presence of Jewish artists. His concern to show the participation of Jewish artists, which differentiates Kaufmann from, for example, Bezalel Narkiss, is entirely due to his embattled position as a proponent of the art of a nation supposed to be without it, a position that Narkiss, centered in Jerusalem, does not occupy.[58]

Kaufmann's rhetoric also supports his main theme: that the illustrations were made by the scribes, who welcomed the relative freedom they offered from the strictures that normally circumscribed them when they wrote the text.[59] The freedom offered by this relaxation of constraints contrasted to the very real difficulties under which the artist-scribes worked. He occasionally dramatized his discussion of these triumphs over artistic constraints with reference to constraints emanating from another source: "A selflessness [*Opferfreudigkeit*] that did not know how to let up, seemed to extend the bounds of the art, which the outrage of religious persecution, the catastrophe of Jewish expulsion, only too often interrupted in the performance of its task."[60]

In his effort to show that Jews illustrated their own manuscripts, Kaufmann discussed occasions where Christians collaborated with Jews. Since these moments when a Christian became involved with Jewish illuminations were noted in the texts themselves with pride, Jewish manuscripts must generally have been illustrated by Jews.[61] Elsewhere, he sought to claim Jewish sources for Christian art, identifying, for example, Jewish liturgical, if not artistic, sources for the imagery of the Roman catacombs.[62] Christian art related to Jewish art, he noted, similar to the way early Christian liturgy related to that of the Jews: abandoned and forgotten aspects of Jewish liturgy lived on in the rites of the Early Christians.[63] Such reflections, which threatened to blur the boundaries between Judaism and early Christianity, served to refute the charge that Jews did not make art.

They did not, however, prove the existence of Jewish art. The interpenetration of Jews and Christians in his methodology meant that he had to contend with a narrative problem that still faces scholars writing about Jewish art today. This is nowhere more true than in his lengthy and complex study of manuscript painting. He sought to preserve Jewish art as his subject, yet he addressed Jewish art within national boundaries and in relation to art conceived on national lines. Thus he held two narratives simultaneously in play. Within each section, he divided his discussion into national groups, pausing to demonstrate that Jews had contributed to Italian and to Dutch art. Even so, however, he primarily sought to tell one story about Jewish art, not several stories about German, Italian, or Spanish art. Therefore, his overall structure was divided into categories of manuscripts, tracing separate developments of Haggadah, Machzor, and other genres. The result is repetitious and disjointed.

Certainly, Kaufmann was limited by his lack of expertise in art historical scholarship (*Kunstwissenschaft*). He failed to recognize (or at least to point out) the Christian origins of the well-known motifs in some manuscripts, such as the representation of winter as an old man warming himself by the fire, which appears in Christian calendar illustrations that themselves borrowed pagan motifs.[64] Yet his exposition suffered from a rhetorical difficulty as well: the difficulty of making Jewish art equal to Christian art while keeping it different. He concentrated his efforts on proving its existence. But he could only validate it with reference to an attractive resemblance to normative (Christian) art. In a discourse of art based on nationalism, it was not enough to prove that Jews participated in art making.[65] To leave Jewish art indistinctive in this fashion, whether intentionally or not, erased it exactly where he wished to prove its existence. He was trapped by the national paradigm.

The Cosmopolitan Nationality

Kaufmann probably regarded the prejudice against Jewish art as essentially the same as other manifestations of anti-Semitism, since the strategy that he employed against it – that is, the practice of validating Jewish qualities and achievements by equating them with Christian qualities – was essentially the one applied to most objects of anti-Semitism by practitioners of the Wissenschaft des Judentums. Certainly the Second Commandment, shared by the two religions, could be seen as a unifying principle, since to accept it would seem to risk an iconophobic interpretation. But Kaufmann had honed the strategy of equating Jews and Christians for years in both secular and popular journals, in pamphlets and newspapers, where he battled outspokenly against anti-Semitism and fought for the academic recognition of the Wissenschaft des Judentums. Failure to acknowledge the Wissenschaft des Judentums in the academic community allowed inherited prejudices to persist, he argued, echoing Zunz, not just against the Wissenschaft des Judentums itself but against all of Jewry, since it prevented the emergence of knowledge concerning Jewish contributions to medieval and modern culture and the conditions under which Jews had lived and realized their accomplishments.[66] His activism against academic anti-Semitism caused him difficulties. For example, his angry response to an attack on Jewish scholarship by the anti-Semitic professor Paul Lagarde spelled the end of his relationship with the *Göttinger Gelehrte Zeitung*, to which he had previously been a frequent contributor.[67]

In his attacks on anti-Semitism, Kaufmann adroitly compared Judaism with Christianity, Jews with Christians. Judaism, Kaufmann argued, possesses everything Christians accuse it of lacking. In a pamphlet published anonymously in 1880, Kaufmann countered the anti-Semitic accusations of Adolf Stöcker (1835–1909), court chaplain of Berlin, by mitigating them and turning them back on Christians. In calling Jews foreigners, he argued, Stöcker himself violates the laws of the land, since Jews, like Christians, have citizenship. Similarly, Christians, like Jews, have among their number some who are less than upstanding; Jews are only as proud of their religion as Christians are of theirs; and so on.[68] Embracing Christianity along with Islam in one ecumenical messianic partnership, he proclaimed that "the deepest thinkers in the Middle Ages among the Jews, Juda Halavi and Moses Maimonides, openly recognized Christianity and Islam as assistants in the messianic task."[69] Unfortunately, this offer of an assistantship for Christianity under the direction of Judaism seems to have had little attraction for Stöcker, who, besides his activities as a preacher, was the founder of the Christian Social Worker's Party, a party with an anti-Semitic platform.[70]

Kaufmann's battle against anti-Semitism was intimately connected to his expressions of ecumenicalism in his academic work. In his first important academic work, a study of teachings about the attributes of God in medieval Jewish philosophy, he folded Islamic sources and Jewish religious philosophers into a searching inquiry into the gradual triumph over anthropomorphism in religious thinking.[71] His study of concepts of the senses in medieval Jewish thinkers rings with ecumenical sentiments like the following, connecting the Arabic, Christian, and Jewish worlds: "That which the Middle Ages understood as science was a universal one, which the diversity of the lands, yes, not even the oppositions of religions, could change. Islam, Judaism, and Christendom resound with the same wisdom. Therefore the study of one literature is not more important in this context than the study of the others."[72] Showing how Hebrew words for the eye adapted both Latin and Arabic roots and brought together concepts from each realm, Kaufmann repeatedly equated Judaism, Islam, and Christianity, softening the contours of each disarmingly.[73]

The contradiction between Jewish uniqueness and Judaism's communality with the different nationalities within which it found itself may have been resolved, for Kaufmann, by Zionism. Kaufmann's attitude toward Zionism was not easily discernible. Although his reply to Stöcker argued for Jewish citizenship in European countries, other works suggest an attraction to Jewish nationalism that was not uncommon among many practitioners of the Wissenschaft des Judentums, even when they expressed little enthusiasm for Zionism. Kaufmann was an early enthusiast of Hess's *Rom und Jerusalem* (1862).[74] In 1877, he greeted with warmth George Eliot's novel *Daniel Deronda* for its treatment of the Jewish longing for the homeland. Such a longing was not, Kaufmann argued, inconsistent with love for the "foreign lands within which Jews found themselves." Rebuilding of the land of Israel, he thought, could only strengthen the Diaspora and its influence.[75] He deliberately distanced the nationalism of the Jews of his time from the universalism of the late eighteenth century: "How different [from Nathan the Wise] in 'Deronda'! Here the Jew demands the rights pertaining to his race, and claims admittance into the community of nations as a legitimate member."[76] In this statement, Kaufmann's ecumenicalism becomes cosmopolitanism.

When Herzl founded the political Zionist movement, Kaufmann held an increasingly ambiguous position. For a planned publication, he translated into German Herzl's English summary of *The Jewish State*, which the *London Jewish Chronicle* published four weeks before the first German edition of the pamphlet was published.[77] Yet when Moritz Güdemann published his objections to Herzl's Zionist movement in 1897, Kaufmann sent him a supportive, although not uncritical, postcard. Concerning Güdemann's idealized account of the role of Jerusalem in Judaism, Kaufmann wrote: "In your hands, Jerusalem almost turns into 'jerus-shel-malah' (Jerus-a-bove)."[78] Yet he appreciated Güdemann's depiction of the exalted mission of the Diaspora. He praised highly the sections of Güdemann's pamphlet that treated Christianity's debt to Judaism's universalizing mission.[79] Kaufmann's approach to Zionism suffered from the same ambiguity as his art historical narrative: his acceptance of nationality as his organizing principle caught him between the dual national claims of Jews.

Symptomatic of the precariousness of Kaufmann's attempt to balance the demands of the Jewish and the secular Christian worlds was his friendship with Franz Delitzsch. Delitzsch, a Christian, was a prominent Hebrew scholar at the University of Leipzig. He won steadfast loyalty from many Jewish scholars through his unbiased devotion to Hebrew literature, his outspoken opposition to anti-Semitism, and his cooperative ventures with Jewish scholars, who regarded him as their defender in the academic world. Yet Delitzsch put his Jewish friends' loyalty to a severe test, for he was also committed to converting Jews and in 1880 helped found the Institutum Judaicum, later called the Delitzschianum, to do so.[80] Kaufmann's obituary for Delitzsch conveys with warmth his appreciation for his friend's advocacy of Hebrew literature and Jewish causes; it also conveys his distress at the extent to which these were connected with demeaning efforts to convert Jews.[81] Delitzsch's son would upset the balance between his father's philo-Semitism and his proselytizing energy. Also a scholar of Oriental philology, Friedrich Delitzsch authored the notorious study of ancient religion *Bibel und Babel* (1902) as well as the openly anti-Semitic *Die grosse Täuschung* (1920).[82]

Multinational allegiance was perhaps conceivable for Kaufmann because the state to which he was subject was the Hapsburg Empire, an entity that constantly had to adjudicate the demands of its various peoples, among them Czechs, Poles, Germans, and Hungarians. Kaufmann was himself an example of its cosmopolitanism. Having been born in a Czech province, he returned from studies in Germany to make his career in Budapest, where he successfully added Hungarian to an already vast linguistic repertoire.[83] He cited with approval the angry words of another subject of the empire, Adalbert Stifter, foretelling a dire end to Prussian domination of German unification.[84] As much as he praised Stifter for his "ardent patriotism [*glühende Heimatliebe*]" for Austria, however, Kaufmann probably understood, as has been suggested, that Jews were the most enthusiastic supporters of Hapsburgian multinational character.[85]

Competing forces, however, imposed themselves on his thinking, just as they did on other similarly positioned Jewish thinkers, such as those who advocated assimilation.[86] Indeed, despite the mild, ingratiating language of his essays on art, his desire for recognition of Jewish art partook also of his nationalist ambivalence toward assimilation and his anger against anti-Semitism. These are the most salient characteristics of his earliest writings on art. His interest in art must have begun early, since he was already writing on the subject by 1878. It appears in the letters he exchanged with Leopold Zunz, to whom he confided that he had gone to Paris in order to "become acquainted with the library and the exhibition and very likely, in the process, with the city as well."[87] By "the exhibition" he meant the Paris World's Fair. He had already seen the one in Vienna in 1873. By the time he wrote Zunz he had visited the exhibition in Paris twice. He was surprised to note that the prize for church painting had gone to a Jew, Henri Leopold Levy. Kaufmann had heard that Levy complained that he could not use Jewish subject matter for his history paintings. Zunz responded tersely that Levy could find enough Jewish subject matter, just not enough Christian buyers. But Kaufmann's interest in Levy was based on the painter's potential to refute anti-Semitism. He saw Levy's success as disproving the contention, which Kaufmann attributed to Ernst Renan, that Jews could not make art. "You talk too much about Renan," Zunz replied.[88]

The experience of the World's Fair, which also included a fine exhibition and illustrated catalog of Jewish ritual art, marked the inception of Kaufmann's battle for Jewish art.[89] Regarding Levy, however, he imbibed some of Zunz's cynicism. In a manuscript published only after his death, he subtly accused Levy of excessive assimilation for his canvas of Saint Denis. Kaufmann understood that as a "national" artist, by which he meant not a Jewish one, it might be easier to turn to subjects that have traditionally been crowned with glory.[90] Kaufmann, however, suggested that by turning away from tried-and-true subjects of the passion and taking up others, such as the Maccabees, Levy might be able to achieve greater independence. Seeking to turn the acculturation of both artists and collectors to the advantage of Jewish art, he suggested that the collection of Jewish art would be a way for the "great" among the Jews truly to imitate the "great" of the nations, as they so very much love to do.[91] He expressed the same sentiment, less cynically, in the published article.[92]

As soon as he was able, Kaufmann followed his own recommendation. After his 1881 marriage to an offshoot of the wealthy Gomperz family, he amassed a large collection of Hebrew manuscripts, including many important chiefly for their illuminations (see figure 31). The collection would become the material at the core of his study of Jewish manuscript illumination. Perhaps appropriately, the fourth volume of the Center for Jewish Art's *Index of Jewish Art* is devoted to this collection,

31. *The Parting of the Red Sea*, Kaufmann Haggadah, manuscript, 14th century. MS Kaufmann A 422 f.58r. Oriental Collection, Library of the Hungarian Academy of Sciences, Budapest. Courtesy of the Getty Research Library.

bequeathed by Kaufmann's widow, Irma Gomperz, to the Hungarian Academy of Sciences in Budapest, where it is housed in the Oriental library.[93]

Kaufmann remained just as marginalized as the other proponents of the Wissenschaft des Judentums, whose ghettoization he opposed vigorously. This amazingly erudite and wide-ranging prolific scholar taught for his entire career in the rabbinical seminary in Budapest and published few articles likely to find readers outside the confines of the Jewish intelligentsia.[94] His essay in the edition of the Sarajevo Haggadah was as close as he ever came to membership in the wider art historical community. But even this effort did not win unmixed acceptance for the artistic branch, or *Kunstwissenschaft*, of the Wissenschaft des Judentums. His lengthy essay, of fifty-six pages (longer than that of Schlosser), was relegated to an appendix. His honorarium, he commented wryly to a visitor, consisted of one copy of the completed edition.[95]

Kaufmann's Legacy

While not all scholars of Jewish art are in a strict sense Kaufmann's heirs, many of them faced similar problems and found related solutions. They were spurred on by the discovery of far more evidence of Jewish art than Kaufmann ever enjoyed: by monuments such as the synagogue at Dura-Europos, excavated from 1928 to 1932, for example, and by the growing evidence of manuscript illumination. Yet they still found themselves desirous of bringing Jewish art history closer to Christian, and the study of Jewish art closer to the mainstream. They achieved these aims, however, with the help of better training in art history. By the 1970s and 1980s, the history of Jewish art was eagerly pursued by devotees in the United States and Israel. The great mass of this scholarship, however, was still produced under Jewish auspices, unlike the scholarship of Christian art, which found itself a home in secular universities. A master's program in Jewish art has been offered since the mid-1990s in conjunction with the Jewish Theological Seminary and the Jewish Museum in New York; and the Center for Jewish Art at the Hebrew University in Jerusalem, founded by Bezalel Narkiss, has produced copious scholarship on the subject since its founding in 1978. At

Narkiss's instigation, the Art History Department at the Hebrew University began offering bachelors and masters programs in Jewish art in the late 1960s.[96]

The success of such institutions as the Center for Jewish Art, which culminated in the awarding of the Israel Prize to its founder, was rare and reflects the heritage of Bezalel as much as it does that of Kaufmann. More modest studies, in more difficult conditions, were typical. For years, the standard work on Jewish art was a history whose brief first edition was written by the director of the Jewish Museum in Berlin in 1935.[97] Removed from his professorship at the University of Breslau, Franz Landsberger found himself forced to limit his research to Jewish subjects. After time spent in a concentration camp, he emigrated to Cincinnati, where he taught at Hebrew Union College and published his book *A History of Jewish Art* in an expanded English edition.[98]

But the extent to which the professional scholar of Jewish art in the mid-twentieth century inherited Kaufmann's problems is perhaps best exemplified by the career of the art historian Joseph Gutmann. Gutmann began his career with studies at Hebrew Union College when Landsberger was still teaching there, but he turned his attention to Jewish art in studies, under other Jewish émigrés, at the Institute of Fine Arts in New York. The "so-called Second Commandment" has preoccupied Gutmann, just as it had Kaufmann.[99] Titles such as "The 'Second Commandment' and the Image in Judaism" and *No Graven Images* attest to a prolonged engagement with the commandment.[100] Some differences between the two men are attributable to different religious orientations. While any attempt to historicize scripture was strictly proscribed in, for example, the Seminary at Breslau, where Kaufmann studied, the reform rabbi Joseph Gutmann could and did freely historicize the scriptures to speculate on when the biblical text might have been written or altered, and why later writers might have invented and projected Bezalel, the desert artist, back into the years of wandering.[101] Changing interpretations of the Second Commandment also play an important role in essays that envision a "dynamic Judaism which, in the course of its three-thousand-year history, has given rise to many diverse types of life-style and expression, each with a different view of the biblical prohibition."[102] Reform Judaism, because of its "unfettered pursuit of the truth," can "work hand in hand with contemporary artists, who also strive for universal values and attempt to unite man through a universal language."[103]

But many of Gutmann's arguments resemble those of Kaufmann. To refute the iconophobic claim, Gutmann, like Kaufmann, used historical arguments that interpreted iconophobia as a local, historical matter.[104] Like Kaufmann's, his explanation also included a reassuring use of Christianity as the standard to which Judaism conforms. From the similarity between Saint Bernard of Clairvaux's dislike of the "ridiculous monsters sculpted in the cloisters" to the pronouncement by the thirteenth-century Rabbi Meir ben Baruch of Rothenburg against distracting animal and bird figures in Jewish prayer books, he concluded that "the dogmatic insistence that Judaism has always repudiated the image does not take into account the fact that there frequently exists a wide divergence between the verbalizations of religious leaders in a particular society and the practice actually adhered to by large segments of their followers. This holds true for Christianity as well as Judaism."[105] Three-quarters of a century after Kaufmann, it was still necessary to point out further that Christians and Muslims were bound by, and thus had to interpret, the Second Commandment as well as Jews.[106]

Accordingly, Gutmann's research, like that of Kaufmann, centers on the relationship between Jewish and Christian art. Presumably, it was his enhanced ability to keep Christianity the focus of Jewish art history that made it possible for Gutmann, unlike Kaufmann, to make the transition between seminary and university. In fact, he confined his teaching to Christian art altogether; his few attempts to offer courses in Jewish art ended in disappointment when few students registered.[107] With little institutional support, Jewish art history maintained a timid profile, and Gutmann could justly complain as late as 1990 that "Jewish art history, unlike its related discipline Jewish history, is still largely moored in the Wölfflin and Panofsky schools of thought and has not yet fully absorbed the newer approaches of contemporary art history."[108]

Gutmann's frustration with the field of Jewish art demonstrates the limits of the pursuit that I have been calling the (Kunst)Wissenschaft des Judentums. The efforts of scholars such as David Kaufmann to create the category of Jewish art and gain recognition for its scholarship had little effect on the wider world of either scholarship or art. Not Kaufmann's enthusiastic acceptance, but Schlosser's dismissive approach and Goldschmidt's cautious reaction would be typical for twentieth-century art historical scholarship. While Islamic art, tied to distinctive geographical centers, began to find coverage in art historical surveys, Jewish art sacrificed its section in surveys to the growing secularization of culture and its liberal Protestant critique.[109] With the exception of the synagogue at Dura-Europos, it now merited barely a mention. A new appreciation of ethnic diversity was occasionally the justification for a specialized study of Jewish monuments by mainstream art historians, but they were still self-consciously marginalized as, for example, the "cultural context" that "helps us to understand the special qualities of the masterful creation."[110]

The marginalization of both the early practitioners of what I have called the (Kunst)Wissenschaft des Judentums and better-trained successors like Gutmann suggest that Kaufmann's limitations were not due only to lack of training. He suffered the difficulties of trying to put an end to a discourse while speaking within it, or, as current terminology would put it, being positioned by it. Had he been in the center of the art historical community, would he have been better able to transform the discourse of Jewish art? I now turn to a thinker whose training in celebrated departments of art history brought him much closer to the center of the profession: Martin Buber.

CHAPTER FOUR

Martin Buber

Jewish Art As Visual Redemption

How idle indeed is the debate over whether there is a Jewish art! Certainly there is none in the sense that there is, for example, a Dutch art. But those are only categories, and the great historical miracle is the fact that there are Jewish artists at all, and also, that in their vision, in their handling of form, very quietly and covertly, something of an essentially Jewish character is stirring, something of the hereditary character of the pure blood that flows around their optical nerves, the muscles of their hands.
Martin Buber in *Die jüdische Bewegung*

Richard Wagner could still deny to the sensory intuitive powers of the Jews the ability to produce creative artists. At the time, the validity of his assertion held up almost entirely in the face of an insignificant pack of imitators. If we can point to some Jewish artists today, we are obliged to inquire into the causes of that former sterility.
Martin Buber in the introduction to *Jüdische Künstler*

Toward an Aesthetic Haskalah

The Jewish philosopher Martin Buber (1878–1965) is best known for his groundbreaking contribution to the philosophy of dialogism, beginning with his seminal work, *Ich und Du* (I and Thou), first published in 1923. He is less well-known for his writings on visual art. His 1901 speech to the Fifth Zionist Congress in Basel, however, in which he argued that having their own land would make it possible for Jews to develop a national art, made an impression on the delegates and added to the momentum that helped establish the art school Bezalel in Palestine in 1906.[1] This speech was an episode in Buber's brief but remarkable flirtation with the concept of Jewish art.

Buber's interest in Jewish art began in 1900, when he founded a department for Jewish art and science in the Berlin Zionist organization.[2] Within Zionism, he represented a wing supporting Cultural Zionism, which, using a cultural definition of nationhood, worked to promote national consciousness through a Jewish cultural renaissance. In 1902, he and the writer Berthold Feiwel founded a publishing concern called the Jüdischer Verlag (Jewish Press). Its projects included the *Jüdischer Almanach*, published in 1902 and 1904 for art and literature in an effort to win the intelligentsia to the cause of Zionism. Buber wrote essays on Jewish artists Hermann Struck and Lesser Ury for literary Zionist journals such as *Ost und West*, and in 1903, he edited an anthology of Jewish artists for the Jüdischer Verlag, which celebrated the art of well-known Jewish artists such as Liebermann and Josef Israels along with less-well-known artists more identified with Jewish subjects and publications, such as Ury, E. M. Lilien, and Jehudo Epstein (see figure 32).[3] Until 1906, he championed the cause of Jewish art in these undertakings and, as we shall see, in other ways. Thereafter, while he continued, albeit infrequently, to make penetrating references to the visual arts throughout his life, these were usually relegated to the background of his philosophical concerns.

Like earlier proponents of the (Kunst)Wissenschaft des Judentums, Buber advocated art as a component of a larger effort to champion Jew-

32. E. M. Lilien, *Jesaia* (Juda). From *Ost und West* 1 (1901): 519–20; also reprinted in *Jüdische Künstler*, ed. Martin Buber (Berlin: Jüdischer Verlag, 1903). Courtesy of the Asher Library, Spertus Institute of Jewish Studies.

ish culture. Like them, he made his case by universalizing ideas that he associated with Judaism. Unlike them, however, Buber did so in a Zionist context. Given these credentials, he could not be expected to follow David Kaufmann's example and seek to win recognition for Jewish art by integrating it into the art of surrounding peoples. His underlying premise was more integral, almost visceral, than Kaufmann's. He thought that a Jewish national art should seek to express the soul of the Jewish people. But Buber hardly seems to have chosen an effective means of distinguishing Jewish artistic contributions. He began his essay on Jewish art by accepting Richard Wagner's premise of Jewish artistic sterility and assuming the task of tracing its history. In fact, unlike David Kaufmann but very much like Julius von Schlosser, he founded his call for Jewish art on the acceptance of the very characteristics that were supposed to disqualify Jews from pursuing the visual arts.

Buber's contribution to the concept of Jewish art signified an important moment both for the recognition of Jewish art and for his own development. Buber was among the first influential spokespeople to support contemporary Jewish art qua Jewish art, and in this context, he first publicly discussed Hasidism, the Jewish mystical movement that was to play an important part in his early career.[4] The relevance to the present context of Buber's case for Jewish art, however, rests on the negative premises with which Buber began. His championship of Jewish art represents an important strategy of subverting negative stereotypes that has seen repeated service in the reevaluation of minority arts and cultures. Buber's reevaluation and ultimate subversion of Jewish stereotypes set a pattern in the discourse of Jewish art, giving Buber's crusade for a new Jewish art a significance greater than that of a brief episode in his early career.

The particular character of Buber's struggle to come to grips with the concept of Jewish art draws heavily on the art historical preparation that led up to it, and this preparation also allowed him to transcend the issue of Jewish art. David Kaufmann was not burdened by art historical training, at least of any self-conscious, theoretical sort. Consequently, he did not worry, at least not in print, about what constituted a national art.[5] Whether "Jewish art" need distinguish itself from "Christian art," for example, did not exercise him. Buber, however, knew too much. He was stuck in the mud of an art history that made "Jewish art" theoretically impossible and that could prove that impossibility through formal analysis. The methodology of his attempt to write and rewrite the history of Jewish art, to integrate it into art history, comes from within the discipline itself. Buber found himself in the precarious position of one who attempts to change the position of a ladder while standing on it, in order to reach a different part of the ceiling. This confrontation with the negative construction of the concept of Jewish art, beyond its contribution to the discourse of Jewish art, was crucial to his attempt to reconcile Judaism and modernity, or more precisely, modernism, understood as the set of concerns and values that underlie cultural endeavors. His use of formal analysis to create a place and an ethos for Jewish art had an effect on his development as a philosopher as well. The project proved formative in the emergence of his dialogic philosophy.

While he was writing on Jewish art, Buber was also finishing his doctoral studies in Vienna. He began these studies in Vienna as well, during the winter of 1896–97, a year before Julius von Schlosser published his edition of the Sarajevo Haggadah, with Kaufmann's appendix. That year, Buber registered in Schlosser's introduction to art history.[6] Buber's studies concentrated on philosophy, but he displayed an intense interest in visual art throughout his university career. In his first semesters in Vienna, besides Schlosser's course he registered in a course on Dutch art with the innovative art theorist Alois Riegl and in one on the origins of naturalism in art with the art historian Franz Wickhoff (1853–1909), whose edition of the *Wiener Genesis* details ancient Roman precedents for impressionist painting.[7] In two semesters in Leipzig he continued his study of Dutch art (in a course on Dutch and German art), participated in the seminar of the art historian and theorist August Schmarsow, and studied cultural history with the mentor of several influential art historians, the historian Karl Lamprecht.[8] In 1901, he continued his art historical studies in Vienna with Franz Wickhoff's course on Albrecht Dürer. Thus his studies brought him into contact with at least five of the foremost theorists of art in his time. Buber took Rigorosen, exams required for the doctorate, in 1904. His major subject was philosophy, but, in accord with the normal range of a doctoral program at the time, his minor subject was art history. His examiners were Riegl and Wickhoff.

Unfortunately, Buber failed the exam. Only on a second attempt, with Wickhoff and the classical archaeologist Emil Reisch, did he manage the undistinguished passing grade of *genügend* (satisfactory).[9] Nevertheless, either because Buber received sufficient encouragement in his studies of art or because he was unusually tenacious, he spent the year 1905–6 in Florence in an effort to complete a substantial scholarly study with an art historical theme.[10] This *Habilitationsschrift,* if completed, would have qualified him to teach art history at a university.[11] Art history, in other words, was not a minor interest.

During his university years, Buber displayed not only a concern with art history but an interest in secular literary and philosophical avant-garde movements and in the new field of sociology. When he first arrived in Vienna to attend the university, Buber immersed himself in the symbolist aesthetic of the Viennese avant-garde. Among the themes that preoccupied this group of writers were the evanescence of life and the instability of human identity.[12] Buber found these concerns, as explored in drama, poetry, and essays, fascinating, but perhaps bordering on the morbid, for his first publication responded to them. This essay, written in Polish at the age of nineteen, addressed not a Jewish issue but the writings of four major writers of this movement: Peter Altenberg, Hugo von Hofmannsthal, Hermann Bahr, and Artur Schnitzler.[13] Buber evaluated these poets of Jung Wien (Young Vienna) appreciatively but not uncritically. His essay explores their attitudes toward love and truth to self, interpreting their words as direct mirrors of their souls. Their inability to find, or accept, a stable center concerned him poetically and personally.

His university career also reflected the interests of the Viennese avant-garde, particularly in philosophy. He began to study philosophy in Vienna and pursued it in travels that took him to universities in several other cities in Germany and Switzerland, returning him to Vienna in 1901. Friedrich Nietzsche and Arthur Schopenhauer, favorite philosophers of Jung Wien and other avant-garde movements of the fin de siècle, attracted his attention at first. He devoted to them his earliest writings in German, some of them published.[14] In 1897, his second semester in Vienna, Buber registered in a course with the physicist Ernst Mach. Mach's perceptual theories, expounded in the 1885 book *The Analyses of the Sensations,* provided Jung Wien with theoretical support for its views challenging the unity of the ego.[15] Later studies in Leipzig and Berlin brought Buber into contact with the psychological theorist Wilhelm Wundt, the sociologist Georg Simmel, and the hermeneutic scholar Wilhelm Dilthey.

When, toward the end of his studies, he turned to medieval Christian mysticism, these studies transposed into the Christian realm the issue of the individual in its particularity and in relation to the world, which had begun with his readings of Hofmannsthal and Schnitzler and his studies of Nietzsche and Schopenhauer. In mysticism he appeared to find a path to the center he thought missing in the writings of Jung Wien. Buber contributed to this discourse in a Viennese literary journal. His essay on the thought of Jakob Böhme found Böhme's mysticism reflected in the yearning for a bridge between the individual and the world, which Buber saw in his contemporaries. Feelings of cosmic unity stirred by the taking of food and wine, the yen to embrace trees and commune with animals, and a heartfelt identification with the "maturing and fading of the most distant stars": all of these are part of Buber's understanding of that which brought his own contemporaries close to the world of Böhme, St. Francis of Assisi, and the Vedanta at this early stage in his career.[16] His more sober dissertation, completed in Vienna in 1904, considered the work of Nicholas Cusanus and Böhme in the context of the development of modern individuation.[17]

Although his reference to the Vedanta reveals Buber's interest in non-Western mysticism, a subject that would continue to preoccupy him, Judaism never came up in these early studies.[18] His essay on four poets of Jung Wien did not mention that three of them, Hofmannsthal, Altenberg, and Schnitzler, came from Jewish backgrounds.[19] But once Buber began to participate in the Zionist movement, in 1898, he stayed active in Jewish affairs throughout most of his studies, with the only possible exception of one year in which he tried to curtail his Zionist efforts to study for his exams.[20] Indeed, his Zionist activities paralleled his literary efforts. Buber's Cultural Zionism, in representing Jewish nationalism through the advocacy of a Jewish cultural renaissance, consisted of bringing together specifically Jewish cultural and religious ideas with modern culture so as to appeal to and inspire secular Jewish culture, just as Böhme's Christian mysticism could be made to satisfy secular cravings of the avant-garde.

Buber's preoccupation with Hasidism made the parallel complete: his Hasidism consisted in a Jewish analogue to the Christian mysticism he studied at the university, and it similarly promised to bring the past to bear on a contemporary avant-garde. He translated Hasidic tales and wrote several essays on the subject of Hasidism, publishing his first book on the topic, a collection of the stories of Rabbi Nachman of Bratslav, in 1906.[21] Hasidism and art could together serve Buber's Zionism because they formed a continuum between the Jewish past and the Jewish future. The revitalization of interest in Hasidism served to give Judaism a positive national identity rooted in the past, while art was part of Buber's plans for a Jewish cultural renaissance. Even Jakob Böhme, after all, had spoken to a similarly nationalist sentiment, as a potent symbol of German unity.[22]

A secular identity was vital to Buber's attempt to span past and future. Twenty-six years younger than David Kaufmann, Buber was less strict in his practice of Jewish ritual than Kaufmann, yet his appeal was at least as spiritual as Kaufmann's, if not more so. His approach resembled that of the Jewish artist E. M. Lilien, who reassured Max Liebermann that to be a Zionist he would not have to keep kosher or wear "tzitzis."[23] Lilien's art, which supplemented a style modeled on Aubrey Beardsley with Hebrew characters (in both senses of the word), made Judaism attractive, offering contemporary aesthetics in Jewish clothing (see figure 32).[24] Similarly, Buber's writings on Hasidism made this mystic strain of Judaism accessible to young, antibourgeois aesthetes who wished a return to spirituality without a return to Jewish ritual. His approach to the acculturated Jews of his day avoided the appearance of dry scholarship. It enabled him to combat the stereotype of Judaism, accepted among Jews and gentiles alike, as an arid religion of law.[25] Buber's appreciation of Jewish mysticism addressed a complex spiritual need of secular Jews uplifted by mystical ideas. If, as Güdemann stated, "in the synagogue, nothing mystical happens," that did not mean that there could be nothing mystical in Judaism.[26]

The mixture of the secular and the religious engaged Buber in another respect as well. Buber grew up with a direct experience of the tension between German culture and Jewish learning. Buber's father was a secular Viennese businessman. Buber was raised, however, in Galicia by his grandfather, Solomon Buber, a successful businessman who was also an important talmudic scholar. As Buber characterized him in the dedication of his tales of Rabbi Nachman, he was "the last master of the old Haskalah [Jewish Enlightenment]," a movement instrumental in reconciling Judaism with the modern world.[27] The equilibrium Buber evolved reflects the particular mixture of the secular and the religious that he developed in his formative years. Buber could be considered a master of the new Haskalah. In the new Haskalah, there was a role for visual art.

Judaism's Mystic Art

The publication of Buber's adaptation of the tales of Rabbi Nachman in 1906 initiated Buber's successful insertion of religious Judaism into the discourse of secular mysticism. This book, and the following one of the tales of the Baal Shem Tov, Hasidism's founding master, inspired a wave of enthusiasm for Hasidism among Jewish youth, which, as in Buber's own case, sometimes provoked conflicts between the young enthusiasts and their parents.[28] Buber's work first led Gershom Scholem to study Jewish mysticism.[29] Although Buber carefully distinguished the historical Hasidism he admired from its present-day "deteriorated" form, his work led to a resurgence of interest in Hasidism that motivated others to search for, and sometimes become disciples of, present-day Hasidic masters in Eastern Europe.[30]

But to build one bridge was to burn another. The timing of Buber's move to Hasidism is worth dwelling on, because when Buber committed himself to the serious study of this Jewish mystical movement he ceased writing about Jewish art. His first publications on Hasidism appeared during his stay in Italy, where he was to write his *Habilitationsschrift* in art history. Buber's ambition for a *Habilitation* in art history, assuming he actually entertained such a plan, certainly did not involve a Jewish subject.[31] Without baptism, he could in any case have anticipated little success in attaining a professorship in art history.[32] Whether he abandoned the *Habilitation* because of lack of support from the academic community or from his own family, the Jewish topic he took up in its place was irreconcilable with a secular academic career. His departure from secular academia, for the time being, may have given him the freedom to study Jewish themes; conversely, his disillusionment with a Jewish student's prospects for an academic career could have motivated him to retreat to his own tradition. The turn to Hasidism, however, began in the midst of his preoccupation with Jewish art and found its first expression in visual terms. Poignantly, his art historical training contributed most productively to his thought as his art historical ambitions came to an end.

Buber first publicly mentioned Hasidism in the introduction to his volume on Jewish artists, a text that is also his most serious discussion of Jewish art. Until then, he had applied to Zionism current ideas that linked culture and art to nationhood, blood, and soil. The "Renaissance" in "Jüdische Renaissance" (1900), for example, referred not to a rebirth of classic, universal values but to a creative use of "the specific characteristics of blood-related tribe [*Blutstammes*]," which should create an internal homeland before the achievement of an external one.[33] His conception of culture, defined in an early essay, was nourished, like his philosophical interests, directly by the philosophy of Nietzsche and in turn resembled the *völkisch* ideas of German nationalists, which contrasted a nationally based "culture," expressing the soul of a nation, to an internationalist and strictly utilitarian "civilization."[34] Jewish art played a part in this "renaissance" because of the symbiotic relationship between nationalism and art. Art needs a nation from which to grow; Zionism needs art to express Jewish nationality.

But Buber found art as a Jewish pursuit more problematic than other aspects of the Jewish Renaissance. Jewish literary ability was uncontested, but Buber had no reason to question the received wisdom about the nonexistence of Jewish visual art. The essay "Von jüdischer Kunst," an address to the Fifth Zionist Congress in 1901, began with a lament for the thousands of years that Jews had lived without art. The complete lack of visual art was a symptom of a centuries-long illness that was deleterious to Judaism's religiosity. The Diaspora was the original cause, but emancipation and enlightenment only worsened the condition by encouraging assimilation. "Thus for centuries, indeed for thousands of years the eternal task of Judaism has remained stifled [*blieb . . . ertötet*]."[35] The straightforwardly Zionist cure was Eretz Yisrael. Once the Jews had a land of their own, art was certain to flourish: "A national art needs a land to grow out of, and a sky toward which it blossoms [*entgegenblüht*]."[36]

These two essays, different as they were, were followed by a third, the preface to *Jüdische Künstler,* which took yet another tack. Although the book appeared under Zionist auspices, Buber did not emphasize in it the necessity of moving to a national homeland. Far from resuscitating an ailing Jewish culture, in fact, the homeland shouldered much of the responsibility for the artistic deficiencies of its inhabitants. Buber's harsh opening lines, with their direct reference to the anti-Semitic composer Richard Wagner, accepted Jewish nonvisuality and attributed it to "racial characteristics."[37] While he explicitly limited his reference to race to climate, conditions, and social structure, his characterization of Jewish life in ancient Israel comes directly from anti-Semitic stereotypes that equated the aridity of Jewish culture with the desert landscape from which they emerged; the desolation of the land corresponded to the desolation of the art.[38] The consequences were explicitly visual. The optical effects of the Middle Eastern sun prevented Jewish art from flourishing. Its blinding light "pushes the objects in the distance, dissolves the third dimension, and permits no harmonious nuances of color."[39]

Buber went on, however, to describe the specific problems and obstacles to Jewish art and their later remedy, not in nationalistic but in philosophical, social, and religious terms. The main obstacle to art was the inability of the Jew to grasp the "Einzelding": "Everything remains relation; the substances do not become evident. Only the relation is evident. Nothing is seen in itself; everything is seen in relation."[40] The Jews' inability to visualize, he argued, constricted their *Weltanschauung* (world-view) to "I-relationships," or function, making it impossible to see "perceptual absolutes in the individual [objects]" like the Hindus of the time, or the "closed form" like the Greeks.[41] In the Diaspora, the limitation of Jews to money dealing stifled emerging visual as well as spiritual yearnings. Rabbinic law, of which Buber clearly disapproved, owed its severity to these economic conditions. "This is when religious law first became all powerful. The human body is despicable. Beauty is an unknown value. Seeing is a sin. Art is a sin. . . . Everything creative is smothered at its first appearance."[42]

Hasidism, not Zionism, played the role of the redeemer, a role it was to reprise many times in Buber's writings. As an agent of Jewish spiritual rebirth, it initiated a restructuring of the Jewish faith that enabled Jews to view the human body as the "devotion of the world. . . . Vision became union with God."[43] The Jewish racial character did not change; it only took on a favorable cast. Art enabled Jewish relationality to reach new forms of expression, giving it a positive value.[44] Emancipation, fruit of the Enlightenment, was also necessary so that the transformation begun by Hasidism continued to develop freely, and even Haskalah, Hasidism's rival, contributed. The decisive step, however, had been taken when the Jewish mystical movement united man with God through vision. The end result was the transformation of Judaism from the enemy of art into an art-loving people who, by the beginning of the twentieth century, were poised to participate prominently in a future avant-garde, "on the threshold of an epoch, whose essence seems everywhere to be the dissolution of substance into relationships and its transfiguration into spiritual values."[45]

Buber's portrayal of Hasidism's redemptive mission continued in his retellings of the Hasidic tales of the late eighteenth century's Rabbi Nachman of Bratslav and later those of the founder of Hasidism, the Baal Shem Tov. These stories were paradigmatic of Buber's means of incorporating Jewish culture into modernity by reconnecting Judaism to a religious past. The youthful Nachman, who died in his thirties in the early nineteenth century, left a small number of deceptively simple, symbolic stories in the form of fairy tales, committed to writing by a faithful disciple. His life and his fables were the stuff of legend, lending themselves to Late Romantic interpretations.[46] Buber drew out all manner of such interpretations from Nachman's brief life and his suggestive tales, frankly revising them to improve their form, which he described as "confused, verbose and . . . vulgar [*verworren, weitschweifig und . . . unedler*]."[47] In Buber's hands, Nachman's laconic tales would have been as comfortable in the German literary and artistic journal *Pan*, in company with such authors as the late symbolist poet Stefan George, as they were in the Jewish periodical *Ost und West* or in the slim volume in which they were eventually collected. Their surroundings were in any case reminiscent of *Pan*: the modest decorations were by the artist Emil Orlik, a Viennese Secessionist with whom Buber had become friendly as a member of the Berlin Donnerstagtisch (Thursday society).[48]

The most extensively revised tale was published first. "The Rabbi and His Son" appeared in *Ost und West* in 1905.[49] In the version transcribed by Nachman's disciple, "two young men" commend to the lad a Hasidic *zaddik*, or holy man, but the Rabbi refuses to let his son visit him because the *zaddik* is less educated and of an inferior family background.[50] In Buber's much more elaborate version of the tale, the father objects to the young men as well as to the *zaddik*, regarding all Hasidim as "fanatics and dreamers [*Schwärmern und Phantasten*]," while the son, for his part, hopes that in his friends' manner, "wild and headstrong as it was," something of his own dreams might be realized.[51] Buber's narrative makes much of the son's "unfulfilled yearning [*ungestillten Sehnsucht*]," giving him an overlay of anxious, searching youth that evokes less the Rabbi's son or even the early-nineteenth-century teller of the tales than the generation gap as experienced by the young adapter of the tales and his audience in the early twentieth century.[52] True to Buber's mystical propensities, the son reaches the "small light" not by performing a "mitzvah," or commandment, as he does in the original story, but through a mystical experience.[53] While the messianic explanation that ends both versions purports to elucidate fully the mystery of the youth's feeling of incompleteness, Buber's version, which ties the youth's feelings for nature to his admiration for the spirited Hasidim, gives the tale the character of a contest between intellect and fantasy, dry learning and life, in a manner that would have been foreign to the Hasidism of the eighteenth century but was very much at home in the antirationalism of the fin de siècle.

Without mentioning visual art as such, Buber imparts to the tale a visual element wholly absent in the versions transcribed from Rabbi Nachman. While Nachman's story relates without elaboration that the boy, who spent his days studying in an upstairs room, felt something lacking without knowing what, Buber's boy is distracted specifically by visual stimuli. The boy's room is small and confining, and while he tended "to spend time and to submerge himself, all his senses concentrated, in the mysteries of the [holy] writings," he found that "his gaze did not stick to the infinite surface of the small, stiff letters, but glided repeatedly out over the yellow waves of grain to the dark streak of the distant fir trees."[54] While Buber may seem to interpret the boy's glance away from his book as simply disobedient to the biblical injunction "do not follow your eyes," the story in fact stresses the visible materiality of the inscribed surface from which his gaze strays. The flatness and nearness of these "small, stiff letters" give way to a rippling yellow plane with a distant brush stroke reminiscent of a broadly painted landscape. Two modes of contemplation correspond to two modes of visual perception. The opposition shapes the difference between reading and looking.

Buber's art historical education had accustomed him to view humankind through such perceptual categories. Karl Schnaase had imported into art history a concept of Jews as "relational people [*Beziehungsmenschen*]," understood in terms of the way in which Jews see individual objects fading quickly in and out of the dark.[55] But a systematic attempt to transform the dialectic of relationships into a formal theory of art came about in the work of the scholar Alois Riegl, one of the professors who would administer the doctoral exam for which Buber may have begun preparing while writing his essay.[56] Riegl specified in great detail the way in which he thought the formal properties of art represent worldly and spiritual relations, augmenting his formal analysis with richly suggestive comparisons between art, society, and nature. In several works published in the years just prior to Buber's essay on Jewish art, but especially in his recently published book *Spätrömische Kunstindustrie* (1901), Riegl constructed a narrative that led art from a notion of material flatness and separation to a relation immaterial and even spiritual in nature. Concentrating on ornament, he began by attributing to ancient Egyptian art a concentration on the material nature of the flat surface. Greek art developed isolating entities, Buber's "closed form," which partially broke free of the material surface while never denying its rootedness in it. The book concentrates, however, on Late Roman art's project of dissolving material entities and replacing them with a spatial relation, conceived as ever more pervasive (see figure 33). In the stage reached by Late Roman art, the solid, material plane of near vision ultimately gives way to the freedom offered by the optical flatness of the distant plane, an analysis in which the flickering effects of light played a key role. Both Wickhoff and Riegl used current theories about near and distant vision to explain epistemologically the formal effects of paintings. Near vision, Riegl wrote, suggests the sense of touch, which, according to recent perceptual theory, identified individual objects. Distance creates an optical effect that dissolves the plastic particularity of objects, an effect exacerbated by the brilliant sun in Buber's Middle East.[57] Art must articulate these two concepts.

33. Frontal side of a marble sarcophagus with Adonis's farewell, departure, and wounding. Lateran Museum. From Alois Riegl, Die *Spätrömische Kunst-Industrie nach den Funden in Österreich-Ungarn* (Vienna: Kaiserlich-königlichen Hof-und Staatsdruckerei, 1901), figure 15. Courtesy of the Getty Research Library.

But Riegl's ideas were not only formal. Tying artistic form to other cultural manifestations, Riegl postulated that the development he traced paralleled that of scientific explanation, which began with mechanical explanations assuming individual entities, progressed to magical notions of causality in which the entities do not touch one another, and, in modern times, evolved into the idea of insubstantial "chemical relations disseminated everywhere as though traversing space in all directions."[58] Such statements may have impressed Buber, as he tried to tie Jewish art to an impending "dissolution of substance into relationships and its transfiguration into spiritual values."[59] Riegl, too, formulated his theory in spiritual terms, imagining that mankind was on the threshold of a new world-view with mystical overtones that would see entities dissolve into unity.[60]

In this light, Schnaase's notion that Jewish art overlooked the individual in favor of the (causal) relations into which it entered could be construed positively. Buber united mysticism, formal analysis, and ethical notions of Jewish identity in an essay on Lesser Ury. Calling Ury an "ecstatic," he explained Ury's use of color in terms of color's ability to unite objects into a whole. "The form says nothing about the interrelation, the interaction of things. This, however, is what is essential. The thing is nothing in itself, [but] everything in the All. The thing is effect, not substance. Close it off, and you take away its life. What is most personal lies in the relation to the other. Tie a being to all beings, and you draw out that which is most personal to it [*sein Eigenstes*]."[61] In a 1901 article on Lesser Ury, Buber identifies Judaism with a "more planar way of seeing, starting from a general mood [*Stimmung*] and directed more toward the relationship between things than toward their forms."[62] Ury, who embodied this way of seeing, had made the transition to modern art, foreseeing it and creating it ahead of time.[63] The Rabbi's son, too, by abandoning the small stiff letters of the endless plane of the Torah for the waving grain and dark strokes of optical flatness in the distant landscape, not only recapitulated the progress from Egyptian to late Roman and modern art, he effected an important epistemological shift not noticed by his shortsighted father. Perhaps Buber's professors were equally myopic when they failed to recognize Buber's creative transformation of their own ideas.

The Ethics of Perception

The ethical ramifications of Buber's perceptual imagery were inherent in the art historical source of its perceptual theory. Riegl elaborated his formal ideas in such terms in a course on Dutch painting he offered in the autumn semester, 1896–97, where he first began work on the thesis of what would become his pioneering study, *Das holländische Gruppenporträt* (The Dutch group portrait).[64] In the book, and in the course, Riegl was grappling with theories of art like that of the philosopher Konrad Fiedler (1841–95) as he worked from his own theory of realism to a theory of artistic volition.[65] The world, according to Fiedler, does not stand over against the viewer as an independent object. Rather, the viewer forms the world through perceptions. The artist, in representing the world, in fact creates the visual in its own material. While Fiedler's notion of art as an exploration of reality appealed to Riegl, he found such theories pessimistic, along with the Kantian philosophy from which they stemmed, because they appeared to strip art of both its epistemological and its ethical functions.[66]

Riegl argued that art seeks not to reproduce or create the world but to relate to it. In the seventeenth century, he argued, the Dutch used the work of art to perform relationships with the beholder by including the beholder in the work.[67] To make this argument, he elaborated a theory according to which the object of art was to permit the beholder to relate to the work of art in the way the beholder wished to relate to the world. The theory united the ethical and the artistic, conceiving the work of art as a being with which the beholder may interact. Artistic activity focuses on the quality of the interaction, not of the object in isolation. Similarly, the power of the desire that underlies art is not contingent on the type of relationship desired, be it one of dominating power, where one partner is subsumed into the other, or of mutual dependence. Riegl thought Dutch art sought to create a relationship of mutual respect. The young future author of *I and Thou* was registered in the course in which Riegl first proposed these ideas. The ethical consequences Riegl drew from this relationship may have spoken to him and encouraged him to continue to pursue the study of German and Dutch art in Leipzig.[68]

The themes sounded by Riegl regarding the ethics of social and visual relations may have been reinforced and extended to other fields of inquiry in Buber's later studies in Berlin with Simmel and Dilthey, from whom he took courses in philosophy, sociology, ethics, and aesthetics. The *Lebensphilosophie* represented by the two philosophers was consistent with Riegl's ethical ideas, and their contribution to Buber's thought has been remarked upon.[69] Like Riegl's aesthetics, Simmel's sociology explored the role of the gaze in human reciprocity.[70] Riegl's notes, however, are already replete with striking images of trees and nature speaking as individuals similar to the ones that would reverberate in Buber's essays, stories, and art criticism and later in the pages of *I and Thou*. Riegl repeatedly depicted the ways in which light creates a unity embracing landscape and viewer in Dutch art. He invoked the trees in Dutch landscapes as individuals capable of communion with the beholder, who senses behind them the presence of a "world soul."[71] Riegl, conscious, as Buber would be, of the sun's capacity to blot out form, made his students aware of the limitations of broadly rendered landscapes: "How should a tree appear to us as an animate [*beseeltes*] individual if we only perceive the irregular outlines of a spot of color?" he asked them.[72]

When Riegl spoke of the broad brush strokes that destroyed the individuality of the tree, he had in mind not only the effects of certain Dutch landscapists but those of their admirers. The French Impressionists sought, as he understood it, to capture the effects of natural light but threatened the individuality of the objects, hence their ability to interact with the beholder. Riegl thought salvation lay in the finely individualized trees of Jacob Ruisdael, through their interaction with the beholder. "Ruisdael speaks to us namely through his trees, which greet us as individuals."[73] He reprised and extended the idea in an article published in the journal *Graphische Künste* in 1902: "One sees almost nothing but trees, but each one of them approaches us as an individual" (see figure 34).[74] Even the sky communes with the beholder "with hundreds of eyes."[75] Buber similarly evokes the souls of Lesser Ury's trees in their continual metamorphoses.[76] He also stresses interrelationships, however: "All things concern one another, arouse one another, help one another evolve."[77] His essay ends with a description of the deepest mission of the [Jewish] people of whom Ury is but one fragment: "Not simply nature, *natura naturans* is everywhere: in me, in you, from me to you, from you to me" (see figure 35).[78]

The unstable interchange between the individual and the relations into which it enters was often played out in changing estimations of the nineteenth-century catchword "Stimmung," an untranslatable term lying between the English "mood" and "atmosphere" and carrying the harmonious musical connotation of being "in tune." *Stimmung*, to which Riegl devoted an essay published in a well-known art journal in 1898, called up images of eternal harmony as well as transitory flights of fancy and seemed to unite the inner "mood" of the individual with the "atmosphere" of the environment.[79] Riegl, like some of his contemporaries, thought *Stimmung* central to modern art but vacillated between regarding it as the emanation of the world soul and as the omen of a dangerous subjectivism, which attracted and repelled him, much as it did the writers of Jung Wien.[80] Shifts in the evaluation of *Stimmung* can be measured against shifting attitudes toward identity.[81]

Buber, too, contended with the concept of *Stimmung*. Like Riegl, he associated it in his essay on Lesser Ury with flatness and relation. In 1905, he combined Zionist longings with fin-de-siècle art theory when he applied the term "Stimmung" to landscapes of Palestine by the artist Hermann Struck. Struck's drawings included distant views of Jerusalem as well as individual monuments (see figures 26 and 36). Buber's nuanced use of the term "Stimmung" to suggest the evanescence of the moment as well as the more permanent union of souls in the homeland suggests Jung Wien. Buber did not merely apply a fashionable term to a Jewish artist, however; he sought to appropriate *Stimmung* as a specifically Jewish phenomenon. No other than Theodor Herzl, he wrote, proclaimed *Stimmung* as the most powerful element of life in an essay written eleven years previously. Buber argued that Herzl could have written that it was the most powerful element of Jewish life.[82]

Buber's desire to ground spirit in the material world provided art with its significance for his vision of a Jewish Renaissance. Literature and philosophy could help Jews to renew their ties to religion and to life. Only art, however, would embody this renewal in material form. When Buber developed his understanding of the world in terms of relations in his early studies of Hasidism, he had already had the advantage of thinking through the concept of relationships in the visual forms of art, and he used arguments he had first developed in the context of art.[83] The two paths to relational redemption came together in his concept of Jewish art.

34. Jakob van Ruisdael, *Der Grosse Wald*, c. 1660. Kunsthistorisches Museum, Vienna.

35. Lesser Ury, *Landschaftsstudie*. From *Jüdische Künstler*, ed. Martin Buber (Berlin: Jüdischer Verlag, 1903).

36. Hermann Struck, *Jerusalem*. From *Ost und West* 5 (1905): 127–28. Courtesy of the Asher Library, Spertus Institute of Jewish Studies.

This visual conception of relational redemption suggests that Buber placed weighty expectations on visual experience. Others, too, expected the redemptive power of spirituality to appear in visual form. Alois Riegl followed his 1901 formulation of the "spatial relationships disseminated everywhere" with a spiritually oriented diagnosis of modern relationality in 1903.[84] Buber's close friend Gustav Landauer was among the first, in his *Skepsis und Mystik* (1903), to acclaim the seminal "Chandos Brief" (1901), by the poet Hugo von Hofmannsthal.[85] This fictional letter, which appeared the year in which Buber published his article on Jakob Böhme, made visual experience central to a position that Hofmannsthal later termed that of a "Mystic without Mysticism."[86] Hofmannsthal's letter writer acutely describes the inability of language to impart unity to a life he has previously experienced as fragmentary. Ultimately, he finds salvation in images. Although Hofmannsthal is less invested in the apparent opposition between words and vision than in the opposition between conceptual and metaphorical language, the images he describes are intensely visual, such as the sight of a bug swimming in a watering can, through which Chandos senses the presence of the infinite.[87] In another work, a returning Dutch traveler finds deliverance from a similar state of moral confusion directly in art: in the rendering of individual objects in the paintings of Van Gogh.[88] Visual experience, especially as expressed artistically, grounds the spiritual in the world. Hofmannsthal does not contrast mystical experience to the small, stiff letters of the printed page, yet in his images, visuality nevertheless suggests the superiority of vision to language. Moreover, Francis Bacon, the recipient of Chandos's fictional letter, appears distressed not because of Chandos's refusal to speak but because of his "complete renunciation of literary activity," or writing.[89] For both Buber and Hofmannsthal, reuniting the fragments of experience consisted in turning from a secular religion of dry law to (an equally secular) one of body and feeling. By the time Buber retold Rabbi Nachman's stories, he was sharing bibliography on mysticism with Hofmannsthal, who in turn became an enthusiastic reader of Buber's tales of Rabbi Nachman.[90]

The need to characterize peoples in terms of perceptual categories preoccupied Buber throughout a series of studies of Jews, Hasidim, and Orientals. In his essay on Jewish art, he distinguished Jews as aural, as opposed to visual, an adaptation of the anti-Semitic trope that Graetz had subverted in his adage "Paganism sees its god, Judaism hears Him."[91] Repeatedly, Buber analyzed the motion-centered Oriental, a concept Schnaase had earlier adapted to art, adding further refinements from perceptual theory.[92] According to his essays on Hasidism, Jews do not perceive through the senses. The Jew feels the "special relation between the cosmos and the psyche" but not the "full reality [*ganze Wirklichkeit*] of the tree."[93] In later writings, different sensory experiences determine the distinctive character of the "Oriental." The Oriental, he wrote, perceives with all his senses and "experiences the world less in the separate, diverse, isolated existence of things than in their amalgamation."[94] He is to be contrasted to the sensory-type Western man, "under the preponderant influence of the most detached, most independent, most objective [sense]; the sense of sight."[95] In Buber's concept, the sense of sight provides knowledge of the objective, isolated existence of things rather than, as in Riegl's system, the sense of touch. Yet Buber's interpretation of perception, which preserves the notion of the nonvisual Oriental, incorporates Riegl's perceptual adaptations of unity and separation.

The notion of the artistic relationship adapted itself to new preoccupations after Buber's aspirations became universal. When he developed his thoughts on relationships into a theory of dialogism, in the formulation of his 1923 work *I and Thou,* he grounded his ideas in the secular, universal realm. By *I and Thou,* Buber had come to see the dark side of *Stimmung*. Like Riegl, he rejected the model of nature that corresponded to the broad brush strokes of French Impressionism: "The tree," he wrote in *I and Thou,* "is no impression [Eindruck], no play of my imagination, no atmospheric value [*Stimmungswert*], but it is bodied over against me and has to do with me, as I with it."[96] *Stimmung,* which implies selfless immersion, was ill-suited to render a relationship of respect.

Art, on the other hand, grew out of such a relationship. Buber not only formulated a concept of the relation of art to its beholder, he reconceived the origin and genesis of art in terms of relations. Art comes into being when a form encounters the artist and "through him wants to become a work" (13). Stressing the separateness of the form from the artist, Buber describes the genesis of the work as a process whereby the work comes into existence as the artist realizes the form and speaks to it. He conceived the form as a presence that forms a relation to the artist and explicitly opposed it to the outpourings of an artist's own mind (13–15).

Not until many years later, however, in "Man and His Image-Work," did Buber seek to probe deeply into the dialogical relationship of man with his art. The essay, one of a series on the anthropology of knowledge, builds on his previously articulated dialogic vision of the origins of art. "Man has a great desire to enter into personal relation with things," he wrote in his essay "Urdistanz und Beziehung" (Primal distance and relation), "and to imprint on them his relation to them."[97] In "Man and His Image-work," Buber mined a quotation from Dürer to the effect that the artist tears art out of nature for its relevance to modern life, a quotation that served as a caption for the watercolor by Dürer that served as the cover of the first publication in English of Buber's essay (see figure 37). This late essay, however, despite references to modern physics that situate it in the mid-twentieth century, remains in the conceptual milieu of the fin de siècle. It brings to bear on Dürer's statement Buber's response to the ideas of Konrad Fiedler. Buber had the same problem with Fiedler as did Riegl and solved it similarly by postulating that the artist does not try to produce or reproduce the world but is, like the lover or the true believer, motivated by the "demand for the perfect relation."[98] "The artist," he wrote, "whose meetings with x are of an intensity peculiar to himself, is not content to behold that which the world of the senses, which humanity holds in common, makes perceptible to him. He wants, within the sphere of that one sense to which his art is oriented, to experience and realize the relation to the substrata of the things of the senses in its perfection: through figuration in vision and in the work."[99]

The standpoint is borne out concretely in several essays on the artist Leopold Krakauer. Krakauer, a recently deceased architect, was also an accomplished painter and draftsman. Buber's initial essay commemorated the thirtieth day after the death of his friend, but versions of it appeared for several years thereafter in expanded forms and different languages. Krakauer's engagement with the landscape around Jerusalem concerned Buber now, as Hermann Struck's confrontation with Palestine had concerned him many years before. In contrast to the *Stimmung*

37. Albrecht Dürer, *Lilie*, watercolor, c. 1508[?]. Kunsthalle Bremen, Germany.

he admired in Struck's drawings, however, Buber used the essays on Krakauer to discuss a personal relationship with nature.[100] Krakauer's encounter with Jerusalem's landscape corresponded to Buber's dialogically conceived "meeting"; the solitude of the landscape encountered and transformed that of the artist. The artist could grasp internally the "dynamic of its solitude, which corresponded to and answered to his own."[101] Although Krakauer, like Struck, often took distant hillscapes by Jerusalem for his subjects, Buber focused on Krakauer's studies of isolated natural objects. Describing "the inner tension, that works out the restless and yet so closed form of the thistle," Buber interprets Krakauer's *Thistle* in the formal language of Riegl's time (see figure 38).[102] Buber appreciated Krakauer's anthropomorphic olive trees, like Riegl appreciated Ruisdael's beckoning trees, because they conveyed the sense of the confrontation with nature as the encounter with a being rather than the representation of an object (see figure 39). The balance had shifted from *Stimmung*'s distant view to an intense personal encounter in closeup.

The essay on Krakauer shows how far Buber had departed from his early years, when the drawing of Palestine operated only as a harbinger of Zionism. Not only had Buber's attempt to incorporate art into Judaism and Zionism given way to other interests, the reality of Zionism and the State of Israel had robbed him of whatever hopes he may have had that the mere return of Jews to Palestine and the emergence of the Jewish state would bring a Jewish art into existence. Yet these late philosophical formulations on art remained in the circle of fin-de-siècle Vienna that had enabled him to conceive of a Jewish art early in his career. The secular spirituality of fin-de-siècle Vienna allowed Buber to negotiate between Judaism and modernity, giving Jewish artists an opportunity to take their place in the forefront of modern art while giving expression to the relationality that Buber regarded as their essential nature. A seemingly nonvisual people could contribute to art in an immaterial age.

But Buber could only hope to propagate the idea of a spiritual Jewish art among acculturated Jews who liked to think of themselves as participants in the artistic culture of the gentiles surrounding them. The 1903 volume on Jewish art, therefore, served Buber's project to reconcile Jewish tradition and contemporary European culture. While his

38. Leopold Krakauer, *Thistle*. From *Die Kunst und das Schöne Heim* 3/62 (December 1963): 114. Courtesy of the Getty Research Library. Reproduced with the permission of Dr. Trude Dothan.

39. Leopold Krakauer, *Ancient Olive Tree*. From *Ariel* (winter 1964–65): 7. Courtesy of the Getty Research Library. Reproduced with the permission of Dr. Trude Dothan.

characterization of the Jewish race could only be intended for a Jewish audience, the call for a spiritual art was part and parcel of what would make Buber an ambassador from the Jewish to the gentile world. That is, the same project – the reconciliation of Jewish spirituality with modernity – that gave *I and Thou* its aura of universality, and his tales of Rabbi Nachman their appeal, also governed his views of art.

Faced with the difficulty of bringing art into a society that he thought had lived without it, he reached for an alternative notion of Judaism that valued the life of the senses, and visuality above all. The art that served this vision discarded the representation of sensory data in favor of a relationship to them. While the Jewish culture of the past did not provide Buber with a precedent for such art, he could draw on the Hasidic movement for permission to let the senses form a relation to God. Similarly, he could use his art theoretical training to help him conceive an art of relations reconcilable with Jewish artistic limitations. Art theorists in fin-de-siècle Vienna conceived modern art as an art of relations. For Buber, however, the concept of art in terms of relationships rather than objects made possible a mode of art suited to a people without art.

CHAPTER FIVE

"Jewish Christians" and "Early Christian" Synagogues

The Discovery at Dura-Europos and Its Aftermath

> The Synagogue [at Dura-Europos] brings to vivid expression the vigor and the piety, the high aspiration and the dignity of a relatively small and unimportant Jewish community of the eastern Dispersion in a frontier garrison city. At the same time through this one structure we can look out into a vast panorama of historical development and relationships, finding new insights suggested everywhere. Here we find new suggestions for an understanding of the growth and development of synagogue architecture. Here the history of Jewish piety and of the development of its interpretative tradition is freshingly illumined. Here the ancient Jewish use of art is restored to its rightful place in the total picture of ancient Judaism. Here we see in a new light the common front which Christianity and Judaism held against paganism, and the relationship between Jewish and Christian art. **Carl H. Kraeling** in *The Synagogue: The Excavations at Dura-Europos*

Who Is a Jewish Art Historian?

Nationality, in art history, is a function of one's field of study. An "American art historian" studies American art, while a "French art historian" studies French art. Dual or triple nationality accrues to the scholar who concentrates on any combination of Italian, French, and German art. But there is an exception. Jewish art historians are defined not through their material but through matrilineal or patrilineal descent, conversion, or marriage. A Jewish art historian is a Jew who studies art history.

The prospects of Jewish art historians – by this definition – improved dramatically in the early twentieth century, when most art historians, whatever their "nationality," spoke German. At the turn of the century, only Adolph Goldschmidt was able to procure an art historical professorship without a baptismal certificate, once as much of a prerequisite as a doctoral degree.[1] Fervent German patriot though he was, Goldschmidt's first Ordinariat, in Halle in 1904, necessitated a governmental dispensation; by 1912, he was the Ordinarius in Berlin, a position in which he was highly successful until he retired in 1929.[2] By then, however, the field had opened to Jews, and two, Erwin Panofsky and Paul Frankl, pursued art historical careers successfully. Others, such as Aby Warburg and his followers in Hamburg, had an impact on art history through the new directions in scholarship and theory that they inspired. Art historians of Jewish heritage took part in the intense theoretical debate that characterized art history in German-speaking countries in the 1920s and early 1930s.[3]

As suggested above, the prospects for scholars of Jewish art improved less dramatically.[4] The most prominent Jewish art historians rarely studied Jewish art. Goldschmidt wrote nothing on the topic, while later scholars of his caliber, whether European or American, wrote little. Neither Erwin Panofsky nor Meyer Schapiro, for example, contributed notably to the scholarship of Jewish art.[5] Those progeny of David Kaufmann who concentrated on Jewish topics remained marginal to the field as a whole. Some art historians who did make important contributions to the study of Jewish monuments were – perhaps accordingly – doubly marginal. They were women – for example, Rachel Wischnitzer, in Germany, and, somewhat later, after her emigration to England, Helen Rosenau, who worked tirelessly to further scholarship on Jewish art, writing a second doctoral thesis on synagogue architecture in 1940.[6] By 1930, however, when Wischnitzer gave her assessment of the state of the field, there were a few major publications for her to mention and an upcoming generation initiated active research into Jewish monuments.[7] Cecil Roth began his studies of Jewish art; Rudolf Hallo added to the literature on Jewish art and organized exhibitions on the subject at the Hessisches Landesmuseum.[8] In 1927, Richard Krautheimer completed his *Habilitation* on medieval synagogues.[9] That same year, the first ambitious publication of a Haggadah since Julius von Schlosser's edition of the Sarajevo Haggadah appeared. The two-volume publication, *Die Darmstädter Pessach-Haggadah*, reproduced an entire medieval Haggadah in facsimile, along with several studies, including a stylistic analysis by L. A. Mayer.[10] Ernst Cohn-Wiener was the first of several to publish an ambitiously conceived, book-length attempt at a general history of Jewish art.[11] Contemporary Jewish art, too, became a subject worthy of publications and exhibitions. The critics Karl Schwarz and Waldemar George published widely on Jewish artists.[12] In France, where a community of Jewish artists took part in the avant-garde, a series of monographs on individual Jewish artists appeared between 1928 and 1932.[13] It began to look as though the concept of a Jewish art historian would come to mean more than an art historian born of Jewish parents.

None of the scholars engaged in these activities made an academic career solely out of the study of Jewish art. Roth, a professor of Jewish studies, wrote on many subjects besides art; Hallo, also a man of wide interests, died young in 1933; Cohn-Wiener was an Islamist. Richard Krautheimer turned his attention to other matters and dismissed his early work on synagogues.[14] In 1944, he rejected an offer to become director of the newly founded Jewish Museum in New York. But these scholars' work demonstrates at least a willingness on their part to work on Jewish subjects in the art historical field of the 1920s. Krautheimer, for example, used the position he did accept and briefly occupy at the Jewish Museum, that of director of research, in an effort to establish a research center at the new museum, which would have focused on the scholarly study of Jewish art.[15]

Late in the 1920s, important new discoveries of Jewish monuments made their scholarship appear current and vital. The excavation of ancient synagogues in Palestine, Beth Alpha foremost among them, revealed mosaic floors that provided new evidence for the existence of Jewish figural art (see figure 40).[16] In 1932, these finds were eclipsed by the discovery of elaborate representational murals in the third-century synagogue at Dura-Europos in Syria (see figure 41). Jewish art historical studies, like Jewish art historians, seemed poised to make an impact on the field of art history. Not the German art historical community, therefore, but the Franco-American team led by Clark Hopkins, of Yale University, who discovered the Dura paintings, may provide an answer to the question "Who is a Jewish Art Historian?"

The site at Dura-Europos, excavated beginning after its discovery by British troops in 1920, was remarkable for its conjunction of pagan, Christian, and Jewish houses of worship, all located in close proximity. Their decorations, immediately datable through inscriptions, and through the well-documented destruction of the city by the Parthians in 256, were executed within decades of one another. The pagan and Christian discoveries caused great excitement. But the most momentous discovery was that of the Jewish frescoes. Decades later, Hopkins described evocatively the moment late in 1932 when the painstaking labor of his crew laid bare the elaborate figured murals of the synagogue.

> We stood together in mute silence and complete astonishment. A casual passerby witnessing the paintings suddenly emerging from the earth would have been astonished. If he had been a Classical archaeologist, with the knowledge of how few paintings had survived from Classical times, he would have been that much more amazed. But if he were a biblical scholar or a student of ancient art and were told that the building was a synagogue and the paintings were scenes from the Old Testament, he simply would not have believed it. It could not be; there was absolutely no precedent, nor could there be any. The stern injunction in the Ten Commandments against the making of graven images would be sufficient to prove him right.[17]

But the paintings were more than oddities. The man who discovered them was convinced of their artistic value as well. He had no doubt that "the devout artist who designed the tremendous series of paintings at Dura was a genius who magnificently fulfilled the challenge presented

40. *Sacrifice of Isaac,* mosaic pavement, detail. The Synagogue at Beth Alpha, 6th century. From Eleazar L. Sukenik, *The Ancient Synagogue of Beth Alpha* (Jerusalem: University Press; London: Oxford University Press, 1932), plate xix.

41. Tora niche and wall decoration from the synagogue at Dura-Europos, 3rd century, National Museum, Damascus. Courtesy of Bildarchiv Foto Marburg.

by the great bare walls of the Synagogue."[18] Hopkins readily accepted the paintings as a great monument of Jewish art.

Not everyone has shared this assessment. While the historical significance of the paintings has made them the first existing Jewish religious monument to enjoy a secure place in surveys of art history, the writers of these surveys have generally denigrated either their Jewish or their artistic credentials. Scholars account for Dura, as Julius von Schlosser accounted for the Sarajevo Haggadah, in terms of canonical, non-Jewish developments. In his book *The Story of Art*, E. H. Gombrich proved himself a true student of Schlosser in his justification for the study of the paintings with the comment that "similar considerations [to those raised by Dura] began to influence art when the Christian religion spread from the East and also took art into its service."[19] The necessity to categorize the paintings caused other anomalies. While H. W. Janson put the paintings in a chapter on Roman art, two other popular surveys placed Dura under the rubric of Early Christian art (without, of course, intending to allude to any Christianizing activity that did take place in synagogues), thus implicitly creating the phenomenon of "Early Christian Synagogues."[20] The category does not result only from knotty problems of organization. Since it fails to engage the literature on the transition from synagogue to church in early Christianity, it is safe to assume that it results from an unthinking interpretation of the Jewish religion as only the superseded – and static – forerunner of Christianity. This interpretation, ahistorically Christian or teleologically Hegelian, reverberated even recently, when an important scholar of late antiquity labeled the third-century synagogue's visual interpretation of the Crossing of the Red Sea "pre-Christian."[21]

It was also possible to deny the Jewish character of the paintings by turning them into an example of assimilation conceived negatively, as in the following passage written by a critic: "With all due deference, and subject to correction, I would suggest that the murals at Dura are to be classed with other visual art done by Jews in forms alien to them: . . . The Jewish artists who executed this work had become masters of a craft; but in carrying out that craft they renounced their Jewishness."[22] At least one critic seems to have found it necessary to baptize the monument in order to bring it into mainstream art history. Even one of the most famous, and earliest, responses to Dura, that of Erwin R.

Goodenough, cited Dura's use of images to argue for the existence of a Hellenistic Jewish mystic cult far from "normative Judaism."[23] The paintings were an aberration.

The standard surveys of art history approached the monument with at least tacit acceptance of the notion of a ban on images in Judaism, for they found it necessary to comment on the contradiction between a religion that forbids images and the figured decorations on a synagogue. Gombrich's survey was the only major one to propose an explanation for the presence of paintings in an imageless cult. Far from singing the praises of the "genius" who designed them, as had Hopkins, Gombrich tried to excuse the deficiencies of the artist who designed the "humble" paintings: "The artist was doubtless not very skillful. . . . But perhaps he was not really much concerned with drawing lifelike figures. The more lifelike they were, the more they sinned against the Commandment forbidding images."[24] The explanation links two tropes about Jewish art: Jews' lack of artistic skill reduces the risk of violating the tendency to violate the commandment forbidding them to make images.

Annabelle Wharton, whose artistic opinion of the paintings (gained firsthand in Damascus) resembles that of Hopkins more than that of Gombrich, has written eloquently of the prejudice against Dura, identifying signs of Orientalism in the scholarship of the monument as well as a pervasive tone of diminution in the discourse around the paintings, including the tendency to reduce the thriving metropolis of Dura to an outpost. Even specialized scholarship, she recognized, suppressed the Jewishness of the paintings and located Dura's significance to scholarship in its relation to Early Christian art. She recognized Goodenough's intention, in de-Judaizing the paintings, to bring Judaism closer to Early Christianity and reenergize the myth of a Judeo-Christian tradition.[25] The major art historical text on the synagogue, by Kurt Weitzmann and Herbert Kessler, she writes, locates its importance in (a) its role as a predecessor of later Christian monuments and (b) its impetus in earlier Hellenistic manuscripts, thus omitting the Jewish mo[nu]ment that falls between its past and future. Indeed, the very title of Weitzmann and Kessler's book suggests an effort to keep its focus Christian: *The Frescoes of the Dura Synagogue and Christian Art.*

Wharton's observations constitute the beginning of a new understanding of the scholarship of Dura-Europos. The threat posed by the discovery of works such as the paintings at Dura to the art historical paradigm that needed the nonexistence of Jewish art has indeed given rise to neutralizing strategies like those she describes, as well as to the subtly modified yet persistent continuation of the trope of Jewish art outlined in chapter 1. But the reception of the paintings in the synagogue at Dura involves complexities beyond the suppression of ethnicity and Jewish religiosity. At the moment of their startling discovery, the paintings found not only the well-worn tropes of Jewish art but a set of counterdiscourses ready for their insertion. Evoking these discourses, scholars could mobilize the paintings narrowly as an art historical support for the concept of Jewish art or, more broadly, in the service of a form of art historical resistance to fascistic nationalism. The paintings in the synagogue at Dura-Europos, perhaps more than any other Jewish monument, have inspired ambitiously comprehensive visions of the role of Jewish art in a Christian world. And no monument has had a greater impact on what it means to be a Jewish art historian.

Humanist Discourse Meets German Nationalism

These counterdiscourses were not designed for the purpose of Jewish defense. Long before the synagogue at Dura provided a convenient focus for fighters for Jewish rights on the artistic front, the same climate that gave rise to Julius Langbehn's anti-Semitic appeal to Rembrandt's educational role, and to Josef Strzygowski's venomous attacks, disrupted the rarified atmosphere of academic humanism, a scholarly discipline that stressed the study of classical philology and literature. Humanists were already an embattled group, hurt by the emphasis, in the late nineteenth century, on science. But ethnic conflicts hurt them as well. One front against the Humanists, for example, was the field of German prehistory. Its fortunes having been advanced by patriotic ardor in the aftermath of German unification, it competed successfully for funding and academic positions against the universalistic humanism of scholars of classical philology and archaeology. The extremist Gustav Kossinna, for example, explicitly directed the study of German prehistory against "the men wearing the blinkers of a *Gymna-*

sium education," where they would have studied Latin and Greek.[26] The accusation labeled Humanists, themselves once beholden to German Romanticism, as blind to Germanic interests.

Beginning in the 1880s, when the altar from Pergamum entered the Berlin museum and other important Hellenistic works entered European museums, scholars could use the cross-cultural, disseminating role of Hellenistic art on the front lines of the battle between pan-Germanic nationalism and the multinational empire of which Vienna was the center. Aware that the unity of the empire was threatened by the nationalism of groups such as Slavs and Germans, whose empires bordered on Austria-Hungary, as well as the ethnic nationalism of smaller subgroups such as Bohemians, Austrian scholars battled ethnic isolation, arguing for the contribution of each nationality to a larger multiethnic entity and to history conceived as a worldwide development.

Some probably acted from opposition to racism. In public, Jewish art historians rarely acknowledged their own ethnic identities, and Christian art historians seldom used a public forum to attack the anti-Semitism that they wrote about in private. Yet art historians then as now wrote for multiple interpretive communities that were doubtless often aware of the political or social nuances of their scholarship. The same scholars who condemned the anti-Semitism of the art historical community in private correspondence often argued against pan-Germanists in their publications. Friedrich Portheim, the young scholar who objected to assigning an observant Jew the topic of the baptism of Christ, led the art historical assault on the pan-Germanists in his 1886 book on Hellenistic art.[27] Portheim flatly denied the notion of primeval German traits, attributing all of them to pan-Hellenism instead, and dismissed Celtic ornament, supposedly the revered expression of primeval Germans, as a derivation of early Christian art.[28] Colleagues from his days as a student of Moriz Thausing, a much-maligned professor said to have been of Jewish descent, supported him and similarly attacked German nationalism in key areas, such as the veneration of Greek art and identification with Rembrandt and Dürer as quintessential Germans.[29] Alois Riegl valued the contribution of Oriental to Greek art in antiquity and of Italian to Northern art in the sixteenth and seventeenth centuries.[30] He thought nationalism too narrow-minded a motive for historical preservation.[31] Others fought the battle of North and South in handwriting. Patriotic Germans claimed Fraktur as their birthright; humanists dismissed it as an illegible derivation of Carolingian miniscule.[32] It is surely no accident that the *Protest deutscher Künstler,* whose anti-Semitic overtones were discussed above, used Fraktur, while its opponents published their response in Roman type.

Pan-German scholars and multiculturalists attacked one another not just on the basis of their conclusions; they implicated their methodologies as well. The imbrication of method and politics comes out clearly in an exchange of the 1930s between the French art historian Henri Focillon and Josef Strzygowski, whose earlier anti-Semitic scholarship was discussed in chapter 1. The letters, dated 1932 and 1934, appeared in 1935 under the auspices of the Institut International de Coopération Intellectuelle, a committee of the League of Nations. An exchange between Rabindranath Tagore and Gilbert Murray represented East and West, while Strzygowski and Focillon represented the "Génie du Nord" and "Latinité," respectively.[33]

The subject of the letters originated in several exchanges between Focillon and Strzygowski in a centennial symposium on Johann Wolfgang von Goethe, published under the same auspices.[34] In his letter to Focillon, Strzygowski explicated his "comparative method" of formal analysis. His method was superior to the philological approach of classical archaeologists, he argued, because it was applicable to the reconstruction of evidence that has not survived.[35] In practice, Strzygowski based his argument about the nature of the northern genius on his derivation of the Greek temple from wooden "blockhouses" of the North and on the northern origin of interlace.[36] He compensated for the lack of material evidence for these derivations with conjectural evidence based on the northerner's all-consuming need for protection against winter.[37] These northern, perishable arts, he argued, were transformed into monumental architecture on the shores of the Mediterranean.[38] But he did not content himself with architecture nor limit himself to prehistory. He returned to the subject of the previous symposium, Goethe, whom an understanding of the North reveals to have been a "pioneer of modern landscape painting."[39] Strzygowski concluded, in an unmistakable reference to National Socialism, that the evolution of humanity always depends on the migrations of northern peoples.[40]

Strzygowski's arguments recall those of archaeologists influenced by the architect Gottfried Semper, a name he invoked more than once.[41] Semper theorized that artistic styles were determined by functions, materials, and techniques. Neo-Semperian archaeologists sought to establish the ethnic origins of peoples through their stylistic responses to Semper's determinants.[42] Their work often had the effect of establishing the racial purity of Greek art. When proposed in the late nineteenth century, this determinism drew the fire of scholars like Alois Riegl, who argued for artistic freedom and who presumably disliked their conclusions as much as their methods.[43]

Focillon's reply went beyond the revulsion that he must have shared with many fellow art historians to the overt National Socialism in Strzygowski's letter, especially those who, like Focillon, were to be active opponents of Nazism.[44] Identifying Strzygowski's conclusions with his methodological strategy, Focillon criticized the assumptions inherent in the comparative method. Strzygowski's formal method, he argued, entailed biological determinism, and his concern for sources was nothing other than a concern for race. Focillon's own cosmopolitan formalism sought to determine not the origin of an artistic style but the way in which an artist develops it, whatever its origin. "That the barbarians had a wooden model [for the column] is not at all contested," he wrote, "and it is not that that must be admired, but rather the mathematical care with which it is measured and its parts articulated."[45] Gothic architecture is not a development of wooden architecture or an expression of the northern genius, but a solution to the problems of stone, created by an urban bourgeoisie.[46]

Where Strzygowski saw only race, Focillon insisted on seeing universally human potential. "How just and well founded seems to me your remark on the necessity of interrogating the popular arts," he wrote, "not as a national or local expression, but as a common treasure!"[47] The significance of an invasion is not in the mixture of races to which it gives rise but in the encounter it makes possible between two "states" of man.[48] The baroque style has no native country; it is a "moment in the life of forms."[49] The phrase alludes to the title of the book that Focillon published the year of his answer to Strzygowski.[50] In *The Life of Forms in Art* (*Vie des formes*), Focillon argued fervently that art is animated by a kindred spirit of forms, not of nationality or ethnic identity. Distinct chauvinistic implications echo even through Focillon's rhapsodic discourse, yet the dependence on methodology for the construction and refutation of nationalistic arguments was never made clearer than in Focillon's demonstration that the origin, fixed forever, is essentializing and antihistorical, while development, to the contrary, is always open. "If we were condemned always to resemble a rigorous anthropological pattern," Focillon wrote, "civilization would be without a past and without a present."[51]

The Scholarship of Resistance

The discovery of the synagogue at Dura-Europos not only was the most dramatic of the discoveries of Jewish art but also came at a critical moment, October 1932, just a few months before the Nazis came to power in Germany. By the time news of the discovery spread, the study of Jewish art had been relegated to newly opened Jewish museums in Berlin and Frankfurt and other Jewish cultural organizations. To be sure, through these organizations a number of art historians who had never previously studied Jewish art were temporarily "encouraged" to do so by the loss of their academic positions (Franz Landsberger, mentioned in chapter 3, was among them).[52] But the promise of Jewish art to emerge as a respectable field of research was gone, and even Nazi-sponsored outlets were eventually threatened along with the livelihoods and lives of Jewish art historians. A glance at Hopkins's enthusiastic presentation in the *Illustrated London News* of the monument and its significance for Christian art, in the company of an article about an anti-Nazi demonstration by Jews in Hyde Park and a cover story about a proposal to offer British citizenship to Albert Einstein, makes clear that the symbolic power of this evidence of Jewish religious art resides as much in its timing at a crucial moment in Jewish history as in the intrinsic artistic or scholarly worth of the find, immense though it was.[53]

One of the most important scholars to be influenced by this discovery was the Byzantinist Kurt Weitzmann, a student of Adolph Goldschmidt. He learned about the discovery of the paintings in the Dura synagogue in 1933, when a Christian theologian, Hans Lietzmann (1875–1942), told Goldschmidt about it at the Prussian Academy of Sciences. A French archaeologist, Franz Cumont, had informed Lietzmann about the discovery in great excitement, beginning in October 1932.[54] On the basis of a complete set of the photographs given him by Professor P. V. C. Baur, of Yale University, Lietzmann decided to offer a seminar on the topic in Berlin that academic year, 1933–34.[55] Weitzmann, already a post-doctoral student, enrolled.

Weitzmann's account of the incident does not impute to Lietzmann any but academic motives for offering the course. Surely it was astounding enough to discover an important cycle of wall paintings by a people hitherto thought to lack representational art. Furthermore, Lietzmann had already written about representational images in Jewish catacombs.[56] It is hard to believe, however, that no political motivations came into play in Lietzmann's decision to focus on their art during the year following Hitler's assumption of power. In fact, the gesture of holding a seminar on the decoration of a synagogue corresponded to the tenor of Lietzmann's acts of resistance, or at least of stubbornness, during the Third Reich. He belonged to the Wednesday Society (Mittwochs-Gesellschaft), a venerable, conservative society of about sixteen intellectuals and government officials. Among them were some of those who planned the attempt on Hitler's life in July 1944; several members of the society would eventually be imprisoned, executed, or driven to suicide in its aftermath. In the early years of the Third Reich, however, they practiced a seemingly milder course of passive resistance consisting mainly of disregard, among themselves, for the intellectual and social strictures around them.[57] Lietzmann's actions, until his death in 1941, accorded with this pattern. He supported academic colleagues dismissed from their posts for ideological or racial reasons; he delivered papers that, sometimes subtly, challenged Nazi ideology and sought to oppose Nazism's threat to the Protestant churches and the universities. In the Mittwochs-Gesellschaft, he chronicled the failed attempts of the Protestant Church in 1934 to work with the National Socialist regime, and in a historical talk about Constantine, he discussed the beginnings of the problem of Church and state, a thinly veiled reference to the situation of the moment.[58] His vote against a resolution to apply the government's Aryan Paragraphs to the employment of pastors within the church earned the University of Berlin a letter from the district leadership of the Nazi Party requesting his dismissal.[59]

The seminar on the synagogue at Dura-Europos conforms to this paradigm of quiet opposition, to which Lietzmann's continued interest in the paintings of the synagogue throughout the 1930s contributed. The second volume of his *A History of the Early Church*, published in 1936, referred to the paintings and raised the possibility of Jewish models for early Christian iconography.[60] A stipend for travel to the Holy Land enabled him to visit the excavations in Dura and to see the recently installed murals in Damascus. While the minutes of his report to the Academy of Science on his trip east do not mention the synagogue, elsewhere he stressed its importance for Christian art and speculated on the existence of a Jewish illustrated Bible.[61] In a review of early monographs on the paintings, he emphasized the significance of Jewish art for Byzantine art and, like Annabelle Wharton, found the published reproductions inadequate to the experience of the originals.[62]

Kurt Weitzmann dated his preoccupation with the relationship between ancient Jewish and Christian art to his encounter with the paintings in Lietzmann's seminar, calling it an "event... which was to change my life."[63] It did so in a more than academic sense by giving him the opportunity to move to the United States. Lietzmann, impressed with Weitzmann's work, promised him the support of the Prussian Academy for an edition of the Byzantine Octateuchs. Weitzmann's consequent attempts to procure photographs of the Octateuchs from Princeton University led to an invitation from Charles Rufus Morey to collaborate with him in Princeton for a year on another project.

Weitzmann accepted the invitation because he could not find suitable employment at a university in Germany. He was not Jewish, but he was devoted to his Jewish professor. Weitzmann's years-long collaboration with Goldschmidt, the first of many extensive collaborations with colleagues, brought him into the home of the elderly professor for several hours almost daily. This relationship did not bring him the academic opportunities it might have had it come earlier, given the success enjoyed by many of Goldschmidt's students.[64] Albert E. Brinckmann, Goldschmidt's successor in Berlin, rejected Weitzmann for a *Privatdozentur*, an early step on the academic ladder, telling him that he would accept no pupil of Goldschmidt, whatever his qualifications. Weitzmann then found another position, with the aid of Hans Jantzen, a former student of Goldschmidt who had joined the Nazi party, only to discover that acceptance would require submission to a one-year indoctrination in Nazi ideology.[65] He declined yet another offer, from the Kaiser-Friedrich-Museum, because it meant replacing a curator, Wolfgang Fritz Volbach (1892–1988), dismissed because of "a 'wrong' grandmother." [66] In 1933, Weitzmann had begun editing a *Festschrift* for Goldschmidt's seventieth birthday. For fear of political consequences, however, some of Goldschmidt's students withdrew their contributions before the *Festschrift* appeared in 1935.[67] Only after accumulating several such experiences did Weitzmann finally accept Morey's offer and leave Germany for Princeton in 1935. A permanent position soon materialized.

While in Princeton, Weitzmann continued his interest in Dura. He established a close friendship with Carl Kraeling, the author of Yale's reports on the synagogue. The Dumbarton Oaks annual symposium of 1945 consisted of seven lectures by the two men on the synagogue. According to Weitzmann, an understanding with Kraeling, whose final report appeared in 1956, prevented Weitzmann from publishing anything substantial on the paintings until 1990. When, however, he finally coauthored *The Frescoes of the Dura Synagogue and Christian Art* with Herbert Kessler, he dedicated it to the memory of Lietzmann and Kraeling.[68]

The first discussions of Dura recognized its potential to unravel the mystery of the relationship between Christian and Jewish art.[69] Beginning with his paper on the painting of the Crossing of the Red Sea, read in Lietzmann's seminar, Weitzmann eagerly took up the theory, initiated by David Kaufmann, that Christian art could be traced to Jewish sources. The synagogue decorations served to support the theory that Jewish manuscripts must have existed and functioned as sources for Christian manuscript cycles. With more science than Kaufmann, but along similar lines, Weitzmann and other scholars argued that theme after theme in Christian art originated in illustrations that adorned now-lost Jewish manuscripts in the Hellenistic period. Their confidence that Jewish manuscript illumination existed in Hellenistic times depended entirely on the excavations at Dura-Europos. These were nearly the only Jewish illustrations brought to bear on a complex argument that postulated the existence of a rich tradition of Jewish illustrated manuscripts, from midrashim to the Hebrew Bible, all lost.[70]

Weitzmann's arguments depend not on the discovery of a trove of ancient manuscripts but on the validity of his application to visual images of a philological method initially developed by nineteenth-century German scholars for textual criticism.[71] The philologists assumed that all existing copies of a text are corrupted copies of older manuscripts. The scholars constructed ideal "recensions" that ordered these manuscripts according to the earlier copies from which they must have descended, in order to approach the reconstruction of an original, pure text. In the late nineteenth century, the classicist and colleague of Goldschmidt Carl Robert (1850–1922) and the Viennese art historian Franz Wickhoff proposed theories of the historical development of narrative art in antiquity. Weitzmann used these theories to construct recensions of manuscript illuminations similar to those philologists constructed for texts. The cycle of images in Dura, because it involved narrative techniques that Weitzmann associated with Hellenistic art, seemed to prove the existence of Hellenistic Jewish illustrated Bibles. Weitzmann traces the Dura panel of the *Finding of Moses* to five scenes in its putative model (see figure 42).[72] Following this method, scholars who identified illustrations of Jewish midrashim in Christian manuscripts could point to Dura to trace these illustrations to lost Jewish Hellenistic manuscripts.

The search for the origin of a motif might seem to commit Weitzmann and his followers to value the primeval identity of an originating culture, whether German, French, or Jewish, placing them on Strzygowski's side of the controversy with Focillon, despite the use of philological methods that Strzygowski would have rejected. Weitzmann's preoccupation with sources, however, is misleading. To investigate the effect on art of diverse influences from different places was to value community and diversity, which were the abiding themes of Weitzmann's work on Jewish and Christian art. Weitzmann allied himself with such classical archaeologists as Otto Jahn, Carl Robert, and Ulrich von Wilamowitz-Moellendorff. He criticized Josef Strzygowski directly for his antagonism to Greek culture, his failure to appreciate the role of Hellenistic art in the creation of illustrated books, and his disregard of the contributions of classical archaeologists, while regarding Strzygowski's admiration of the Persians (or Aryans) with suspicion.[73] But more importantly, Weitzmann must have been aware of the implications of the search for origins, for immediately after the war, in the definitive statement of his philological method, he distinguished his work from

42. *Finding of Moses*, wall painting, detail, from the synagogue at Dura-Europos, 3rd century. Courtesy of the Yale University Art Gallery, Dura-Europos Collection.

that of the philologist who seeks to reconstruct a lost original in order to find a superior text. "Paradoxical as it may sound," he wrote, "iconographic corruption and artistic improvement can coincide in one and the same miniature, depending on the scale of values for different periods.... It is this interplay of two overlapping time factors which gives to the study of miniatures its peculiar richness and variety and makes the history of a miniature recension appear as a process of organic growth rather than a process of gradual fading as in text transmission."[74]

An understanding of Weitzmann's search for origins as a means to reveal change illuminates an interpretive property of Weitzmann's work: its tendency, by analyzing Jewish works in terms of Christian and Hellenistic rather than Jewish art, to obscure their specifically Jewish character. If the aim of studying a monument is to determine its originality, to isolate it from the mainstream of history, and to render it an object of contemplation, then Weitzmann could be accused of having marginalized Jewish monuments. Yet Weitzmann's strategy of placing Jewish monuments in a mainstream artistic development, in the context of canonical monuments, was designed not to hide the ethnicity of a monument or to denigrate its art, but to break down barriers between Christian and Jewish monuments and, by extension, between Christians and Jews.

Originality was less important to Weitzmann than the nature of the community that enabled transmission. By placing the Dura synagogue in relation to Christian art, rather than merely to lost libraries of Jewish art, Weitzmann invents a vast community for Dura. This imagined community, in which Christians and Jews lived in harmony, contrasts markedly with the community in which Weitzmann first learned about the paintings. Given the strained relations among Christian and Jewish professors in Germany, it must have been a relief to return to this ancient world. The importance of postulating not only a relation between Christians and Jews but a close and friendly one is evident throughout his work. His introduction to the 1977 exhibition catalog *The Age of Spirituality* glows with discussions of an "atmosphere of tolerance" that went so far in antiquity as to enable burial chambers to depict the symbols of different religions side by side, as well as "the coexistence and mutual tolerance of a variety of religious establishments within the same community" and the creation of an "ecumenical style" developed by no single religion but shared by pagans, Christians, and Jews.[75] In Dura, he rhapsodized, "the various religious groups commissioned the painters without asking about their religious affiliations," an extraordinary third-century exercise in equal opportunity employment (xxv). His section of the book on the Dura paintings ends by evoking the close-knit Jewish and Christian communities in the "small garrison city," which would have been able to share manuscripts borrowed from Antioch, because "the availability of the same model with David scenes in the synagogue and the Christian chapel speaks for the existence of a climate in which Jews and Christians were on good terms with each other."[76]

To trace the narrative technique passed on by Jewish manuscripts not to Jewish but to Hellenistic sources does not detract from the importance of the Jews; it adds to their community. Hence the significance of uniting the story of Dura with that of Hellenistic art and the later Christian Middle Ages. When Weitzmann spoke of his intentions in studying Dura, he used words that are at home in the social realm: "The agreements of the Dura synagogue iconography with that of miniatures in various Byzantine manuscripts and the dependence of both Jews and Christians on a common Greek Hellenistic tradition *frees* the art of the Dura synagogue of its splendid isolation and *integrates* it into the mainstream of biblical art shared by Jews and Christians alike."[77] Weitzmann's ecumenical interpretation accords with his emphasis on the moment of coexistence between paganism, Judaism, and Christianity, rather than the eventual supremacy of Christianity. His methodology itself would not have ruled out competition. Indeed, the competition prompted by the coexistence of several religions is the focus of some important recent studies of the monuments. According to this free-market model, the zeal with which religions competed with one another for converts gave rise to a desire for an ever more fervent assertion of identity by each religion in an exhibition of religious vibrancy and power as dynamic as a modern Madison Avenue campaign.[78] While Weitzmann's students have not been reticent about examining the competitive aspects of influence, Weitzmann himself continually emphasized cooperative aspects of the relationship between religions.[79]

Weitzmann's discussions of Dura repeatedly refer back to the roots of his interest in Dura in the early 1930s. He reminds the reader on the first page of *The Frescoes of the Dura Synagogue and Christian Art* of the place and time that he first heard of the paintings and supports his argument about the friendly relations of Christians and Jews with reference to Carl Kraeling's 1932 description of the "harmonious coexistence" and mutual Christian and Jewish respect in Antioch.[80] Yet Weitzmann never made explicit the relationship between his Nazi surroundings, the insecurity of his position in Germany, his relationship with his Jewish teacher, and the belief in the significance of the paintings at Dura-Europos for Christian art. He may have had to blind himself, or others, to such connections in order to protect the scientific basis of his research.[81]

Others self-consciously introduced race into the rhetoric around Dura. The French associate director of excavations, Comte du Mesnil du Buisson, based his initial identification of the "truly Jewish painter [*peintre véritablement israélite*]" on the fact that the figures were painted from the back, "perhaps because of religious scruples," while another painter was "doubtless not an Israelite" because he omits the ritual fringes at the corner of the garments. One painter was Persian; another was Greek.[82] In the preliminary report from Yale, Carl Kraeling showed himself sensitive to possible racial implications of the find, anxiously chiding du Mesnil for seeking to distinguish the painters of the synagogue on the basis of race. "Only this question may be raised," he wrote, "whether it will not be wise to refrain from using in an artistic discussion terms that have a racial but not an artistic significance."[83] In du Mesnil's 1939 book on the paintings, he praised Kraeling's report and avoided remarks that could be interpreted racially.[84] The introduction by Gabriel Millet to this volume alluded to the timing of the discovery. Characterizing the Jews as a people without idols and ruled by the law of God, he concluded: "And this precious, unique monument merits the attention of all high-minded men who regard as the supreme good the dignity of the human being and safeguard it in the respect for a law of righteousness."[85] André Grabar, whose interest in Dura began when he was asked to review du Mesnil's work, was even more explicit in retrospect, placing his early studies of the paintings in the context of the outbreak of war: "Astonished by the mural paintings of this distinguished monument, I undertook a deeper study of them, while, around me, the systematic degradation and persecution of the Jews began."[86]

Meanwhile, a Viennese academic couple never even attempted to separate the two unpopular struggles, for the theory of the Jewish origin of Christian art and against the dictator who oppressed Jews. Kurt and Ursula Schubert made the study of Jewish art and culture a continuation of the resistance they initiated with their studies of Hebrew and in activities within the Catholic Church during the Nazi occupation of Vienna.[87] Kurt Schubert, after teaching Hebrew and Aramaic at the University of Vienna from 1945, was able to found the Institute for Judaic Studies there in 1969. Later, he founded the Austrian Jewish Museum in Eisenstadt, whose series Studia Judaica Austriaca has published works about the persecution of the Jews in Austria as well as Jewish contributions to world culture. Ursula Schubert's book about the contribution of Jewish art to Christian art in late antiquity, which follows Weitzmann's model, was the second volume in the series.[88] They continue actively to proselytize for the existence of Jewish art.[89] Even Weitzmann referred to their scholarship in the same breath as their resistance to Hitler.[90] Their two-volume work on the Jewish art of the book begins by evoking "the burning of books and the burning of people [which] succeeded one another in Jewish history up through National Socialism in our so-called 'progressive' century."[91]

The Jewish Art Historian Defined

The Schuberts are part of a trend. Almost since the beginning of the assault on the idea of Jewish art by anti-Semites, Christians have tried to convince anti-Semites, and sometimes Jews, that Jews have art. "Jewish art," in fact, has always found Christian champions where Jewish ones are wanting, as Jewish artists noted as early as 1901. "The Jewish artist," complained the painter Lesser Ury, "finds more support among Christians than Jews. The rich Jew shrinks from any documentation of his origins, wants to distract the thoughts of his visitor from these, and heaps up works of all kinds except Jewish ones, while many non-Jews know how to value and admire the young offshoots of the three-thousand year old tribe."[92] The following year in the same journal, E. M. Lilien pleaded for Jewish patrons to support Jewish art.[93]

The Christian campaign to reclaim Jewish art began in the nineteenth century. In 1858, the classical archaeologist Felicien de Saulcy sought to prove the existence of a highly developed Jewish art through a close examination of scripture.[94] In 1878, David Kaufmann's friend Franz Delitzsch's discussion of terms for color in the Talmud indirectly defended Jewish visuality against the accusations made against it on the basis of ancient writings.[95] The paucity of ancient references to the color blue derived from cultural values, not from a physical deficiency, he argued. Talmudic rabbis saw blue in the sky but did not regard blue as the sky's defining characteristic. They valued the sky for its white light. He concluded by citing a midrash according to which God created man in the colors red, black, and white. To the rabbis these colors symbolized universal humanity. The fact that they also stood for the German Reich enabled Delitzsch to end his speech, a fund-raiser for a victory monument, with a plea for brotherhood.[96]

Other Christian scholars supported Jewish art directly. Despite its racial assumptions, Julius von Schlosser's work on the Sarajevo Haggadah can be seen in this light. The director of the Düsseldorf Museum of Applied Arts, Heinrich Frauberger (1845–1920), played an even more active role. He became interested in Jewish art after an architect consulted him about Jewish motifs for an iron trellis around a gravesite. Frauberger was dismayed that he had so little to show the architect: of thirty thousand sheets in the museum's collection of patterns, only five showed synagogues. Thousands of them showed Catholic and Protestant images, and the collection was "rich in models for the Mohammedan and Buddhist cults, although neither Mohammedans nor Buddhists lived along the Rhein."[97] The incident impelled Frauberger to begin research that led him to establish the Gesellschaft zur Erforschung jüdischer Kunstdenkmäler (Society for the Study of Jewish Artistic Monuments) in Frankfurt. In founding the society, Frauberger encouraged research on Jewish art and sought opportunities to encourage its production. Indeed, Frauberger's society supported some of the important research of the 1920s, including that of Richard Krautheimer.[98]

Most of this philo-Semitic activity was directed toward the world of scholarship, but with the exception of Frauberger's Jewish community, to the extent that its audience is religiously identifiable, it was primarily Christian (both Catholic and Protestant). The Schuberts explicitly direct their defense of Judaism to the Catholic Church. Kurt

Schubert was chair of the Austrian Christian-Jewish Friendship League and was commissioned to eliminate anti-Semitic references in Catholic textbooks and passion plays.[99] He also played a role in the preparatory discussions over the Vatican's formal apology to the Jews for the Catholic role in the Holocaust.[100] Similarly, Weitzmann's description of the ecumenical community in which Christian art existed can be seen as serving a cautionary role for Christians. Certainly he must have envisioned Christians, or those interested in Christian art, as his audience. Both *The Frescoes of the Dura Synagogue and Christian Art* and *Age of Spirituality: Late Antique and Early Christian Art, Third to Seventh Century* retain, in their subtitles, an emphasis on Christian art. Only a brief section in *Age of Spirituality* is devoted to Jewish art; in the other work, Weitzmann expressly leaves to others the paintings' ties to Judaism.

But the influence of Dura on Christian art could convey a very different message to Jews. Certainly Dura was important to many Jewish scholars. Rachel Wischnitzer's dissertation on the subject, published in 1948, concentrated on messianic themes.[101] But much interest for Jews, as for Christians, concerned the nature of the ties between Christian and Jewish art. Influence can, after all, cut two ways. It can, for example, be negative. Richard Krautheimer, one of the first professionally trained art historians to devote an important study to Jewish art, used the concept of influence to shift the blame for Jewish iconophobia, attributing it to the influence, first of Christianity and then of Islam.[102] Similarly, Cecil Roth blamed iconoclasm, after "the heyday of religious enthusiasm under the Maccabees," on non-Jews, limiting it to periods "under the influence of the Byzantine iconoclasts, or during the era of Islamic domination."[103] Jews influenced Christian book illustration, but Christians caused Jewish iconoclasm and then blamed it on Jews.

The relation of influence is a relation of power. Jewish empowerment was implicit in the notion of ancient Jewish illustrated manuscripts, in which the relation to Christianity is always at stake. Hence Jewish influence on Christian art became a rallying cry of the strain called the (Kunst)Wissenschaft des Judentums in chapter 3. Cecil Roth, discussing illustrations in the Smyrna manuscript of the writings of Cosmas Indicopleustes, used a rhetoric of strife reminiscent of Josef Strzygowski in accounting for the images: "This seems to show," he wrote, "how powerfully the Jewish pictorial tradition impressed itself on Christian iconography, which, unable to escape it, endeavored to adapt it."[104] Jews, for Roth, flexed their muscles and influenced Christian art. The influence that Strzygowski viewed as disastrous, Roth, like Alois Riegl, could greet enthusiastically.

It was also possible to use Dura-Europos to make claims for Jewish autonomy. One early essay on the paintings, by Theodor Ehrenstein, while it did not fail to notice Lietzmann's implication that Jewish art may have had an influence on Christian, used the paintings primarily to establish Jewish autonomy.[105] Ehrenstein wished to interpret the paintings as part of an independent Jewish art favoring narrative and emanating "Shalom," or peace.[106] Ehrenstein even tried to subsume the Sarajevo Haggadah into this genre, denying the derivative character that Schlosser had ascribed to it: "As little as the frescoes of Dura borrowed from any contemporary work of art, so little did the miniatures of the Sarajevo Haggadah take any other manuscript as a model with respect to style."[107]

Perhaps the most startling outcome of the discourse that began with Dura is the change it made in the reception of Josef Strzygowski, one of the most anti-Semitic of art historians. The vicissitudes of Strzygowski's reception make his career a measure of the ways in which art historical methodology was implicated in the struggle for and against nationalism in art history. In 1886, when David Kaufmann reviewed Strzygowski's early work on the iconography of the baptism of Christ, he criticized him for his infelicitous style but had no reason to cite him for anti-Semitism.[108] Early on, however, many of Strzygowski's contemporaries recognized his anti-Semitic agenda, which emerged from a battle over ethnicities that engaged the entire European art historical community. After World War II, scholars again tended to ignore the anti-Semitism of Strzygowski's early writings, even when they condemned the express xenophobia of the later ones.

For many historians of Jewish art, however, Josef Strzygowski was a pioneer of the field. Beginning in almost the first scholarly accounts of Dura, Strzygowski became one of the most frequently cited forebears of the notion that early Christian art derived from Jewish art. The Schuberts, who, after all, lived in Strzygowski's home base, Vienna, understandably do not mention him. But barely another article on this subject fails to include an admiring reference to Strzygowski's role in the reevaluation of Jewish art. E. L. Sukenik, the archaeologist of Beth Alpha, the sixth-century synagogue in Palestine discovered in 1928, visited Dura in March 1933. In his book on ancient synagogues in Palestine, he cites Strzygowski for his theory of the origin of Christian art from Jewish sources, crediting him with speculations from catacomb paintings actually made previously by David Kaufmann.[109] Rachel Wischnitzer makes Strzygowski part of the canon of Jewish art historiography, quoting his *Origin of Early Christian Church Art* (1929) in a 1967 essay on Jewish art historiography; and Joseph Gutmann refers to Strzygowski's "brilliant surmise," in Strzygowski's 1901 work *Orient oder Rom*, "that the ultimate source of many Old Testament scenes in early and medieval Christian art may be rooted in pre-existent Hellenistic Jewish illustrated manuscripts."[110] Even Weitzmann, who was thrown out of one of Strzygowski's lectures in 1925–26 for laughing out loud at his overt racism, felt obliged to credit him with recognizing the Jewish source for the miniatures in the Ashburnham Pentateuch (see figure 6).[111] Strzygowski himself referred to his discussion of the Ashburnham Pentateuch in reference to the wall paintings in Dura, although he did so only to deny Jewish influence on Christian art.[112] In 1964, Joseph Gutmann inquired of Martin Buber whether he had ever studied with Strzygowski and whether Strzygowski was Jewish. Buber answered laconically in the negative to both questions.[113]

Strzygowski did not mean his designation of the illuminators of the Ashburnham Pentateuch as "Jewish Christians" to be a compliment. But it appealed to some historians of Jewish art not only because it could be utilized in an argument for culture contact, but because it guaranteed the survival of a Jewish element that could be identified in later, non-Jewish art. Accordingly, like many anti-Semitic assertions of Jewish power, intelligence, and wealth, the assertion of Jewish artistic power could be subverted. It inspired scholars of Judaica, whether or not they were Jewish, to look for evidence of Jewish artistic activity. This search, which gained momentum in 1932 with the discovery of the figural murals in the synagogue at Dura-Europos, changed what was at stake in philo-Semitic and anti-Semitic positions. While the desire to right an injustice against the Jews inspired Delitzsch, and the Austrian scholars at the turn of the century sought to foster what they regarded as the multicultural mission of the Austro-Hungarian Empire, the desire to find an example of a harmonious society innocent of Nazi anti-Semitism propelled Weitzmann and the Schuberts into their studies of Jewish art. The ardor of art historians who looked for origins as signs of irreducible Jewish essences, however, posthumously transformed the anti-Semite Strzygowski into a champion of Jewish art.

Although Weitzmann was vague about his own motives, he made the point about art historical methodology clearly in reference to his teacher Adolph Goldschmidt. Weitzmann's memoir of Goldschmidt's last years makes visible the dissonance between the oppression Goldschmidt suffered in Germany and his patriotic attachment to German culture, which he demonstrated by his continued residence in Germany and his unwavering study of German manuscript painting. Goldschmidt remained in Germany long after Weitzmann had left. When his successor refused to let him into his office at the university, Goldschmidt continued his work at home. He worked until the libraries closed their doors to him: first the manuscripts, then the books. Only in 1938, after Max Planck came personally to urge him to resign from the Prussian Academy of Sciences, did Goldschmidt decide it was time to leave. Goldschmidt, after all, wrote not about Jewish art but about German art. He left "the East" to Weitzmann.

Goldschmidt lectured to the Academy of Sciences for the last time in 1937. In his memoir, he identified his topic as the influence of Italy, France, and England on German art, and the changes wrought by Germans on these foreign models. If so, the topic was timely, because the German universities were at least giving lip service to the idea that art historical positions should be filled with professors "whose gaze is turned more toward the Germanic world than the Italian."[114] With satisfaction, Goldschmidt reported on the positive reception accorded his lecture and that of a colleague (probably Mittwochs-Gesellschaft member Eduard Spranger) to the effect that a German race did not exist, only a German people, Goldschmidt's account melding the two lectures into one triumphant evening.[115] It is possible that the evening or evenings did not progress exactly as he remembered them, since nothing in the published synopsis of his talk "German Painting and Sculpture under the Saxon Emperors" mentions foreign art, and Spranger's lecture actually took place nearly a year later.[116] According to Weitzmann, Goldschmidt's talk was about Albrecht Dürer.[117] Dürer's greatness, Goldschmidt argued, was owing to his exposure to the Italian art of Andrea Mantegna. Weitzmann did not misconstrue the significance of the topic; he called it "Goldschmidt's answer to the limitation, propagated by the Nazis, to indigenous, national sources."[118]

Whatever the subject of his talk to the academy, Goldschmidt did publish an essay about English influences on the art of the continent in a safer, American venue in 1939, and at least his memory showed that, when pressed, he would turn to the same cosmopolitan position as Riegl and Focillon, countering nationalism with an argument for the beneficence of foreign artistic influences.[119] Perhaps in these writings, Goldschmidt the Jew was a "Jewish art historian."[120] If he was, then so was the Christian Henri Focillon in his reply to Strzygowski. But where does that leave Weitzmann, who directed his attention for decades to the interdependence of Christian, Jewish, and pagan art? Perhaps his efforts can be summed up in the reproach "We are all Jewish art historians."[121]

PART THREE

Abstaining from Jewish Art

In the nightmare of the dark
All the dogs of Europe bark,
And the living nations wait,
Each sequestered in its hate
W. H. Auden, *In Memory of W. B. Yeats*

CHAPTER SIX

C[lement] Hardesh (Greenberg)

Formal Criticism and Jewish Identity

–What is your nation if I may ask? says the citizen.
–Ireland, says Bloom. I was born here. Ireland.
James Joyce, *Ulysses*

The Dilemma of the Jewish Critic

The "national arts" to which Jewish artists contributed were never stable entities. They were defined in constantly changing and often contradictory ways, modeled by internal efforts to shape national "imagined communities" and by external efforts to interact with the imagined communities of one's neighbors. Beginning in the 1920s and 1930s, the complex interplay between a developing international style and the rise of German nationalism in its National Socialist form made for a tense climate in which Jews had to negotiate between increased opportunities to contribute to the discourse of art and exclusion from the same discourse as foreigners. We have seen the effect of the allegiance to the international style on the artists who began in 1935 to remake the Bezalel School of Arts and Crafts in Jerusalem as the New Bezalel. In Europe during the same period, decisions as to whether to include or exclude "foreigners" in national arts had a new urgency, not only in Germany, and were made on both practical and ideological grounds. An exhibit of French artists that took place in Berlin in 1937 included only native-born, "Aryan" artists, while an exhibit in Paris that year was "happy to honor at the same time these artists from the School of Paris, who had come from all points of the world, Parisians before anything else."[1] The political situation, which surely shaped the wording of that French catalog, also found its way easily into the stylistic and theoretical speculations of art critics in those days of intense self-examination and lively art theoretical debate. The critic of art could not fail to respond to the pressures of that fraught theoretical and ideological climate.

Hard choices faced art critics who addressed Jewish art in the years preceding and following Hitler's rise to power in Germany. The French critic Waldemar George, for example, a Jewish immigrant from Poland who had already established his career in Paris when he began to consider Jewish art in the late 1920s, made successive, contradictory choices. In a move reminiscent of Martin Buber, his first pronouncements on the subject turned anti-Jewish stereotypes on their head to secure Jews a central place in modern art. In the introduction to the catalog of a

1929 exhibit of contemporary Jewish artists, *Jüdische Künstler unserer Zeit,* Waldemar George concluded that while formal traits do not link Jewish artists, "a community of sentiments, of ideas, of aspirations, presides over their labors."[2] The community of ideas is suited to a people without art for it is based on sacrificing form for expression: "Jews are Goths. They sacrifice form to the expression of internal life; they spiritualize it" (8–9). George, who wrote not in Buber's symbolist era but in that of the international style, could consider it a positive boon to lack a nationality. "The art of the Jews is international, even supranational," he wrote. "It communicates to the world its dynamic principle, . . . its 'nervousness' [*nervosisme*], its anxious character, its instability and its exaltation" (9). If Gothic represented Christian Europe, then Europe was now Judaized.[3] The stereotype of the nervous, excitable Jew, in Waldemar George's hands, became a valued emblem of universality.

Seven years later, internationalism did not seem such a blessing. In 1936, captivated by Josef Strzygowski's description of the spirit of the North, and under the influence of Italian fascism and nationalist movements, George changed his evaluation of a Judaized world.[4] He now condemned the characteristics of Jewish art he had once praised, supporting instead the classical art of Giorgio de Chirico. He found support for de Chirico's painting in Alois Riegl, to whom he erroneously attributed the position that Late Roman society had "ceased to believe in the reality of physical matter."[5] After the war, however, George again became a supporter of Jewish art. In his contribution to Cecil Roth's *Jewish Art,* "The School of Paris," he accused nationalism of causing art historians to narrow their horizon and lose sight of the unity of Western art.[6] In contrast, the "rare quality of universality" is once more for Waldemar George the primary contribution of Jewish artists (642). Some peoples are more universal than others.

Other critics, however, thought some peoples more individualistic than others. The topic "Is there a Jewish Art?" at the Jewish Museum in 1966 presented the art critic Harold Rosenberg with a difficult rhetorical problem, which he initially tried to solve, following Jewish custom, with reference to food. The highlights of his grandmother's cooking were virtuoso noodle cutting and cleverly fashioned challah in the shape of a bird.[7] But as tangible (edible?) evidence of Jewish artistry, these starchy works did not amount to much. For one thing, his grandmother's best cooking days were probably over even before Willem de Kooning's best painting days began, making Jewish art seem dated. For another, if we leave aside the noodles, her "bird bread" was solidly representational, while modern art was moving in nonrepresentational directions. An identifiable style was Rosenberg's criterion for the nonculinary visual arts, and although a number of important present-day American artists were Jewish (he listed several), they created as individuals, not as Jews, and thereby "helped to inaugurate a genuine American art," rather than, presumably, a Jewish one.[8]

Rosenberg wrote cogently about Jewish identity in other areas of endeavor, particularly literature, and the essays show that he took the subject of Judaism seriously.[9] Although he probably never read Martin Buber's essay on Jewish art, he showed that he was a reader of Buber, having reviewed Buber's recently translated book on Hasidism in 1948.[10] But while Buber's Hasidim conformed to the modernity of the turn of the century, in Rosenberg's hands they became even more up-to-date, turning into upholders of the radical individualism of the American literary world in the middle of the twentieth century. Rosenberg found in the Hasidim the radical individualism he celebrated in the American action painters. It has been observed that Rosenberg thought there was something Jewish in the very individualism of these artists.[11] But that did not promote a "Jewish art" for Rosenberg. Even when the painter Barnett Newman used explicitly Jewish subject matter, Rosenberg took pains to disassociate him from it, carefully distinguishing Newman's interest in the Kabbalah and his design for a synagogue from an identification with Judaism, even though elsewhere Rosenberg espoused an ethnic definition of Jewish identity by referring to the Jews as Newman's "tribe."[12]

His reticence concerning Jewish art, however, is not surprising given that most of his audience probably assumed that he was right when he said that American Jews tend to express themselves in the visual arts as individuals, not "as Jews." The Jewish artists championed by Rosenberg might have agreed; few of them advertised their religious identity. Other art critics were no more revealing. Clement Greenberg, Rosenberg's great rival for the position of spokesman of the abstract expressionists, also wrote on Jewish subjects, although less often than did Rosenberg. Yet he rarely dared tackle the question of Jewish art directly.

The silence about Jewish identity in the discourse of art criticism appeared natural and inevitable, Rosenberg's and Greenberg's reticence on the topic a purely personal matter.

If it had been only personal, the omission might not be worth remarking, despite the significance of their contributions to high modernism. But their relative silence on the subject of Jewish art is significant. Greenberg's few remarks represent a recognizable position in the discourse prepared and conditioned in the discipline of art history. The example of the critic Waldemar George, and even that of Martin Buber, suggests that a concerted effort to consider Jewish identity within the purview of modernist criticism would have been hard put to avoid anti-Semitic rhetoric. The hesitation of prominent critics such as Rosenberg and Greenberg to discuss Jewish art therefore not only represents a footnote to a body of influential criticism but locates certain difficulties that the theoretical and historical map of art history placed in the way of postwar American Jews and, by extension, other ethnic minorities. With a discourse vacillating between individualism and universality, there is little space for the identification with small, ethnically defined groups.

Purity in Art and Race

Although he never devoted an essay to Jewish art, Greenberg did touch on the subject occasionally, and uneasily. For example, on the eve of Israeli statehood in March 1948, he reviewed an exhibit in New York's Jewish Museum of the paintings of the then-director of New Bezalel, Mordecai Ardon. Greenberg appreciated Ardon's "apocalyptic" landscapes, particularly his *Mount of Olives* (1938), for the nearly abstract surface created by their texture: "an expressionism modified by cubism" (see frontispiece). His attempt to explain the affinity to the Old Testament that he sensed in them, however, created one of those awkward moments when the normally glib, articulate critic found himself at a loss for words. "Far be it from me to see an eternal Jewish soul any more than an eternal Anglo-Saxon one," he began, continuing "but . . ." without, however, replacing the "eternal soul" with a more insightful explanation.[13]

Greenberg rarely mentioned an American Jewish artist's religion, but when he compared the American painter Arnold Friedman stylistically to Ardon, he added that he is "also a Jew," as though intending gingerly to open the possibility that Jewish artists have stylistic similarities, a possibility he does not, however, develop.[14] He does, however, allude to it again, comparing Friedman with Camille Pissarro and Chaim Soutine because, like them, he "took himself for granted as a Jew."[15] Otherwise, Greenberg's vast output contains few references to Judaism in the visual arts. No wonder. Greenberg could only account for Jewish art within an established art historical framework, that of formal analysis as conceived and established by scholars in the late nineteenth and early twentieth centuries.

Jean-Paul Sartre, in *Anti-Semite and Jew*, offered a tool for understanding the function of formalism in relation to ethnicity.[16] According to his paradigm, the myth of universal humanity and the practice of "abstraction" enabled Jews to deny the reality of their own oppression. His scheme would attribute this potential to artistic formalism as well because, like the symbolist movement in art and literature, it was a response to a crisis of artistic representation. It attempted not, as is sometimes assumed, to abolish or denigrate subject matter in art (and it was never against content), but to provide it with a more unassailable basis.[17] It placed formal considerations above subject matter in order to discover universal truths beyond academic conventions and denied differences to search for a common denominator beneath them. Formalism's potential support for the idea of universal humanity led Jews and other internationalists or even anti-nationalists to embrace it, just as they later embraced the international style and abstract art.

Within Sartre's framework, formalism can be seen as a form of denial. Unlike international Marxism, which Sartre thought would remedy anti-Semitism by changing the social structures that led to it, the formalist *internationale* offered a comfortable refuge, making art appear a pure realm of visuality, free from specific racial, ethnic, or political agendas – and religious ones. Art offered Christians as well as Jews a secular religion to replace faith lost in the Enlightenment, or conversely, an expansion of religion beyond narrow denominationalism. For Jews, the opportunity to ignore iconography in favor of formal analysis allowed them in addition to worship at Renaissance altarpieces without the necessity of a formal conversion. Even better, it opened nonreligious art to devotional purposes, opening the field to rich religious imagery in praise of abstract paintings, often made by secular Jews.[18]

Although formalism helped Greenberg and others handle Christian art and even surrealism, whose iconography he disliked, it let him down in the face of Jewish art. Formalism, for example, trapped Greenberg into resorting to an "eternal Jewish soul" when seeking to explain the relation between Ardon's "apocalyptic landscapes" and the Old Testament because it forbade an explanation based on traditions of biblical landscape or imagery.[19] These might have helped him. Even though Ardon's explicitly kabbalistic images would only come later, we have seen that the "Pillar of Absalom" in the landscape that Greenberg regarded as the strongest of the group was a landmark whose biblical associations were so well-known that objects of Judaica such as Etrog containers were modeled on it (see figures 26 and 27).[20] It was not surprising that Greenberg ignored an association he might well have seen on a postcard, since even Rosenberg, after all, was enough of a formalist to insist on style as the only reliable criterion of Jewish art (see figures 43 and 44). Similarly, Greenberg's discussion of Marc Chagall's origin, in "the Jewish enclave in the provinces of Eastern Europe" far from Paris, emphasized differences in painterly traditions but not culture.[21] His rhetoric posed "visual logic" against a "murky, indeterminate *fond*" and set a picture that "happens to repeat Chagall's previous success with royal blue" against "the large and unresolved *Crucifixion* with its yellowish malaise" (see figure 45).[22] But it ignores the subject matter of these works, replete with references to Jewish experience in the Holocaust.[23] He mentions "crucifixions and monsters" only to make more precise his reference to Chagall's "more ambitious or more surrealist subject matter."[24]

The reference to Ardon's "eternal Jewish soul," even though Greenberg rejects it, illuminates the way in which formalism, Greenberg's route to universalism, could fuel anti-Semitism. This could happen because formalism grounded representation in the universality of nature, rather than the arbitrariness of conventional codes. Greenberg contributed to the "naturalization" of formalism in such essays as "The Role of Nature in Modern Painting" (1949).[25] He also understood art on the biological basis of the senses and appropriated from earlier formalists

43. Tomb of Absalom, postcard, before 1948, Levant Picture Publishing. Collection Sanford L. Aronin. Reproduced with permission.

44. Mordecai Ardon, *Mount of Olives*, oil on canvas, 38 x 51 ins., 1938, detail. Collection Alex Marx. Reproduced with the permission of Professor Michael Ardon.

45. Marc Chagall, *Yellow Crucifixion*, 1943. © 2000 Artists Rights Society (ARS), New York/ADAGP, Paris.

the perceptual rhetoric that Alois Riegl had pioneered of "optical" and "tactile."[26] Biology, in the mode of perceptual psychology, naturalized formalism, just as in the mode of racism it naturalized nationhood.

Because biologic formalism erects standards and identifies deviations, racism was always a temptation, sometimes leading thinkers in directions they would prefer not to go.[27] The insights of Gestalt psychology, for example, which postulated a biophysical relationship between human response to form and internal molecular organization, could also be used to bolster racial stereotypes. Rudolf Arnheim came close on occasion to turning Gestalt into a new phrenology. While he criticized current ways of investigating how the external forms of "homosexuals, sadistic murderers, etc.," as perceived by observers in photographs, might be related to "these pathological manifestations," his objection was not to the endeavor but to the procedure used.[28] Stereotypes according to which, for example, "aquiline noses indicate courage and . . . protruding lips betray sensuality" may perhaps be "so hardy because they are so true."[29] To bolster his call for an examination of the relationship between the "mentalities" of ethnic groups and the configuration of their gestures, he cited a study of Jewish and Italian communities in New York City.[30] Arnheim somewhat misrepresented this study, however. The work of a Columbia University student, working under Franz Boas, aimed at refuting the Nazi science of race by showing that gesture systems are environmentally determined. It cherished hybrid gesture systems created by the conflicting influences of family and the New York environment on immigrant groups and their offspring and would not have suggested similarly measuring "mentalities" to arrive at a biological formula (see figure 46). The author himself lived a hybrid scenario, having been raised in Argentina by Yiddish-speaking Orthodox Jews. It would be difficult, within Arnheim's formalism, to encompass such a complex interplay between the social and the visual.

Arnheim was not the only Jewish formalist critic whose universalism was sabotaged. Bernard Berenson, whose criticism Greenberg admired, espoused universalism during the Nazi years, partly in response to the Nazi threat. With Strzygowski's example specifically in mind, he condemned the search for influence because it is "seldom free from nationalistic prejudices."[31] "My tendencies toward universalism and timeless-

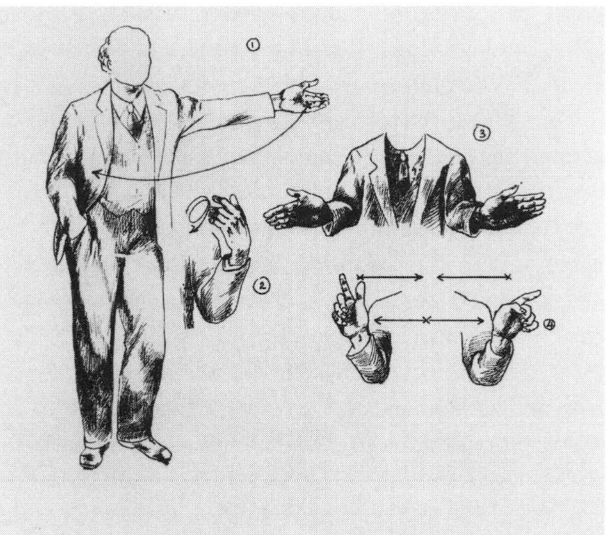

Fig. 80: Schapiro. Americanized Jew. While many of his gestures have a small expressive tempo following the cadence of the thought, characteristic of the traditional Jew, at other times, great breadth of gesture is shown as in 1, in which he says "he creates a fresco of . . . proportions".
2. In its motion describes the evolution of an idea, a kind of symbolic picturization to accompany his speech.
3. "Two views of American History" one sees a kind of mental crystallization of the idea into two distinct forms, one being indicated by each hand.
4. "–Equality–"

46. "Schapiro, Americanized Jew." Sketch by Stuyvesant van Veen, 1941. From David Efron, *Gesture, Race and Culture*, Approaches to Semiotics, no. 9, ed. Thomas A. Sebeok (The Hague: Mouton, 1972). Courtesy of Mouton de Gruyter, a division of Walter de Gruyter GmbH & Co.

ness," he wrote, "have disinclined me to dwell on differences that seem slight, compared with wide and deep resemblances, and have inclined me to look for the same human quality in every individual." Yet he laid a trap for himself when he completed his sentence with the phrase "and furthermore to erect the same qualities into ultimate standards and to appraise societies as well as individuals by the extent to which they have possessed these qualities."[32] Thus, even more than Waldemar George, he took to heart the porcine message in George Orwell's *Animal Farm,* which found some animals more equal than others: he found some societies more universally human than others.

These remarks, in his *Aesthetics and History in the Visual Arts,* appear in an explicitly anti-Semitic (and often cited) discussion of Jewish art.[33] Following the traditional formulas, Berenson consigns Jews to a dismal artistic existence: in some passages they lack a national art; in others they lack art altogether. He appears to forget his own rejection of the cult of originality when he condemns Jews as imitators:

> Neither they themselves nor their forebears possessed any kind of plastic or even mechanical ability . . .
>
> As a matter of fact Israel through the ages has manifested nothing essentially national in the plastic arts, neither in antiquity, nor through the Middle Ages, nor to-day. The coinage of their Maccabaean period is the poorest Hellenistic. . . . In later periods Jews imitated the art of the peoples among whom they were scattered, to the pitiful extent that they made use of art at all. Even in recent years when Jews emancipated from the ghetto have taken to painting and sculpture and architecture, they have proved neither original nor in the least Jewish. I defy anyone to point out in the work of Liebermann, Pissarro, Rothenstein, Modigliani, Messel, Antokolskij, Epstein, Chagall, or Soutine, anything excepting subject matter that is specifically Jewish.[34]

The difficulty of finding anything "specifically Jewish" in Pissarro's art has only been tackled in recent scholarship.[35] Yet Berenson's remarkable leap from Maccabean coinage to the avant-garde movements of his own youth suggests that for Berenson, despite the attack on Josef Strzygowski that forms part of the context for his remarks, the issue is nevertheless a racial one, just as it had been for his target, Strzygowski. Berenson himself entertains this possibility: "The Jews like their Ishmaelite cousins the Arabs, and indeed perhaps like all pure Semites (if such there be), have displayed little talent for the visual, and almost none for the figure arts."[36]

Along with biologism came the fear of miscegenation. Hybridity posed a problem for formalist methodologies because its aspiration for universality did not admit difference. As has been pointed out, abstract art achieved universalist purity through an exclusionary process that often did not admit, for example, women.[37] Ethnic differences were also excluded. In the 1930s and 1940s, when Greenberg was earning his wings, the longing for purity that pervaded modernism often found expression in the abhorrence of "hybrid" styles and mixed genres. Berenson, for example, quotes with approval the remark by the (refugee Jewish) Islamist Ernst Herzfeld that "hybrid" Persian arts appropriating misunderstood Greek form could have historical but not aesthetic interest.[38] Unlike the contemporary enthusiasm for the "hybrid" location of the postcolonial, and the postmodern celebration of mixed media, complexity, and contradiction, these thinkers viewed "hybrid" artistic styles with disdain.[39] Formalism, despite – or because of – its aspiration to universality, could be used comfortably with the nationalistic structure of art history.

Greenberg's early essay "Towards a Newer Laocoon" (1940) demonstrates how a biological view of art accords with a fear of hybridity.[40] In the essay, Greenberg personified art, importing into it the class struggles that concerned him as a socialist: Literature was "dominant," visual art "subservient." When arts become subservient, "they are forced to deny their own nature in an effort to attain the effects of the dominant art."[41] Dominance and subservience are part of Marxist discourse, but the "nature" of these arts are not. The notion that the arts have a nature comes from formal theory, which divides arts according to the senses to which they appeal. Greenberg's emphasis on the "medium" is not simply an expression of his historical materialism; it is at the quasi-biological basis of art.

Acceptance of the physicality of the medium was a ruling metaphor throughout his writings, backed by metaphors of the body and of medicine. In "Towards a Newer Laocoon," the Romantic artist is said to be "ashamed to admit that he had actually painted his picture instead of dreaming it forth" (1:29). The phrasing suggests shame about the body. Elsewhere, health is at issue: "The extreme eclecticism now prevailing in art is unhealthy, and it should be counteracted, even at the risk of dogmatism and intolerance"(1:213). Middlebrow culture posed a danger to the body of art as well: it "attacks distinctions as such and insinuates itself everywhere, devaluating the precious, infecting the healthy, corrupting the honest, and stultifying the wise" (2:257). The metaphors in this constellation do not merely personify art by embodying it; they protect its virtue against cross-breeding. Universalism in art did not extinguish racism in repressing it; it displaced it into another realm.

Greenberg's formalism, like that of the pioneers of formalism, was not ahistorical. Like them, he accepted a universalist notion of history, according to which one current (Greenberg called it a "mainstream") flows at any given time. This totalistic sense of history may also have been informed by Marxism, but the sense of the unity of a culture was more Hegelian than Marxian. His view of Dutch art, for example, was based on a totalistic notion of the seventeenth century, in which space and light were explored through many areas of culture, an idea common among early-twentieth-century thinkers.[42] Like them, he related arts to scientific advancement. "A substantial art," he wrote, "requires balance and enough thought to put it in accord with the most advanced view of the world obtaining at the time" (2:167). Greenberg's lineage of "advanced views," from medieval religion through abstract thought (idealism), was borrowed from nineteenth-century histories. He appreciated the "materialism, or positivism," of the nineteenth century (2:164). By "positivism," he meant a nineteenth-century intellectual movement that stressed empiricism rather than idealism or rationalism.[43] Explaining that Jackson Pollock's art is an attempt to cope with urban life, Greenberg wrote: "It dwells entirely in the lonely jungle of immediate sensations, impulses and notions, therefore is positivist, concrete" (2:166). Positivism also entered into his discussion of the "great change from three to two-dimensionality which modern art has affected in pictorial space – a change that expresses our industrial society's abandonment of Cartesian rationality for empiricism and positivism" (2:203). The corollary of this confidence in advanced science is that while there was a stake in unity in diversity, there was no room for multiple standards in art writing.[44] The public not only should recognize advanced painting, he wrote, but should reject other kinds.[45]

Not only did Greenberg share with his forebears a universal, progressive conception of history, he also accepted their concern for national character. Greenberg several times characterized Klee's nature as "Nordic," and Picasso's as "Mediterranean," although Picasso denied his own nature unsuccessfully by trying to paint like the French (2:150, 297). Greenberg also took pains to determine what was uniquely American in American art. When he proclaimed the victory of New York over Paris, announcing that the main premises of Western art have at last migrated to the United States, along with the center of gravity of industrial production and political power, and that "the future of Western Art depends on what is done in this country," his exultation was patriotic. For the triumph belongs not just to a small group of painters but to the spirit of a people (2:193, 215).

Hardesh: Painting Makes Teshuvah

The triumph did not belong to the "Jewish spirit," however. When Greenberg proclaimed New York the new artistic center, he did not mention that many of the artists that had made it so, Barnett Newman, for example, or Adolph Gottlieb, were Jewish. Their "nationality" was definitively American. In this, Greenberg followed a typical post-Holocaust scenario, in which awareness of the Holocaust tended to promote integrationist, rather than separatist, stances among American Jews.[46] Yet Greenberg's position also accorded with his commitment to a single artistic direction and a single center in which it evolves at any given moment. Any difference from the general population, according to this account, was in danger of falling into the category of the hybrid. Like other minority identities, Judaism enters into his criticism primarily to explain provinciality. Whatever an artist's origins, Greenberg usually identified provinciality with an understanding of cubism (the logic of which "every subsequent master of modernist painting has had to understand"), which is not direct but mediated by another modernist movement. German Expressionism often took this role, since it "seemed to make post-impressionism more accessible to non-Latin outsiders" (2:4). "Picasso's good luck," Greenberg wrote, "was to have come to French modernism directly, without the intervention of any other kind of modernism. It was perhaps Kandinsky's bad luck to have had to go through German modernism first."[47]

C[lement] Hardesh (Greenberg)

Thus the Russian Kandinsky, transplanted into Germany, is as "provincial" as the Palestinian artist Mordecai Ardon.[48] Greenberg's ambivalence about hybridity shows in his assessment of Chagall. While his praise of Chagall's mastery of Parisian art despite his origins in an Eastern European Jewish enclave gestured toward acceptance of hybridity, Greenberg nevertheless worried that Chagall "represented something impure" that made it difficult for his art to become "eligible to take its place in the social order called beauty" (2:84). It went too far in emphasizing his uniqueness. Should Greenberg have believed in the existence of Jewish art, he would have worried about it as well. Lacking a national center, it could only join the mainstream as a hybrid. Israel was too new: it is a country "most of whose cultural products are unavoidably tinged with that provincialism which marks almost all new national self-consciousness" (2:216). A national artistic consciousness must, Greenberg accepted, have a history. The United States, however, was presumably old enough to produce great art.

Greenberg allowed himself to discuss Jewish identity openly in discussions of literature and current events. There, his conflicts are apparent. He disliked the use, by "chauvinist" Israeli Jews, of "Western European standards," which led to the rejection of European refugees and the ideal of Jews as blond and blue-eyed as any Hitler Youth. His grandiose counterconjecture, that "it is possible that by 'world-historical' standards the European Jew represents a higher type of human being than any yet achieved in history," however, does not suggest multiple standards (2:107). Furthermore, although he says "there is much to argue for its possibility," he does not do so. In his first discussion of Jewish issues, he seeks to disassociate "ghetto Jews" from "Orientals," but not because either category is a stereotype. Rather, "the ghetto Jew [was] 'Oriental' perhaps in his poverty and in the denseness of the atmosphere in which he lived but not in his realism and in his abhorrence of hypocrisy" (1:156). In the attribution to Orientals of hypocrisy and lack of realism (often called, disparagingly, "fantasy"), we can now recognize the same Orientalist rhetoric that, as we saw in chapter 1, entered art historical texts in the nineteenth century.

Occasionally, Greenberg appears to regret the loss of what he regarded as traditional Jewish ways. His review of Peggy Guggenheim's book *Out of this Century,* which he signed "C. Hardesh," the Hebrew neologism for "Green Mountain" ("Berg," in German, and "Har," in Hebrew, mean "mountain"; one of the meanings of "desh" in Hebrew is "green"), is a lament for the "martyrs of bohemia." Guggenheim's "martyrdom" was due to her unquestioned acceptance of bohemia, which allowed her to be victimized by it. Her fall was, however, directly linked to her Jewish origins. She tried to escape "moneyed, bourgeois, claustrophobic stuffiness. And it was for fear of being recaptured and returned to it somehow – the unconscious conviction that she would be, simply because Jews are forced to remain bourgeois in spite of themselves – that she threw herself so unreservedly into bohemia and has dwelt in it so unqualifiedly, recklessly, and gullibly" (2:98).

Bohemia is hard on Jews: "In the list of martyrs of bohemia, Jewish names stand out, the names of gifted Jews, too, not merely aberrated ones – beginning with Simeon Solomon in Pre-Raphaelite England and continuing through Modigliani, Pascin, and even Soutine, in Paris. In proportion to the size of the Jewish contingent in bohemia – which is smaller than one would expect – the martyrs are too many, and examples like Miss Guggenheim's too frequent" (2:99). The cause of her downfall, Hardesh speculates, is her abandonment not of modern bourgeois ways but of traditional Jewish ones. "As a Jew I am disturbed in a particular way by this account of the life of another Jew. Is this how naked and helpless we Jews become once we abandon our 'system' completely and surrender ourselves to a world so utterly Gentile in its lack of prescriptions and prohibitions as bohemia really is?" (2:98–99).

Guggenheim's story, as related by Greenberg, is a tragedy of assimilation, with the twist that the heroine is a member of the mainstream bourgeoisie and the group she wishes to join is on the fringe of society. He investigates the topic of assimilation further in the essay "Under Forty," about American Jews and literature (1:176–9), and later in the essay "Jewish Self-Hatred" (3:45–58). In the latter essay, the "ultra-assimilationist Jew," like painting trying to achieve the effects of the dominant art, does violence to himself "because he tries to make himself more typically English, French, or German than any Anglo-Saxon, Gaul, or Teuton ever is" (3:56). The earlier essay, however, made Jews indeed an extreme case of a general modern phenomenon. Like Sartre, Greenberg ascribed the tendency of Jews to abstract, to conceptualize, and to marvel at the "sensuous and sentimental data of experience" to their status as wanderers and outsiders, a typically capitalist plight, which Jews exemplify to an extreme (1:177). Writing serves as a means of access to the general culture. While the nonwriting Jew is integrated into American life, accepting suffocatingly "middle-class" ways but having nothing to write about, writers have a code that protects them from the "ravages of Bohemianism" that engulfed Peggy Guggenheim (1:179). But their code is too middle-class to be used to criticize society. Thus in his essays on literature, Greenberg recognizes Judaism as an identity worked out within and against a dominant culture. The Jewish experience turns out to embody the universally modern experience of isolation and alienation in intensified form because of Judaism's special historical circumstances.

He wrote most penetratingly in this respect of Franz Kafka. Greenberg's struggle with Kafka's literary achievement extended for over a decade. Writing searchingly about the Jewish meaning of Kafka's writing, he wished to avoid seeming to esteem it for this "extra-artistic truth." Kafka's hybrid poetry, the lack of purity of his art, what Greenberg calls its "frustrations," all seem to be related to Kafka's Jewishness, and in turn to Greenberg's belief in the necessary separation of art and life. In one of Greenberg's three essays on Kafka, this struggle between poetry and reality made Kafka modern (3:209). In a version revised for inclusion in his collection *Art and Culture*, published in 1961, Greenberg expressed it differently: "Does not art always make one forget what is literally happening to oneself as a certain person in a certain world? And might not the investigation of what is literally happening to oneself remain the most human, therefore, the most serious and the most amusing, of all possible activities? Kafka's Jewish self asks this question, and in asking it, tests the limits of art."[49] Art, which may be based on individuality, was nevertheless irreconcilable with individual experience.

Group identity frightened many in the 1950s and 1960s, years as much of defiant individualism as of group solidarity. It may, however, have frightened Jews more than most. There is an urgency, for example, in Rosenberg's passionate defense of acculturation in the name of individualism before a group of Jewish engineering students in 1950. His lecture, tellingly, was entitled "Jewish Identity in a Free Society."[50] Similarly, Greenberg explicitly favored individual actions against anti-

Semitism on the basis that communal actions fueled "rabid nationalism" (3:53). Given their energetic embrace of American identity, however, their use of the rhetoric of individuality to justify the rejection of an explicit Jewish identity may conceal a fear of identifying openly as a Jew.

Fear of espousing Jewish identity may have been justified. While Greenberg did not seek connections between the New York abstractionists and their Jewish culture, his detailed account of the relationship of the writer Franz Kafka to his Jewish culture gave rise to an acerbic exchange. The presence of Jewish content in Kafka, argued F. R. Leavis, made Greenberg overvalue his achievement. Greenberg understandably took offense at this insinuation that Kafka's relation to talmudic law can be of interest only to Jews. Kafka's "Halachic logic," he wrote, makes him no more parochial than Dante's Christian cosmology makes him. Yet Greenberg perhaps felt vulnerable to the accusation of "Jewish egocentricity," for even as he defends Kafka, the man who signed himself "C. Hardesh" a few years earlier confesses that "[I] am not, in my ignorance of Hebrew and many other things, *that* familiar with Jewish tradition anyhow" (3:213, original emphasis).[51] In an essay about "self-hating Jews" he was honest enough to begin by counting himself among them.[52]

If Hardesh's essay is a tragedy of assimilation, "Towards a Newer Laocoon" could be viewed as a tale of "Teshuvah," an expression for the religious return to Judaism.[53] It registers anxieties that cannot be spoken of explicitly. In reference to the infiltration of literature into art, he writes that the arts "can only be mishandled in this way when they have reached such a degree of technical facility as to enable them to pretend to conceal their *mediums*" (1:24, original emphasis). Like Jews, whom anti-Semites characterize as chameleon-like in their ability to assimilate, arts too have the urge to assimilate into the dominant form and the potential to acquire the skill to do so. Yet, like Peggy Guggenheim in the face of Bohemianism, it is dangerous for the arts to deny their own natures. The biological understanding of painting that Greenberg inherited from Europe, along with its racial underpinnings and the "school of Paris" itself, has been set to work on the issue of identity. The search for identity embroils both painter and painting. It is as important for a painting to be "all painting; none of it . . . publicity, mode or literature" as for a painter to be "his true self" (2:14, 18).[54]

Greenberg's few remarks about Judaism represent the pathos of his enterprise, a pathos at the heart of modernism. In Greenberg's view, modernist art strove for a unity it thought unobtainable in life; the greater the diversity it reconciled, the greater the art. Piet Mondrian achieved such unity. But Greenberg saw expressionism as exploiting tension rather than resolving it to effect unity.[55] Thus expressionism, the artistic practice of Jewish and other provincial artists, was about the longing for unity rather than its achievement. Like other modernists, Greenberg could not celebrate unresolved diversity.

Just as Kafka's Jewishness expresses a universally modernist crisis in extreme form, Greenberg's relation to Judaism exemplifies in its extreme the contradictions and strain in his conception of the relationship between art and politics, even between art and life.[56] Unlike Sartre's apolitical Jews, Greenberg was committed to political engagement both within and beyond the boundaries of his discipline.[57] Yet formalism necessarily saw art as isolated from life, for universal forms took precedence over the necessarily particularistic subject matter of life. As we have seen, however, formalism had its own politics, since its universal standards were founded on those of white, gentile Europe. Within formalism, it was impossible to do justice either to Jewish identity or to political responsibility. The difficulty of reconciling an art conceived as necessarily isolated with a life committed to political, religious, or ethnic issues was, in fact, a defining tension throughout modernism.[58]

Greenberg's attraction to formalism corresponded to his attraction to traditional Judaism; the separation that he struggled to maintain between art and life he thought he saw in traditional Judaism as well.[59] In the old world, he wrote, Jewish culture was totally religious; it ignored secular life insofar as it was independent of religious ends, and it ignored questions of power.[60] In his conceptual scheme, traditional Judaism constitutes a relation, albeit negative, to politics; one could call it a formalist politics. Whether rooted in the Eastern Ghetto or thoroughly Europeanized in Prague, Judaism escapes, like formalism, from the politics, and the history, of the gentiles.

After raising the possibility that by " 'world-historical' standards" Jews might be the highest form humanity has yet evolved, Greenberg continued: "No one, I say further, has any right to discuss the 'Jewish question' seriously unless he is willing to consider other standards than those of Western Europe" (2:107). The remark was more insightful than he thought. By his own criteria, Greenberg was ineligible to discuss the Jewish question in art.[61]

CHAPTER SEVEN

Graven Images on Video?

The Second Commandment and Contemporary Jewish Identity

> Thou shalt not make unto thee any graven image, or any likeness of any thing that is in heaven above, or that is in the earth beneath, or that is in the water that is underneath the earth; Thou shalt not bow down thyself to them, nor serve them; for I the Lord thy God am a jealous God, visiting the iniquity of the father upon the children onto the third and fourth generation of them that hate Me; and showing mercy unto all of them that love Me and keep my Commandments.
> **Exod.** 20:4–6

The Primal Scene

Despite appearances, I have chosen my epigraph not directly from the Bible but from the 1995 video installation *Bordering on Fiction: Chantal Akerman's "D'est."*[1] In the early 1970s, the Belgian filmmaker Chantal Akerman, then barely out of her teens, took part in the New York avant-garde film scene. She made her name after her return to Europe, when feminists acclaimed such films as *Jeanne Diehlman, 23 Quai du Commerce, 1080 Bruxelles* (35mm, 200 min. 1975), about a single mother who works as a prostitute, and *Les Rendez-Vous d'Anna* (Meetings with Anna; 35mm, 127 min. 1978), about a Belgian filmmaker who travels through Germany to Brussels and Paris, encountering friends and lovers along the way and reuniting with her mother, a Jewish refugee. When the films first appeared, critics did not emphasize the significance of her Jewish themes; a long review in *Film Quarterly*, for example, mentions but makes little of them.[2] But Akerman's parents, like those of Anna, were Polish Holocaust refugees, and *Les Rendez-Vous d'Anna* is not an isolated example of the appearance of such refugees and their offspring in her works. The shopkeeper's wife in the frothy musical *Golden Eighties* (aka *Window Shopping*, 35mm, 96 min. 1985), who has been in a concentration camp, and the Yiddish inflection of Akerman's mother's letters in the French version of *News from Home* (16mm, 85 min. 1976), are among many Jewish allusions in her films.[3]

The three-room installation *Bordering on Fiction*, organized by the Walker Art Center in Minneapolis, centers on Akerman's one-and-one-half-hour documentary film about Eastern Europe, *D'est* (From the East; 16mm, 107 min. 1993) made in 1993. The film plays continuously in the first room while visitors wander in and out. The scenes are composed of long takes with a nonmoving or evenly tracking camera and ambient sound, but no voice-over or dialogue. In them, people stand, wait, dance in ballrooms, or walk. The second room is the focal point of the installation (see figure 47). There, visitors wander among eight triptychs of monitors, staggered at approximately eye level. Within each grouping, the film is fragmented into five-minute sequences, after each of which the monitors briefly go blank. In the third room, the visitor sits on a small bench and looks down at a single monitor on the floor, a speaker on each side of it (see figure 48). The video shows a tracking shot down a street at night. As the camera gradually pans up to the sky, the occasional traffic lights or glimpses of lighted buildings become blurry. In a voice-over, Akerman reads a text beginning with the Second Commandment recited first in Hebrew and then in translation. Finally the images fail to reappear, and Akerman's voice continues briefly in darkness. In the background, a cello plays a melody some viewers might recognize as the Ashkenazic melody of the Kol Nidre, a legal formula chanted in synagogues at the late afternoon (or in some Reform congregations, evening) service that begins the Jewish Day of Atonement, Yom Kippur.[4] In case visitors failed to recognize the piece, however, the installation at the Jewish Museum in New York identified it in a plastic-covered handout that also contained a transcription of Akerman's entire text.[5]

The Kol Nidre asks release from vows that one cannot fulfill or that one violates unintentionally. Since in the installation the melody provides the background to a reading of the Second Commandment, the broken vow presumably refers to the commandment. As a filmmaker, Akerman apparently perceives herself as vulnerable to the charge of violating the Second Commandment; she recited it in a short film about herself made in 1984.[6] But the commandment against graven images does not straightforwardly aim at any and all image making. Even if the category of graven images self-evidently included video, the injunctions against idolatry that precede and follow it show that the prohibition pertains to those made for worship, and that its true target is idolatry.[7] Aware of this connection, Akerman raised the issue of idolatry in film in an interview about *Bordering on Fiction*, explaining herself with reference to the "face-to-face" philosophy of Jewish philosopher Emanuel Levinas.[8] "I try to make images that are not idolatrous but in a relation of face to face with the spectator, where the Other is. The spectator ought to be a true Other, the cinema should not be a machine to embrace (*englober*) and absorb the spectator. . . . I think that in my cinema the spectator can never forget himself, so he cannot be in a relation of idolatry."[9]

Akerman's interpretation of idolatry synthesizes Levinas's philoso-

47. Chantal Akerman, *Bordering on Fiction: Chantal Akerman's "D'Est,"* 1993/1995. View of installation, second room. Collection Walker Art Center, Minneapolis. Justin Smith Purchase Fund, 1995.

48. Chantal Akerman, *Bordering on Fiction: Chantal Akerman's "D'Est,"* 1993/1995. View of installation, third room. Collection Walker Art Center, Minneapolis. Justin Smith Purchase Fund, 1995.

phy with contemporary discourse on the gaze. This discourse was powerfully articulated in the 1970s in film theory, with which it remains identified. According to the discourse, film is structured by a male gaze that objectifies and dominates the female. The related notion of suture explained the mechanisms by which the classic Hollywood film, and any film following its influential example, absorbs the spectator, "suturing over" any emerging awareness of the constructed nature of the film, including its technical aspects as well as evidence of its maker's intentions. The filmmakers control audience reaction, determining the characters with which the audience may identify and those it may regard as objects, keeping the audience largely unaware of how it is being manipulated.[10] Levinas's theory, when applied to suture, extends to film an ethical imperative against suture grounded in relations with God: the unknowable "Other" must not be subsumed into the "same." Whether one loses oneself in the Other, or dominates the Other so that the Other becomes part of oneself, the result is the "same": sameness. Levinas himself extended his theory into the realm of sexual relations, where it has had an influence on poststructural feminist theory.[11]

Sexuality often plays into interpretations of idolatry as proscribed by the Second Commandment, although sexual prohibitions and dysfunctional relationships are evoked more frequently than the gaze. Moshe Halbertal and Avishai Margalit, for example, usefully identify several conceptions of idolatry, among which two are relevant to Akerman's understanding of the Second Commandment. Their notion of idolatry as betrayal could be reconciled with Akerman's notion of idolatry as a failure to acknowledge the otherness of the face-to-face encounter.[12] According to their account, idolatry is understood as a dysfunction in interpersonal, sexual relations: the idolater betrays [her] husband, God. God has, after all, just declared his possessiveness ("You shall have no other gods before me") and admitted his jealousy ("for I the Lord thy God am a jealous God"). Halbertal and Margalit argue that God, in his desire for exclusive possession of his bride, Israel, acted like any other jealous husband. He didn't want her to have other gods; he didn't want her to engage in "strange practices"; he didn't want her to yield to the temptation of strangers. Using this rhetoric, the writers of the Bible could harness against idolatry the antipathy they could count on their audience feeling against adultery.

Even after adultery itself loses its power to evoke disgust, idolatry retains uncomfortable associations related to love relations.[13] In spiritual terms, the betrayal of God can be viewed as a failure to recognize God's essential otherness, to fail to commit oneself to a relationship of responsibility with the Other, but to perceive God as an object that can be consumed or exchanged. As Martin Buber might have put it, the exchange of an I-Thou for an I-it relationship constitutes a form of idolatry.[14]

If idolatry amounts to losing oneself in an image or narrative, however, subsuming the other into the same, surely Akerman's installation avoids it. The film it fragments, after all, is already so nonabsorbing in any traditional sense that an assistant curator at one of its venues advised me to skip it (I did not, thankfully). The installation evokes the idea of idolatry, however, if by some stretch of the imagination the supports for the video cameras in the second room can be seen as pedestals. In fact Akerman calls them steles, an interpretation whose funerary associations are compatible with the notion of idolatry.[15] If indeed, as Akerman's use of the term suggests, the steles were intended to bring to mind idolatry without inducing it, that would explain the lack of a stele in the third room, where the Second Commandment is read. From this point of view, however, the installation demystifies rather than exemplifies idolatry, rendering the Kol Nidre unnecessary. If it is necessary after all, perhaps the reason is that to demystify something entails rubbing shoulders with it and therefore risks courting unintentionally the very thing that needs demystification.

Akerman's broken vow, however, does not derive from crossing a line, in her installation, between a dangerous proximity to idolatry and idolatry itself; it does not derive from representing, in violation of the Second Commandment, random objects in heaven or on earth. In her "third room," she recognizes her misstep and tells the viewer the meaning of the standing, waiting figures in the monitors and screen of the first two rooms:

> And slowly you realize that it is always the same thing that is revealed,
> a little like the primal scene.
> And the primal scene for me although I fight against it . . .
> It is far behind or always in front of all images barely covered by others
> More luminous, radiant even

Old images of evacuation
of walking in the snow with packages
toward an unknown place,
of faces and bodies placed one next to the other
of faces flickering between robust life
and the possibility of a death
which would strike them down without their having asked for anything. . . .
Once the film is finished,
I said to myself,
so *that's* what it was:
that again.[16]

Akerman's "primal scene" is the Holocaust. The fact that she inadvertently represented it, in spite of her conviction that such representations were banned, is apparently the transgression that calls for the Kol Nidre. In an interview about the installation, Akerman spoke as though the commandment was written *only* to deal with the Holocaust: "The film was already showing me images that I had in my head and those images were related to the concentration camps. From that idea I went to the idea that you cannot show images of a concentration camp, that in the Jewish religion you don't have a right at all to make images about that. . . . So that's why I wound up doing something very abstract with that text."[17]

The Holocaust-related content of the images with no text in the second room explains the funerary associations of the pedestals; the abstract something that she did with her text in the third room was the slowly blurring nonimage on the screen.

With the representation of the Holocaust at issue, the notion of idolatry as adultery is less pertinent than another conception of idolatry illuminated by Halbertal and Margalit: the notion of idolatry as error.[18] This view assumes that since God is unrepresentable, any attempt to represent God is bound to result in a false image. This image is then fated to be confused with the real thing. If one extends the argument to the Holocaust, the notion of the horrific replaces that of God. It is an error to represent the horrific, because we confuse the horrific itself with our representation. Holocaust idolaters, if there are such, rob the horrific of its horror just as religious idolaters rob God of God's majesty.

In practice, however, the two approaches to idolatry cannot be kept apart so easily. An idolatrous mistake often has an ulterior motive. If a fetish, for example, represents idolatrous *error*, it does so because it "is an object to which people attribute powers that it does not have."[19] But if it is an error, surely it is a Freudian one. Freud himself informed us of the sexual content of fetishes that lead to strange practices with objects other than the real one.[20] The error of idolatry involves desire just as does betrayal. The user of a fetish presumably wishes the representation on which it is based to be of the real thing. Even when an argument ostensibly concerns unrepresentability, it still retains sexual associations.

Desire enters into discussions of Holocaust representation as well. Saul Friedländer has exposed the fascination for death in his analysis of representations of Nazism, literary and filmic. Speaking of the depiction of death in Luchino Visconti's film *The Damned*, he writes: "For the viewer, everything signifies fascination, terror, and ecstasy."[21] According to Geoffrey Hartman, the use of visual images causes complications in the visual representation of the Holocaust beyond those of literary representations because "popular representations emerge that are uncomfortably close to fantasies that may have played their part in the genocide. Thus the problem of limits changes."[22] While the limits he has in mind are those of human empathy, his argument also suggests the issue of the gaze as understood in poststructural theories that link the gaze with desire, for it associates the problem of representing the Holocaust visually with the risk of exciting desire attendant on any visual image.[23] This entailment of desire in visual imagery brings the ban on visual representation of the Holocaust close to the discourse of the Second Commandment.

This formulation owes a debt to Theodor Adorno, who warned against the possibility that any depiction of the Holocaust would risk beautifying it, turning it into a commodity.[24] The same fear earlier fueled – and tempered the interpretation of – his famous dictum "To write poetry after Auschwitz is barbaric," in an essay on the cooptation of cultural criticism by commodification.[25] His aniconism, which he actually focused on image-based literary modes, extended to conceptions of socialist utopia as well, where he explicitly cited the ban on images to unite theology and materialism against idealism.[26] Adorno's union of dialectical materialism and iconoclasm, along with his repudiation of depictions of the Holocaust, has made him a key figure in the discourse on the ban on visual representation and the Holocaust.[27]

The association between the ban on images and the Holocaust takes many forms, but it is especially common in the discourse of film, Akerman's métier. It has often been brought into discussions of Claude Lanzmann's film *Shoah*. As a large and growing number of commentators have reminded us, *Shoah* stays resolutely in the present.[28] Although its numerous interviews focus on the camps and the process of extermination, the film avoids archival footage or recreations. Lanzmann does not quote from the Second Commandment, but by implicitly invoking it, such statements as "there is an interdiction on representation" transfigure the vow to abstain from representing the Holocaust visually into a holy task.[29] When Lanzmann accuses the television series *Holocaust* of transgression, he builds his case on another veiled reference to the commandment. The Holocaust, he writes, "is first of all unique in that it builds around itself, in a circle of flame, the limit that cannot be transgressed because a certain absolute of horror is intransmissible. To pretend to be able to do so is to make oneself culpable of the most serious transgression."[30] As idolatry places other gods beside the one true God, representation "abolishes thereby the unique character of the Holocaust, that which makes it incomparable, and . . . that in which it is worse than all the crimes committed or to be committed."[31] Had he found documentary footage "showing how 3000 Jews, men, women, children, died together, asphyxiated in a gas chamber in crematorium 2 of Auschwitz," he would have destroyed it.[32] Indeed, he attacks *Holocaust* and *Schindler's List* with all the energy of an Abraham smashing idols.

But Lanzmann also objects to the two films on the basis of desire. Filmed Nazis like the ones in *Schindler's List* are too attractive in their uniforms, while Holocaust victims are too weak to be portrayed by actors.[33] The problem is not just truth, but pleasure, desire. We cry in *Schindler's List*, according to Lanzmann, but our tears give us "pleasure," to denote which he uses the word *jouissance*, a loaded term whose list of meanings, including "pleasure" and "orgasm," has nourished French theory's psychoanalytical tendencies.[34] In the hands of Julia Kristeva, *jouissance* stood for a potentially subversive pleasure, often characterized specifically as a female one, that threatened to destroy the symbolic chain at the heart of patriarchal law.[35] As Lanzmann uses it, the term's evocation of an illicit pleasure that should be alienated and repressed suggests the same constellation of meanings as does idolatry.

The same discourse of idolatry that connects the Holocaust to the Second Commandment connects it, in turn, to the purism of high modernism, many of whose most important critics supported non-representational art. Again the pivotal figure is Adorno. In her study of Adorno, Gertrud Koch found a resemblance between high modernism's strict interpretation of the Second Commandment and that of Babylonian and later kabbalistic Gnostics. Although this Gnostic variant was only of marginal significance to the medieval world, which limited the ban on images to the image of God, she argues that it "is linked in a quite astonishing manner to the aesthetics of modernism."[36] Building on Koch's argument, although she ultimately finds the critique of Lanzmann's *Shoah* in high-modernist terms reductive, Miriam Hansen writes that the Holocaust has "radicalized the case for . . . the non-representational, singular, and hermetic *écriture* to be found in works of high modernism."[37] For these present-day scholars, then, the Second Commandment does not just ban images of the Holocaust. After the Holocaust, the Second Commandment came to be seen as upholding the standards of high modernism as well. The artistic applications of the Second Commandment underscore and support one another: Holocaust and modernism.

No Dead Images

The discussions of the Second Commandment and its relationship to the Holocaust and to high modernism that we have just explored suggest how the discourse of empathy, pleasure, and desire unite to implicate the Holocaust in the discourse of the Second Commandment, demonstrating the wide range and significance of the prohibition against graven images in contemporary discourse.[38] With this in mind, it is time to return to the central question: why has the Second Commandment been invoked in the context of the Holocaust at all? We might wonder, for example, why it is used to interdict representations of the Holocaust but not the representation of other horrors. Although I have chosen not to reproduce them here, it is easy to locate horrifying photographs of the atrocities committed by American soldiers in Vietnam. They can be found even in coffee-table books.[39] Yet objections to the coverage of atrocities and violence apart from the Holocaust, when made at all, tend to be on different grounds. Much of the controversy surrounding Robert Capa's famous Spanish Civil War photograph known as the *Death of a Loyalist Soldier* (1936) centers on the issue of whether the man was really dead.[40] Military authorities ordered John Huston to edit out most of his footage of dead and wounded American soldiers, or edit it in a less dramatic fashion, in his film *The Battle of San Pietro* (1944) because of the possibility of weakening morale. The unstated assumption is that no objections were raised to the sight of dead enemies.[41] It is not unusual to draw attention to the undercurrent of condescension inherent in representations of the grief of an Other.[42] But even an issue as close to that of sanctity as, for example, privacy is remarkably rare in the discourse of atrocity.[43] The argument for suppression of horrifying footage is more likely to rest on "compassion fatigue" than on impropriety or idolatry.[44]

But even bracketing other atrocities, it is striking that the Second Commandment should have captured the Jewish cultural imagination as it has. The other commandments are not nearly as ubiquitous in artistic circles. Leading cultural journals have published few articles on the Fourth Commandment, for example, which enjoins keeping the Sabbath. In an appropriate venue, however, a roundtable on the relationship of the Second Commandment to the making of Jewish art might attract a sizeable Jewish audience, even if it were held on a Saturday.

In other words, many of those who find meaning and relevance in the Second Commandment, however they may observe the other commandments (and it is not my purpose to know how Chantal Akerman or other artists may do so), rarely try to apply them to art. It might therefore seem reasonable to ask what the appeal is of this particular commandment, and whether it has the same appeal to Christian theorists. After all, as David Kaufmann and others tried to show, there is no theological reason why the Second Commandment should be seen as Jewish alone. Christians have had to confront the Second Commandment along with the other nine, often with tumultuous results.[45] Iconoclasm comes to mind. Has something happened in the modern world to limit the Second Commandment to Jews?

I will argue that since the Holocaust, the Second Commandment, above and beyond its religious significance, has become significant as a badge of Jewish identity. While Christians may claim to follow or violate the other nine, the Second Commandment is often seen as belonging to the special domain of Jews, where they claim it as their own. The commandment lends itself to functioning as a source of pride: it suggests restraint, self-denial, and antimaterialism. "Thou shalt not covet" has these qualities, too, but its implications (and it has obvious ones for the art market) are more mundane. Among all the commandments, the Second Commandment is the one used most often to distinguish Jews from Christians.

Such an observance must come from tradition. And while perhaps a scholar of religion could make an argument that Gnosticism could present such a tradition, anyone who is reading the present book from the beginning will not be surprised that I do not identify any transmitted religious heritage as the "source" for the iconophobia of secular intellectuals. We recall that even Gertrud Koch was "astonished" at the link between Gnosticism and high modernism. It does not diminish practicing art critics, such as Clement Greenberg, to point out that their grasp of kabbalistic or other Jewish theological arguments was often minimal, and their interest in them almost nonexistent, even if others, such as Harold Rosenberg, did at least read Martin Buber's *Tales of the Hasidim*.[46] But they did know secular discourses about art. Indeed, whatever its religious basis, the historical source through which secular Jewish critics, as well as artists and thinkers, encountered the association between Jews and the Second Commandment, the interpretation of the ban on images familiar to most theorists of art was not Jewish at all but was one I have been tracing throughout this book.[47]

The secular thinker's understanding of the Second Commandment came from the concept of Jewish art that we have seen develop in the discourse of art history. Akerman's strategy, to draw positive consequences from the negative stereotype, is not medieval but modern, one in a century-long series of reactions to the established, mainstream paradigm of Jewish art: the notion that the Second Commandment forbids Jews, alone among the nations, to make art. Her modernization of the commandment for the post-Holocaust West gives us an opportunity to trace the stereotype of the nonvisual, antiartistic Jew, still alive and well nearly to the end of the twentieth century, through its various metamorphoses since Martin Buber first tried to subvert it for the purposes of a symbolist aesthetic.

Twentieth-century art movements such as abstraction and expressionism gave the stereotype new life, since the opponents of these movements could make Jews responsible for them. The tendency to relate abstraction to iconoclasm, and covertly to a negative view of Judaism, was common in twentieth-century theory, even as late as 1981, when Kenneth Clark published his essay "Iconophobia." Clark strives for the evenhanded tone of a gentleman resigned to abstraction, although he knows that it means his old age will be spent with a form of art he believes to be incapable of development. Yet he manages to introduce the ancient Jews into the history of iconophobia and in the process to mouth most of the tropes about uncreative, and even savage, Jews, who "turned their limitation [the inability to make images]" into a "moral and religious principle."[48]

Buber was only the first in a long line of thinkers who, accepting the stereotype of Jewish art, tried to subvert it for the purpose of the avant-garde. These thinkers came from the art world as well as the world of Judaica and pledged allegiance to a variety of avant-garde movements. They found the Second Commandment eminently suitable to an art world dominated by expressionism and later abstraction, where a sense of beauty was associated with dry academicism, and artistic value turned on spiritual content. Earlier reproaches against the Jews for failing to love beauty now gave Jewish artists a heroic appearance. Steven Schwarzschild, for example, pointed out that the Shulchan 'Aruch permits representations in distorted form. In accord with this definition, Jewish aesthetics was well positioned to nourish modern art beginning with Picasso's "one-eyed, three eyed and otherwise distorted human faces."[49] Not surprisingly, the paintings at Dura-Europos could be appropriated for a similar argument. Photographs of them, exhibited at the opening of the Jewish Museum, were displayed near works by modern artists. The catalog made the point that the artists of Dura, who "progress[ed] beyond the naturalistic forms of late Greek art," were spiritual compatriots of "the modern artists [who] advance into realms where the consistency of the human figure becomes questionable in the light of spiritual forces stronger than the quest for bodily perfection."[50]

Abstraction made it easy for Jews to claim a stake in art – hence the notion that Jewish art had the obligation to be abstract, already voiced in Yiddish in 1919.[51] The tendency to make the likes of Clement Greenberg into closet Kabbalists because of high modernism's championship of abstraction comes out of the same set of assumptions. But it was possible to come even closer to the Second Commandment if one dispensed with the object altogether. At the end of Harold Rosenberg's lecture "Is There a Jewish Art," discussed in chapter 6, Rosenberg made a final attempt to answer the question stated in his title, using a different tactic than he had thus far. He enlisted the Bible itself on behalf of Jewish art. Unwilling to let the Jews in his audience go away empty-handed, Rosenberg turned the prohibition against images in the Second Commandment into an artistic manifesto: for antiart. "Jewish art," he wrote, "may exist in the negative sense of creating objects in the mind and banning physical works of art."[52] He also identified an Old Testament provenance for found art. Jews held the "idea that if you inhabit a sacred world you *find* art rather than *make* it."[53] In claiming the ancient Jews as forerunners of the found and conceptual art movements of the 1960s, he can be seen as updating Buber's argument for the benefit of Jews in a contemporary, secular art world who regarded art as intellectual but were less likely to accept spirituality in art, and to whom an antiartistic stance was perfectly acceptable. It was as though the Second Commandment read "Thou shalt make only Conceptual or Found Art." Surely Rosenberg's Second Commandment functioned primarily to reinforce his own Jewish identity and that of his audience.

Since Rosenberg, the commandment has been updated to suit the world of technology. For example, in the Kabbala-influenced holographic poetry of the contemporary Brazilian artist Eduardo Kac, letters float in midair, forming different words or turning into numbers as the viewer moves. The fluid boundaries between numbers and letters recall kabbalistic meditations on the numerical value of the words of the Bible.[54] Kac divided his childhood days between the Jewish day school where his Yiddish-speaking grandparents sent him, and the nearby Copacabana beach. He is not religious, but he readily makes a connection between the avoidance of idolatry inherent in his Jewish identity and the evasion of imagery in his holographic poetry, telecommunications art, and ventures into cyberspace, where recently it was possible to participate in an interactive composition whose structure was modeled on the Kabbala.[55]

In short, by following the precepts of the Second Commandment, Jews end up in the forefront of every avant-garde movement. The Second Commandment proves to be just the kind of self-imposed restraint that helps keep artists fruitful and makes their products multiply. It would seem that the Second Commandment proscribes only tedious academic art, although Rabbi Kook's advice to the Bezalel School in Jerusalem suggests that even that may have had champions.[56]

This will to connect the Second Commandment to contemporary art is a typical Jewish response to anti-Semitism. Jews consistently internalize the marks of Jewish difference attributed to them by anti-Semitic clichés and transform them into proofs of Jewish excellence or virtue, often betraying an underlying insecurity about their own identities.[57] The strategy of dealing with prejudice is not limited to Jews. It closely resembles feminist demonstrations that what was thought to be scatterbrained feminine chitchat is better suited to poststructuralist thought than "phallocentric" law and similarly echoes the strategies of many other minority groups.[58] Jewish attempts to trace the basis of poststructuralism to Jewish talmudic reasoning emanate from the same impulse.[59] The supposed shortcomings of the minority group, whatever group it may be, are transformed into a way of claiming part – usually the best part – of the majority culture for its own.

With the conversion of the Second Commandment into a watchword of avant-garde movements already under way, the Holocaust gave the Second Commandment a new lease on life in the discourse of Jewish art. The Second Commandment's application to the Holocaust was more powerful than other strategies to redeem the commandment because it now could be vested with the moral authority of Jewish suffering and anti-Semitic persecution. Video and computer artist Pier Marton has written: "In my tradition, I interpret the graven image interdiction as the forbidding of any image that would, through its formulaic cliché, lead to the grave; i.e., much of the religious and Holocaust imagery that falls into kitsch, into dead images."[60] Transforming the threat of "dead images" into the threat of death, the Second Commandment could be used to evoke the complexities of Jewish identity as understood in the post-Holocaust Jewish Diaspora.

Teshuvah: Visualized Communities

I would like now to return to the musical background to Chantal Akerman's reading of the commandment. The holiday of Yom Kippur is the traditional moment of Teshuvah, return. The individual returns to God, and the roving Jew has often taken this moment, in fact and fiction, to return to the fold of the Jewish people.[61] Traditionally, the Kol Nidre is repeated three times in the evening service. While the formula is perhaps repeated for legal reasons, it has also been conjectured that the repetition intended to accommodate latecomers.[62] If so, coming late can be a metaphor for return. Whether or not Akerman would fit into this category of metaphorical latecomers, the recitation of the commandment of post-Holocaust Jewish identity to the accompaniment of the music of Teshuvah is a rich symbol of return.

But there is another shade of meaning to take into account. This legal formula, chanted to a beautiful melody, has a history similar to that of the Second Commandment. Since its revision in the twelfth century, the Kol Nidre that is chanted in Ashkenazic synagogues on the eve of Yom Kippur makes a legal statement in the name of the full congregation retracting vows and oaths that will be made in the year to come. The idea that Jews had divine permission to renege on their promises has never been a popular one with rabbis. Even now, the Conservative prayer book prefaces the entire evening service with a "Note on the *Kol Nidre*." It begins: "Our words, and especially our promises, must be taken seriously; our integrity must be unquestioned."[63] It reminds the congregant that breaches of trust against people have to be forgiven by the offended party, that the Kol Nidre applies only to vows made to God. The English version of the prayer adds conditions not in the Hebrew-Aramaic version.[64]

If even rabbis have had trouble with the prayer, it is not difficult to imagine what anti-Semites have made of it. According to the seventeenth-century professor Johann Andreas Eisenmenger, who quotes several preexisting anti-Semitic tracts and whose own contribution to this genre was still being translated and published in the late nineteenth century, the Kol Nidre allowed Jews to swear falsely to Christians.[65] The prayer was routinely used to prevent the admission of Jewish testimony in a court of law or to force the Jew to take special oaths and resort to special humiliating ceremonies in order to have his testimony admitted.[66] In part for this reason, the Reform movement sought to abolish the prayer as early as 1817 and succeeded in 1844. In 1930 the melody was published without any words, but the original text was not restored to the official Reform prayer book until 1978.[67] The legal problems it poses have never been satisfactorily resolved.

The prayer refused to disappear; as early as the sixteenth century, efforts to change it foundered on the reluctance to alter the familiar melody.[68] It has in fact become the musical showpiece of the evening, which is called the Kol Nidre service after it. Max Bruch's 1880 arrangement for cello and orchestra intensified affection for it. Attacks on the Kol Nidre by anti-Semites only contributed to the esteem in which it was held, and ultimately the prayer became identified with solidarity against such attacks. Positive interpretations of the Kol Nidre began to appear. A folk tradition associated it with Jewish martyrdom at the hands of the Spanish Visigoths.[69] In the twentieth century, the (quickly discounted) theory was proposed that the Kol Nidre arose in the first place to nullify forced conversions and other rash actions Jews might have to perform in the face of persecution.[70] A. Z. Idelsohn attributed the touching Ashkenazic melody to the feeling of solidarity with the Marranos as expressed by an Ashkenazic Hazzan (cantor) circa 1500.[71] The idea caught on. "In repeating this prayer," according to the Reform prayer book, "we identify with the agony of our forebears who had to say 'yes' when they meant 'no,'" a meditation not easy to reconcile with the condition, stated two pages later in the "translation" of the prayer, that we are required to make an "honest effort" to keep our vows.[72] Progressively, the formerly embarrassing prayer became a badge of heroism and resistance. Arnold Schoenberg's setting of the Kol Nidre contains an express invitation to "be one with us in prayer," to those Jews who have been "unfaithful to Our People because of fear."[73] Such allusions in the text that Schoenberg wrote with Jacob Sonderling, together with the date of its composition, 1938, gives it connotations of resistance in the Nazi era. Like the Second Commandment, the Kol Nidre came to mark Jews' relation no longer to the Jewish God but to the gentile world in which the Diaspora Jews find themselves isolated and embattled.

Like the Kol Nidre, the Second Commandment articulates the Jew's relation to a monotheistically conceived God. Like the Kol Nidre, it was used to bar newly emancipated Jews from testifying - in the secular artistic realm. Is it now to become a central tenet of a new "Jewish art," based on staking a Jewish identity against a hostile outside world?

Perhaps not. The most readily apparent reason is that excessive preoccupation with the Second Commandment is limited to the Jewish Diaspora. Whether because of the utility of Jewish art for promoting national identity, or because in the Middle East iconophobia is not an effective tool for distinguishing Jews from their surrounding cultures, the Second Commandment plays only a minor role in Israeli art, even in relation to the Holocaust. The most exhaustive book on the visual iconography of the Holocaust barely discusses Adorno's strictures, with little sense that the Second Commandment might be at stake in them.[74]

But I do not wish to end on the theme of the Holocaust or in Israel, like many classic narratives of the post-1945 and post-1948 eras.[75] I would prefer, following another genre, to extend some of the implications of what has gone before to a context beyond exclusively Jewish concerns. Religious constructions of secular art in modern times, after all, are not limited to Jews. They contribute to a discourse of the sacred that informs, and masks, artistic discourse from Romanticism to postmodernism. The discourse of the graven image marks the entrance of denominationalism into the paradigm of art as a sacred practice. Despite the Christian associations of writings such as Wilhelm Heinrich Wackenroder's *Herzensergiessungen eines kunstliebenden Klosterbruders* (Outpourings of an art-loving friar; 1796), and paintings like Caspar David Friedrich's *Tetschen Altar* (1807–8), the paradigm it began suggested rivalry, not identification, with organized denominations.[76] Romantic artists sought to replace the church, rather than unite with it, when they clothed their art in the aura of sanctity and borrowed the rhetoric, visual and verbal, of holiness. Their secular religion of art paved the way for the universalism that helped make it possible for Jewish thinkers to participate in art criticism and scholarship.

The discourse under discussion is no less secular, perhaps more so, than that of the Romantics. Yet it relies, as did theirs, on an opposition between secular (or neutral) spaces and sacred spaces. Greenberg's abstention from Jewish art operated within this context, just as does that of Akerman. These spaces structure social interaction. Sacred spaces are exclusive; only initiates may enter. They reaffirm the identity of a community but do little to prevent hostile communities from remaining hostile. In contrast, secular, or neutral, spaces aim at creating a dispassionate, inclusive ground that allows interchange between groups.[77] Both endeavors run into difficulties, however. Akerman's insistence on a strict interpretation of the Second Commandment extends the realm of the sacred over a wide area. Yet her sacred space houses the huddled community of the persecuted, not a community of the faithful. Greenberg's conception of art as a pure object demanded an expansive neutral space. In practice, however, Greenberg's secular space is not expansive but confining, not to say market driven; his struggle to balance the demand for moral standards against the autonomy of art sent him longing, as he contemplated the conferral of the Bollingen Prize on Ezra Pound, for a sacred space after all.[78]

As a departure from the myth of universalism that has served art history for two centuries, denominationalism complicates the sanctification of art by adding the discourse of identity. Identity, like the sacred, was not unknown in modernist discourse, but it had a different, more uncomfortable character; witness the feeble attempt of Leopold Bloom, in the "Cyclops" section of James Joyce's *Ulysses* quoted in this book's epigraphs, to use his Irish birth to defend himself against the citizen.[79] Bloom's difficulty in defining and claiming his citizenship reveals a tension between space (the same people living in the same place) and time (living in different places, successively). A similar tension appears in most attempts to encompass Jewish art, whether in a general survey book, the *Index of Jewish Art,* an artist's implicit claim to be a Jewish artist, or another's claim to a national or an international identity.

Art historical discourse is frequently plagued by thorny issues of time and space. The tension is less pronounced in narratives of specific European nationalities, most of which can lay claim to at least some unity of place throughout the vast changes they recount, than in narratives of Jewish art, whose long history – over three millennia – takes place in numerous different settings. But the striking difficulty of defining Jewish art as the expression of a nationality should not blind us to similar difficulties in defining other nationalities artistically. The study of concepts of Jewish art is not the only way to cast doubt upon the idea of national arts. National arts make use of arts that date from before the nation-states they are used to define; peoples from other geographical centers contribute forms and styles to them; immigrants, outsiders or exiles, create them. As we have seen, national arts need the art of other nations to define themselves against. They suffer all of the difficulties of the term "nation."[80]

The steady progress of linear, chronological time and the timeless space of unchanging identity are incompatible assumptions upon which conceptions of national history rested in the nineteenth century and into the twentieth. Without the thread of national identity, many art historical narratives, and their associated discourses, institutions, and peoples, would not coalesce. Nevertheless, the designation of national identities introduced into the heart of Western history an ahistorical element. The unchanging character imputed to the exotic Other, static Chinese or "eternal Jew," is just that: unchanging, a prejudice that once encouraged an ahistorical approach to the art of the East. The West, however, was endowed in these narratives with a character just as unchanging, even though this character, it is assumed, causes it to develop rapidly. The linear, developing history of the art historical survey (like the single-minded concentration on the unchanging character of any one of its threads) is tied to, but in tension with, the map of art first created in 1842 by Franz Kugler, a map whose own fixed nature both necessitates and nullifies the category "Jewish art."[81]

Art historical definitions of the nation are in turn dependent upon modernist constructions of the subject. The discipline's ability to articulate its subject into categories depended on a unitary self, both for the work of art and for the artist. In terms of narrative, a modernist trope held that a work of art could speak in one voice only, the authentic voice of the monolingual individual.[82] But as groups of people (nations) are conceived "organically" along the lines of a "body politic," a unitary individual presupposes a nation conceived in the same mold: the counterpart to the unitary individual is a unitary group.

A national art, however, is not a matter of identity. It is not, in fact, "identified" at all but rather is constructed, and not only of indigenous materials. The process involves filtering out the diversity inherent in any group of people, sometimes even filtering out the people themselves. To disguise diversity, "foreigners" must be extracted and sutured over. We have seen that the attempt to define and dispose of a concept of "Jewish art" has the effect of suturing over Jews who make art, turning art history into a seamless series of nationalities. The concept of Jewish art functions to support this view of art by excluding dissonant voices from a national group on the basis of their dissonance, just as connoisseurs exclude uncharacteristic works from the oeuvre of a great master. Exclusion fits out an assortment of individuals with a uniform that validates the concept of a national art and gives these individuals authority over others. If the essence of Indian art, imagination, helped give "rational" Europeans the right to political power over India, the imitative character of Jewish art gave the same Europeans the title to Jewish artistic contributions, homogenizing Europe and giving rise to concepts like that of the "Early Christian synagogue."

Faced with national concepts of these kinds, Greenberg's reluctance to embrace the discourse of Jewish art is understandable. While the Jew in him could object to the bestowal of the Bollingen Prize to the racist Ezra Pound, that same Jew rightly shied away from embracing a nationalism of his own.[83] Similarly, in 1996, when the Austrian Cultural Institute, which often calls on the Viennese émigré art historian Ernst Gombrich to celebrate the city of his youth, asked him to speak on the artistic contributions of the "Jewish culture of fin de siècle Vienna" at the Central Synagogue in London, his response, bristling with an irritation worthy of Bloom at Barney Kiernan's, was to deny the existence of a "Jewish culture": "I used to think I was Viennese," he wrote, "or an Austrian."[84]

Gombrich associated a belief in Jewish culture with racism, a legitimate concern in the 1930s, when he last thought he was an Austrian. Even then, of course, other possible positions toward the relationship of the Jew with his or her surrounding cultures existed. But Gombrich's position reminds us why few Jewish art historians and critics have had a stake in concepts like Jewish art or culture until now. By contrast, his position highlights something new about the culture in and for which the present book has been written. While anyone who has arrived at this point in the book must be far more eager to read about Jewish art than most people were in the immediate postwar period, the difference is due not to a rejection of essentializing concepts but to the function of concepts of national culture and art in a different, more global society. Gombrich viewed such concepts suspiciously. He realized that Austrians could celebrate the contribution of long-vanished Jews to Austria while still denying them the right to be Austrians, pretending that what happened during the Nazi era had left Austrian society intact. The Jews came, contributed, and left. To attribute to Jews their own culture marginalizes them and validates their exile, a scenario in which Zionism appears as pernicious as anti-Semitism. This extremely important concern could not have been alien to Clement Greenberg, Gombrich's age-mate in the United States, for whom the notion of "Jewish art" could only serve to isolate Jews from a "mainstream" culture. This two-edged sword was a concern to diverse members of the same generation, such as Meyer Schapiro and Edmond Jabès.[85]

The tools to promote "Jewish art" were forged by cultural nationalism, art history's primary model, with consequent limitations. Franz Landsberger sited his attempt to create the field of Jewish art history within an interdependent hierarchy, in which Roman art echoes Greek, Japanese echoes Chinese, and "American art is a branch of European art. And yet the art of each of these – the Romans, the Japanese, and the Americans – has always been dealt with as a special field. Why should this not apply to Jewish art?"[86] While this introduction seemed to admit the possibility of defining an art as derivative, accepting the category meant defending its originality after all. "I am fully aware," he continued, "that the question has been frequently discussed as to what extent Jews were able to preserve their original characteristics, those which they possessed when they were still a nation. But it is especially Jewish art, since the Emancipation, which seems to prove that such traits have persisted."[87]

Art history, like most nations today, now needs a more flexible concept of nationhood. Cultural nationalism, on which art history depends, can be contrasted to etatist nationalism (state nationalism, political nationalism, or liberal nationalism). The paradigm of the active original and the passive recipient of influence, which prevails from the level of the individual to that of cross-cultural influence, can move aside to allow the development of an internationalist or cosmopolitan position. The scholars now engaged in uncovering the Jewish share in our artistic vision, however, reversing Christian chauvinist paradigms, would do well to keep in mind the danger of setting up a glorified, essentialized ethnic art in the place of older, national models. Eloquent attempts to reverse the paradigm of originality in art history, from Focillon to Michael Baxandall, face a similar risk of simply relocating the site of originality.[88] In our age, competing ethnicities and globalization call for attempts to understand in new ways the guidelines people use to group themselves into communities, cultures, and nations. The very methodologies used to do so, however, are themselves freighted with significance for politics and ethnicity.

In the year 2001, to write about "Jewish culture" is a way of claiming part – usually the best part – of what Greenberg might have called "mainstream culture" for our own. The conception of what it means to be "in" a culture, however, has changed. There is no longer a homogeneous insider's culture for Jews to contribute to from the outside, nor a homogeneous notion of the Jew, even in Israel. Recent parodies hint that, in the United States, there is nothing self-evident for assimilating minorities to mimic. In order to "pass," the heroine of Susan Mogul's *The Last Jew in America* (video, 1984), hides not only the matzos but the Chinese food as well and buys Wonder Bread, thus mocking both "mainstream culture" and the stereotypical Jewish fixation on food. African American humor makes similar points. The favored place to be is not "in" a culture but outside it, since it is only possible to contribute from the margin.[89] The Other may still be defined out, but those who claim to be at the center are often described as "far right."

"Jewish art" is one of the generalized categories people use when they form themselves into groups. Benedict Anderson called these groups "imagined communities," although the novel and newspaper readers he had in mind might seem unfamiliar to scholars of visual culture.[90] "Visualized cultures," however, and reflections about them, are the context in which discussions of Jewish culture and the image belong. To be an effective and useful concept, a culture must distinguish itself from, and must relate itself to, other cultures by resisting, ignoring, enhancing, and subsuming them. The process of defining a group now faces difficulties within and without – among specialties, genders, national perspectives, and generations.

It is in this context that Akerman's discourse of identity can coexist with those of Greenberg and Gombrich. We need to ask not how the Second Commandment determines Jewish attitudes toward images, but how Jewish attitudes toward images relate to the equally complex attitudes of Others, some of whom are also Jews. Such an inquiry would move beyond the present one. It is necessary, however, if visualized communities are to be made more diverse, so that one day different people might live in the same, or in different, places.

Notes

PREFACE

1. On page 6 of the *Deutsches Volksblatt*, no. 4124, 27 June 1900, one can find a report on "Die Pariser Fahrt der Wiener Antisemiten." The group's visit to Paris began with a tour of locations made famous by the Dreyfus case.

2. "Richard" to Wickhoff, 30 January 1902, Wickhoff Nachlaß, Institut für Kunstgeschichte, University of Vienna.

3. On Wagner's plan, see Peter Haiko, "The Franz Josef-Stadtmuseum: The Attempt to Implement a Theory of Modern Architecture," in *Otto Wagner: Reflections on the Raiment of Modernity*, ed. Harry Francis Mallgrave (Santa Monica CA: Getty Center for the History of Art and the Humanities, 1993), 53–83.

4. Margaret Olin, "Alois Riegl and the Crisis of Representation in Art Theory, 1880–1905" (Ph.D. diss., University of Chicago, 1982).

5. Michael André Bernstein, "Forgone Conclusions: Narrating the Fate of Austro-German Jewry," *Modernism/Modernity* 1 (January 1994): 57–79.

6. Michael Shank, *Unless You Believe, You Shall Not Understand: Logic, University, and Society in Late Medieval Vienna* (Princeton NJ: Princeton University Press, 1988), 171; and communications with the author. The inscription is quoted on page 197 n.117.

7. Portheim to Wickhoff, 22 January 1886. Wickhoff Nachlaß, carton 2, "Briefe von und zu Wickhoff," 4.

8. Wilhelm Bode, another scholar about whom Portheim complained, was known for anti-Semitic behavior. Wolfgang Beyrodt, "Wilhelm von Bode (1845–1929)," in *Altmeister moderner Kunstgeschichte*, ed. Heinrich Dilly (Berlin: Dietrich Reimer, 1990), 32.

9. For a useful discussion and citations, see Joseph Gutmann, "Jewish Art and Jewish Studies," in *The State of Jewish Studies*, ed. Shaye J. D. Cohen and Edward L. Greenstein (Detroit MI: Wayne State University Press, 1990), 193–211.

10. Portheim was from a well-known Jewish family from Prague, who, among other businesses, operated a porcelain factory in Chodau, where Portheim was born. *Biographisches Lexikon des kaiserthums Oesterreich*, s.v. "Porges Edle von Portheim, Moses und Leopold."

11. See Margaret Olin, "Alois Riegl: The Late Roman Empire in the Late Habsburg Empire," in *The Habsburg Legacy: National Identity in Historical Per-*

spective, ed. Ritchie Robertson and Edward Timms (Edinburgh: Edinburgh University Press, 1994), 107–20.

12. Laurence J. Silberstein, *Postzionism Debates: Knowledge and Power in Israeli Culture* (New York: Routledge, 1999).

13. Luce Irigaray, *This Sex That Is Not One,* trans. Catherine Porter (Ithaca NY: Cornell University Press, 1985); Homi K. Bhabha, *The Location of Culture* (London: Routledge, 1994); Judith Butler, *Bodies That Matter: On the Discursive Limits of "Sex"* (New York: Routledge, 1993); Henry Louis Gates Jr., *"Race," Writing, and Difference* (Chicago: University of Chicago Press, 1985); Michel Foucault, *The Archaeology of Knowledge,* trans. A. M. Sheridan Smith (London: Tavistock Publications, 1972).

14. Griselda Pollock, *Differencing the Canon: Feminist Desire and the Writing of Art's Histories* (London: Routledge, 1999); Whitney Davis, " 'Homosexualism,' Gay and Lesbian Studies, and Queer Theory in Art History," in *The Subjects of Art History: Historical Objects in Contemporary Perspectives,* ed. Mark A. Cheetham, Michael Ann Holly, and Keith Moxey (Cambridge: Cambridge University Press, 1998), 115–42; and Kymberly N. Pinder, ed., *Race-ing Art History* (New York: Routledge, in press).

15. For example, by the contributors to Robert S. Nelson and Richard Shiff, eds., *Critical Terms in Art History* (Chicago: University of Chicago Press, 1996).

16. I have taken part in "Prophets and Losses: Jewish Experience and Visual Culture," Southern Methodist University, Dallas, 1995; "Jewish Identity in Art History," College Art Association Annual Meeting, Boston, 1996; and "Icon, Image, and Text in Modern Jewish Culture," Princeton University, Princeton NJ, 1999.

17. Other important contributions that have opened issues of Jewish visuality are Linda Nochlin and Tamar Garb, eds., *The Jew in the Text: Modernity and the Construction of Identity* (London: Thames and Hudson, 1995); and Norman L. Kleeblatt, ed., *Too Jewish? Challenging Traditional Identities* (New Brunswick NJ: Rutgers University Press, 1996).

18. Richard I. Cohen, *Jewish Icons: Art and Society in Modern Europe* (Berkeley: University of California Press, 1998).

19. Kalman P. Bland, *The Artless Jew: Medieval and Modern Affirmations and Denials of the Visual* (Princeton NJ: Princeton University Press, 2000).

20. Steven Fine, "Iconoclasm and the Art of Late Antique Palestinian Synagogues," in *From Dura to Sepphoris: Studies in Jewish Art and Society in Late Antiquity,* Journal of Roman Archaeology Supplementary Series, ed. L. I. Levine and Z. Weiss (forthcoming); Fine, *Art and Judaism During the Greco-Roman Period* (New York: Jewish Publication Society, in press).

21. Catherine M. Soussloff, ed., *Jewish Identity in Modern Art History* (Berkeley: University of California Press, 1999).

1. JEWISH ART DEFINED

1. See under "Marginalized in the Mainstream" (later in this chapter) and chapter 5.

2. Exodus 20:4–5; Deuteronomy 5:8.

3. Boaz Cohen, "Art in Jewish Law," *Judaism* 3 (winter 1954): 165–76; Bland, *The Artless Jew*; Joseph Gutmann, ed., *Beauty in Holiness* (New York: Ktav Publishing House, 1970), 1–14; Kurt Schubert, "Jüdische Kultur als Bildkultur," *Kunst und Kirche* 4/96 (November 1996): 222–25; Avram Kampf, "The Interpretation of the Second Commandment," in *Writings About Art*, ed. Carole Gold Calo (Englewood Cliffs NJ: Prentice Hall, 1994), 45–58; David Freedberg, *The Power of Images: Studies in the History and Theory of Response* (Chicago: University of Chicago Press, 1989), 54–81; and Vivian B. Mann, ed., *Jewish Texts on the Visual Arts* (Cambridge: Cambridge University Press, 2000), which also contains a useful introduction (1–18).

4. Barbara Flagg, "The Transparency Phenomenon, Race-Neutral Decisionmaking, and Discriminatory Intent," in *Critical White Studies: Looking behind the Mirror*, ed. Richard Delgado and Jean Stefancic (Philadelphia: Temple University Press, 1997), 220–26.

5. George W. Stocking Jr., "The Turn of the Century Concept of Race," *Modernism/Modernity* 1 (1994): 4–16.

6. George L. Mosse, *Germans and Jews: The Right, the Left, and the Search for a "Third Force" in Pre-Nazi Germany* (Detroit MI: Wayne State University Press, 1987); Mosse, *Toward the Final Solution: A History of European Racism* (Madison: University of Wisconsin Press, 1985); Peter Pulzer, *The Rise of Political Anti-Semitism in Germany and Austria*, rev. ed. (Cambridge: Harvard University Press, 1988); Leon Poliakov, *The Aryan Myth: A History of Racist and Nationalist Ideas in Europe*, trans. Edmund Howard (New York: Basic Books, 1974); Poliakov, *The History of Anti-Semitism*, 4. vols., trans. Richard Howard et al. (New York: Vanguard, 1965–85). For distinctions between religious and racist varieties of anti-Semitism, see John G. Gager, *The Origins of Anti-Semitism: Attitudes toward Judaism in Pagan and Christian Antiquity* (Oxford: Oxford University Press, 1983), 7–9, 13–34; Rosemary Radford Ruether, *Faith and Fratricide: The Theological Roots of Anti-semitism* (New York: Seabury, 1974); Sander L. Gilman, *The Jew's Body* (London: Routledge, 1991); and Uriel Tal, *Christians and Jews in Germany: Religion, Politics and Ideology in the Second Reich, 1870–1914*, trans. Noah Jonathan Jacob (Ithaca NY: Cornell University Press, 1975).

7. On narratives and nationalism, see Bhabha, *The Location of Culture*, 139–70; on racism and nationalism, see Etienne Balibar and Immanuel Wallerstein, *Race, Nation, Class: Ambiguous Identities*, trans. Chris Turner (London: Verso, 1991), 37–67.

8. See Edward Said, *Orientalism* (New York: Pantheon, 1978), 27–28, 113–23.

9. Mosse, *Toward the Final Solution*, 22–23; John M. Efron, *Defenders of the Race: Jewish Doctors and Race Science in Fin-de-Siècle Europe* (New Haven CT: Yale University Press, 1994).

10. Johann Gottfried Herder, *Auch eine Philosophie der Geschichte zur Bildung der Menschheit* (1774), in *Johann Gottfried Herders Werke*, vol. 4: *Johann Gottfried Herder Schriften zu Philosophie, Literatur, Kunst und Altertum 1774–1487*, ed. Jürgen Brummack and Martin Bollacher (Frankfurt am Main: Deutscher Klassiker Verlag, 1994), 9–108; Johann Joachim Winckelmann, *Gedanken über die Nachahmung der griechischen Werke in der Malerei und Bildhauerkunst* (1755; Stuttgart: Reclam, 1969); see also Mosse, *Toward the Final Solution*, 35–50.

11. Paul Frankl, *The Gothic: Literary Sources and Interpretation through Eight Centuries* (Princeton NJ: Princeton University Press, 1960), 417–28, 447–79; Hans Belting, *The Germans and Their Art: A Troublesome Relationship*, trans. Scott Kleager (New Haven CT: Yale University Press, 1998), 26–28, 41–48.

12. Heinrich Dilly, *Kunstgeschichte als Institution: Studien zur Geschichte einer Disziplin* (Frankfurt am Main: Suhrkamp, 1979); Udo Kultermann, *The History of Art History* (New York: Abaris Books, 1993), 87–94, 103–23; Fritz Ringer, *The Decline of the German Mandarins: The German Academic Community, 1890–1933* (Cambridge: Harvard University Press, 1969), 15–25; Susanne L. Marchand, *Down from Olympus: Archaeology and Philhellenism in Germany, 1750–1970* (Princeton NJ: Princeton University Press, 1996).

13. Franz Kugler, *Handbuch der Kunstgeschichte*, 1st ed. (Stuttgart: Ebner & Seubert, 1842). Kugler later entered the Prussian Ministry of Ecclesiastical Affairs, Education, and Medicine. On Kugler, see Peter Paret, *Art As History: Episodes in the Culture and Politics of Nineteenth-Century Germany* (Princeton NJ: Princeton University Press, 1988), 11–60. On the role of institutions in forming "official nationalisms," see Benedict Anderson, *Imagined Communities: Reflections on the Origin and Spread of Nationalism* (London: Verso, 1983), esp. 80–103.

14. Olin, "Alois Riegl: The Late Roman Empire."

15. Balibar and Wallerstein, *Race, Nation, Class*, 86–106.

16. Hubert Janitschek, *Geschichte der deutschen Malerei* (Berlin: G. Grote, 1890), 4.

17. Sophus Müller, *Nordische Altertumskunde nach Funden und Denkmälern*

aus Dänemark und Schleswig, trans. Otto Luitpold Jiriczek (Strassburg: Karl J. Trübner, 1897–98), 2:308.

18. Ferdinand de Saussure, *Course in General Linguistics*, ed. Charles Bally and Albert Sechehaye, trans. Wade Baskin (New York: McGraw-Hill, 1959).

19. Wilhelm Lübke, *Outlines of the History of Art*, ed. Clarence Cook (1860; New York: Dodd, Mead, 1888), 1:117–18. On the phenomenon of the timeless Other, see Johannes Fabian, *Time and the Other: How Anthropology Makes Its Object* (New York: Columbia University Press, 1983); see also Ronald Inden, *Imagining India* (Oxford: Basil Blackwell, 1990); Prasenjit Duara, *Rescuing History from the Nation: Questioning Narratives of Modern China* (Chicago: University of Chicago Press, 1995), 17–50; and Robert S. Nelson, "Living on the Byzantine Borders of Western Art," *Gesta* 35 (1996): 3–11.

20. Mosse, *Toward the Final Solution*, 38; Sander L. Gilman, *Jewish Self-Hatred: Anti-Semitism and the Hidden Language of the Jews* (Baltimore: Johns Hopkins University Press, 1986).

21. Hans-Georg Gadamer, *Truth and Method* (New York: Crossroad, 1975), 153–92.

22. *Christliches Kunstblatt für Kirche, Schule und Haus* was founded in 1858 and edited by Karl Schnaase and C. Grüneisen, with J. Schnorr von Carolsfeld, until 1877 (continued thereafter under other editors until 1927). Other such journals were the *Zeitschrift für christliche Archäologie und Kunst*, founded in 1856, and the *Zeitschrift für christliche Kunst*, founded in 1888; the *Christlichen Kunstblätter*, founded in 1860, combined in 1971 with the *Ökumenische Zeitschrift für Architektur und Kunst* to form *Kunst und Kirche*, which continues to publish. Its November 1996 issue was devoted to Jewish art.

23. Gregor Stemmrich, "C. Schnaase: Rezeption und Transformation Berlinischen Geistes in der kunsthistorischen Forschung," in *Kunsterfahrung und Kulturpolitik im Berlin Hegels*, ed. Otto Pöggeler and Annemarie Gethmann-Siefert (Bonn: Bouvier Verlag Herbert Grundmann, 1983), 263–75; Michael Podro, *The Critical Historians of Art* (New Haven CT: Yale University Press, 1982), 31–43.

24. Karl Schnaase, *Geschichte der bildenden Künste bei den Alten* (Düsseldorf: Julius Buddeus, 1843), xii. The translation is from Wolfgang Kemp, "Introduction," in Alois Riegl, *The Group Portraiture of Holland*, trans. David Britt and Evelyn M. Kain (Los Angeles: Getty Research Institute for the History of Art and the Humanities, 1999), 10, where, however, the source is mistakenly identified as Schnaase's *Niederländische Briefe*.

25. Kugler, *Handbuch der Kunstgeschichte*, 1st ed., ix. On Kugler's claims, see Dilly, *Kunstgeschichte als Institution*, 87–89.

26. Schnaase, *Geschichte der bildenden Künste,* 1:vii. On Kugler's reaction to Schnaase, see Stemmrich, "C. Schnaase," 278–79.

27. Robert S. Nelson, "The Map of Art History," *Art Bulletin* 79 (1997): 28–40; Mitchell Schwarzer, "Origins of the Art History Text," *Art Journal* 54, no. 3 (1995): 24–29.

28. Franz Kugler, *Handbuch der Kunstgeschichte,* 2nd ed., "mit Zusätzen von Jac. Burckhardt" (Stuttgart: Ebner and Seubert, 1848).

29. Kugler, *Handbuch der Kunstgeschichte,* 1st ed., 4–5.

30. Immanuel Benzinger, *Hebräische Archäologie* (Freiburg im Breisgau: Akademische Verlagsbuchhandlung von J. C. B. Mohr, 1894), 269–71; and Benzinger, "Art Among the Ancient Hebrews," *The Jewish Encyclopedia* (New York: Funk and Wagnalls, 1902), 2:141.

31. Israel Abrahams, *By-Paths in Hebraic Bookland* (1920; New York: Benjamin Blom, 1972), 340–46; and sources cited in Rainer Stichel, "Gab es eine Illustration der jüdischen Heiligen Schrift in der Antike?" *Tesserae: Festschrift für Josef Engemann, Jahrbuch fur Antike und Christentum,* supp. vol. 18 (1991): 93 n.3.

32. Kugler, *Handbuch der Kunstgeschichte,* 1st ed., 78.

33. Kugler also mentioned the boy angels in C. L. Eastlake, ed., *A Hand-Book of the History of Painting from the Age of Constantine the Great to the Present Time,* trans. "a lady" (London: John Murray, 1842), 298.

34. Franz Wickhoff, "Der Stil der Genesisbilder und die Geschichte seiner Entwicklung," in *Die Wiener Genesis,* ed. Wilhelm Ritter von Hartel and Franz Wickhoff (Vienna: F. Tempsky, 1895), 5.

35. Elie Faure, *History of Art,* vol. 1, *Ancient Art,* trans. Walter Pach (New York: Harper and Brothers, 1921), 104–5.

36. Karl Schnaase, *Geschichte der bildenden Künste bei den Alten,* 2d ed., vol. 1, *Die Völker des Orients* (Düsseldorf: Julius Budeus, 1866), 234.

37. Schnaase, *Geschichte der bildenden Künste,* 2d ed., 1:227. For a contemporary architectural theory, see Augustus Welby Northmore Pugin, *The True Principles of Pointed or Christian Architecture* (London: John Weale, 1841). As its title implies, Pugin regarded the honesty implied in his architectural theory as inseparable from its Christianity, contrasting it, however, not with Jewish but with pagan architecture and values.

38. Schnaase, *Geschichte der bildenden Künste,* 2d ed., 1:236.

39. Gotthold Ephraim Lessing, *Laocoön: An Essay on the Limits of Painting and Poetry,* trans. Edward Allen McCormick (1766; reprint, Baltimore: Johns Hopkins University Press, 1984).

40. Schnaase, *Geschichte der bildenden Künste,* 2d ed., 1:236.

41. Exodus 25:10–27:8.

42. Poliakov, *The History of Anti-Semitism*, 3:299.

43. Schnaase, *Geschichte der bildenden Künste*, 2d ed., 1:217 n.1.

44. Helen Rosenau, *Vision of the Temple: The Image of the Temple of Jerusalem in Judaism and Christianity* (London: Oresko Books, 1979); Paul von Naredi-Rainer, *Salomos Tempel und das Abendland: Monumentale Folgen historischer Irrtümer* (Cologne: Dumont, 1994).

45. Georges Perrot and Charles Chipiez, *Histoire de l'art dans l'antiquité*, vol. 5, *Judée, Sardaigne, Syrie, Cappadoce* (Paris: Librairie Hachette, 1887), 241–42. The temple in question is described in Ezekiel 40–43.

46. Perrot and Chipiez, *Histoire de l'art dans l'antiquité*, 5:124.

47. See also Georges Perrot and Charles Chipiez, *Le Temple de Jérusalem et la maison du Bois-Liban, restitués d'après Ézéchiel et le Livre des Rois* (Paris: Hachette, 1889), 83.

48. Perrot and Chipiez, *Histoire de l'art dans l'antiquité*, 5:125.

49. Perrot and Chipiez, *Histoire de l'art dans l'antiquité*, 5:476.

50. Lübke, *Outlines of the History of Art*, 1:86. See also Martin Bernal, *Black Athena: The Afroasiatic Roots of Classical Civilization*, vol. 1, *The Fabrication of Ancient Greece, 1785–1985* (New Brunswick NJ: Rutgers University Press, 1987), 337–99.

51. S[alomon] Reinach, *Apollo: An Illustrated Manual of the History of Art throughout the Ages*, trans. Florence Simmonds (New York: Charles Scribner's Sons, 1907), 28; Lübke, *Outlines of the History of Art*, 83 and n.2.

52. Schnaase, *Geschichte der bildenden Künste*, 2d ed., 1:228.

53. G. W. F. Hegel, *Early Theological Writings*, trans. T. M. Knox (Philadelphia: University of Pennsylvania Press, 1948), 192–93.

54. See Terry Pinkard, *Hegel: A Biography* (New York: Cambridge University Press, 2000), 584–86. I owe this reference to Lydia Goehr.

55. As in Herbert Read, *Art and Society* (New York: MacMillan, 1937), 99. This attitude is often traced to Voltaire. Robert S. Wistrich, *Antisemitism: The Longest Hatred* (London: Thames Metheun, 1991), 48–49. Freedberg identifies an aniconic historiographic tradition transcending Judaism, which, convinced of the moral and spiritual superiority of aniconism, "suppressed the possibility of iconicity at the beginnings of Greco-Roman culture." *The Power of Images*, 65. See also Martin Jay, *Downcast Eyes: The Denigration of Vision in Twentieth-Century French Thought* (Berkeley: University of California Press, 1993).

56. A Dr. Köppe wrote in 1816: "Educated Jews are a cosmopolitan rabble, who must be tracked down and expelled from everywhere." Quoted in Poliakov, *The History of Anti-Semitism*, 3:301.

57. Richard Wagner, "Das Judentum in der Musik" (1850), in Wagner, *Gesammelte Schriften und Dichtungen* (Leipzig: E. W. Fritsch, 1887–88), 5:66–85.

58. On Riegl, see Margaret Olin, *Forms of Representation in Alois Riegl's Theory of Art* (University Park: Pennsylvania State University Press, 1992).

59. For political analyses of Strzygowski's explorations, see Olin, "Alois Riegl: The Late Roman Empire"; and Suzanne L. Marchand, "The Rhetoric of Artifacts and the Decline of Classical Humanism: The Case of Josef Strzygowski," *History and Theory: Studies in the Philosophy of History*, Theme Issue 30: *Proof and Persuasion in History* (1994): 106–30.

60. Alfred Karasek-Langer, "Josef Strzygowski: Ein Lebensbild," in *Festschrift J. Strzygowski 70 Jahre, Schaffen und Schauen* (Kattowitz: n.p., 1933), VIII, 7:36–45.

61. See also Annabelle Jane Wharton, *Refiguring the Post Classical City: Dura Europos, Jerash, Jerusalem, and Ravenna* (Cambridge: Cambridge University Press, 1995), 3–14, which also contains a useful discussion of Giovanni Teresio Rivoira.

62. Josef Strzygowski, *Orient oder Rom: Beiträge zur Geschichte der spätantiken und frühchristlichen Kunst* (Leipzig: J. C. Hinrichs'sche Buchhandlung, 1901), 147.

63. Adolf Bauer and Josef Strzygowski, "Eine Alexandrische Weltchronik," *Denkschriften der kaiserlichen Akademie der Wissenschaften, philosophisch-historische Klasse* 51 (1906): 185. This passage is cited in Josef Strzygowski, *Die bildende Kunst der Gegenwart: Ein Büchlein für Jedermann* (Leipzig: Quelle und Meyer, 1907), 270 n.

64. Josef Strzygowski, "Hellas in des Orients Umarmung," *Beilage zur Münchener Allgemeinen Zeitung* 40/41 (1902): 314.

65. Josef Strzygowski, *Das Werden des Barocks bei Raphael und Correggio nebst einem Anhang über Rembrandt* (Strassburg: J. H. Ed. Heitz, 1898), 121, 125; [Julius Langbehn], *Rembrandt als Erzieher* (Leipzig: Hirschfeld, 1890). See Fritz Stern, *The Politics of Cultural Despair: A Study in the Rise of the Germanic Ideology* (Berkeley: University of California Press, 1961), 97–180.

66. Strzygowski, *Die bildende Kunst der Gegenwart*, 270.

67. Josef Strzygowski, *Europas Machtkunst im Rahmen des Erdkreises: Eine grundlegende Auseinandersetzung über Wesen und Entwicklung des zehntausendjährigen Wahnes: Gewaltmacht von Gottes Gnaden statt völkischer Ordnung, Kirche statt Glaube, Bildung statt Begabung: vom Nordstandpunkt planmäßig in die volksdeutsche Bewegung eingestellt* (Vienna: Wiener Verlagsgesellschaft, 1941), 749; Strzygowski, *Nordischer Heilbringer und bildende Kunst* (Vienna: Adolf Luser,

1939), 209–10. See also Hilde Zaloscer, "Kunstgeschichte und Nationalsozialismus," in *Kontinuität und Bruch 1938–1945–1955: Beiträge zur österreichischen Kultur- und Wissenschaftsgeschichte*, ed. Friedrich Stadler (Vienna: Jugend und Volk, 1988), 283–98.

68. Eva Frodl-Kraft, "Eine Aporie und der Versuch ihrer Deutung: Josef Strzygowski – Julius v. Schlosser," *Wiener Jahrbuch für Kunstgeschichte* 42 (1989): 9, 38, and n.117; Ranuccio Bianchi Bandinelli, *Rome, The Late Empire: Roman Art AD 200–400*, trans. Peter Green (New York: George Braziller, 1971), 333. Joan Hart has informed me of an exchange of letters between Richard Krautheimer and Erwin Panofsky in 1948 and 1958, found in the Archives of American Art, Smithsonian Museum, bearing on the distaste of these scholars for anything based on Strzygowski's theories. On Strzygowski's scholarship and reception, see W. Eugene Kleinbauer, "Prolegomena," in *Early Christian and Byzantine Architecture: An Annotated Bibliography and Historiography* (Boston: G. K. Hall, 1992), lxxi–lxxxi; and Christine Maranci, "Medieval Armenian Architecture in Historiography: Josef Strzygowski and His Legacy" (Ph.D. diss., Princeton University, 1998).

69. Josef Strzygowski, review of *Spätrömische Kunstindustrie*, by Alois Riegl, *Byzantinische Zeitschrift* 2 (1902): 266.

70. Renan describes the Semitic race as a "race incomplète par sa simplicité même, elle n'a ni arts plastiques, ni science rationnelle, ni philosophie, ni vie politique, ni organisation militaire" (An incomplete race because of its own simplicity, it has neither visual arts, nor rational science, nor philosophy, nor civic life, nor military organization). Joseph Ernest Renan, *Oeuvres Complètes*, ed. Henriette Psichari (Paris: Calmann-Lévy, 1947–61), 7:88.

71. Miriam A. Dytman, "Zur Geschichte der Familie Liebermann," in *Was vom Leben übrig bleibt, sind Bilder und Geschichten; Max Liebermann zum 150. Geburtstag*, ed. Hermann Simon (Berlin: Stiftung "Neue Synagoge Berlin – Centrum Judaicum," 1997), 47–66. Heinrich Wölfflin stressed Liebermann's Berlin roots in Joseph Gantner, ed., *Kleine Schriften (1886–1933)* (Basel: Benno Schwabe, 1946), 139. This was probably self-conscious. Wölfflin helped Liebermann get an honorary degree from Berlin University and was careful to recommend Jewish colleagues and students for jobs they could actually get. Joan Hart kindly communicated this information to me. On Liebermann's Jewish identity, see also Jay A. Clarke, "The Construction of Artistic Identity in Turn-of-the-Century Berlin: The Prints and Klinger, Kollwitz, and Liebermann" (Ph.D. diss., Brown University, 1999), 214–95.

72. Alois Riegl referred to Liebermann's art as a typical example of Stim-

mungskunst in Riegl, *Gesammelte Aufsätze* (Augsburg-Wien: Dr. Benno Filser, 1929), 36, illustrating the original publication of the essay (about the concept of *Stimmung* in modern art) with a drawing by Liebermann (in *Die graphischen Künste* 22 (1899): 47). In another place, he seemingly denied Liebermann a "Germanic" nature, writing that he "ebensogut Franzose sein könnte" (could as well be French). Riegl, review of *Die deutsche Kunst des neunzehnten Jahrhunderts: Ihre Ziele und Thaten*, by Cornelius Gurlitt, *Die Mitteilungen der Gesellschaft für vervielfältigende Kunst*, supp. to *Graphischen Künste* 23 (1900): 3.

73. "Man hat ihm gerade als Juden den Vorwurf der Abhängigkeit von Frankreich gemacht. Es ist nicht einmal wahr." Ernst Cohn-Weiner, *Die jüdische Kunst: Ihre Geschichte von den Anfängen bis zur Gegenwart* (Berlin: Martin Wasservogel, 1929), 252.

74. Henry Thode, *Böcklin und Thoma: Acht Vorträge über neudeutsche Malerei* (Heidelberg: Carl Winter's Universitätsbuchhandlung, 1905), 101.

75. Herbert Howarth, "Jewish Art and the Fear of the Image," *Commentary* 9 (February 1950): 147. On Howarth, see also Bland, *The Artless Jew*, 38–39.

76. Carl Vinnen, *Ein Protest deutscher Künstler* (Jena: Eugen Diederichs, 1911), 12 (original emphasis). On the protest, see Peter Paret, *The Berlin Secession: Modernism and Its Enemies in Imperial Germany* (Cambridge: Harvard University Press, 1980), 182–99.

77. Vinnen mentions Julius Meier-Graefe in his introduction; A. Goetz criticizes Max Liebermann intensely; on Paul Cassirer, see especially the contribution of Hans Rosenhagen. Vinnen, *Ein Protest deutscher Künstler*, 14, 54–55, 65–69.

78. Wilhelm Hausenstein, "Mittelstandspolitik," in *Im Kampf um die Kunst: Die Antwort auf den "Protest deutscher Künstler*, ed. Alfred Walter Heymel (Munich: R. Piper, 1911), 108.

79. Kathryn Brush, *The Shaping of Art History: Wilhelm Vöge, Adolph Goldschmidt, and the Study of Medieval Art* (Cambridge: Cambridge University Press, 1996), 42.

80. Olin, "Alois Riegl: The Late Roman Empire," 108.

81. Julius von Schlosser, "Die Bilderschmuck der Haggadah," in *Die Haggadah von Sarajevo: Eine Spanisch-Jüdische Bilderhandschrift des Mittelalters*, ed. David Heinrich Müller and Julius von Schlosser (Vienna: Alfred Holder, 1898), 113.

82. Schlosser, "Die Bilderschmuck der Haggadah," 217 and n.2.

83. Among the Jewish authors cited by Schlosser in his notes were the chief rabbi of Vienna, Moritz Güdemann; Moritz Steinschneider; and Heinrich Graetz.

84. Julius von Schlosser, curriculum vitae written on 2 July 1914, quoted in Karl T. Johns, "Julius Alwin Ritter von Schlosser, ein bio-bibliographischer Beitrag," *Kritische Berichte* 16, 4 (1988): 47. He was not a member of the organization, whose proper name was actually Gesellschaft für Sammlung und Conservirung von Kunst- und Historichen Denkmäler des Judentums, when he published the Sarajevo Haggadah.

85. To argue for the "eigenthümliche Elasticität" that sustained the Jews, Schlosser quoted one of the milder passages from A. W. Ambros, *Geschichte der Musik*, ed. B. Sokolowsky (Leipzig: F. E. C. Leuckart, 1887–1911), suggesting that German Jews sang in a manner resembling Gregorian choral music, which "could occasionally have been considered sublime if the execution had been calmer, more even." Schlosser, "Die Bilderschmuck der Haggadah," 249.

86. See also Schlosser, "Die Bilderschmuck der Haggadah," 240, where he calls Jews "eine der constantesten und dennoch beweglichsten Rassen, die der Erdball trägt."

87. Schlosser, "Die Bilderschmuck der Haggadah," 240–41.

88. Liebermann's name in this context has a double significance, since, as well as a common Jewish name, it was also the name of a leader of the anti-Semitic movement, Liebermann von Sonnenberg, a fact that did not escape the notice of his opponents in the Reichstag. See Dietz Bering, *The Stigma of Names: Antisemitism in German Daily Life, 1812–1933*, trans. Neville Plaice (Ann Arbor: University of Michigan Press, 1992), 92–93. I owe this reference to Lydia Goehr.

89. Ludwig Bossler, "Bericht über die Sitzungen der germanistischen Section der XXVI. Philologenversammlung zu Würzburg, 1. bis 3. October 1868," *Germania. Vierteljahrsschrift für deutsche Altertumskunde* 14 (1869): 127. On *Germania*, see Poliakov, *The History of Anti-Semitism*, 4:18.

90. Schlosser, "Die Bilderschmuck der Haggadah," 248.

91. The source of Schlosser's quotation is Moritz Steinschneider, "Robert von Anjou und die jüdische Literatur," *Vierteljahrsschrift für Kultur und Literatur der Renaissance* 1 (1886): 137.

92. See Salo Baron, "Moritz Steinschneider's Contributions to Jewish Historiography," in *History and Jewish Historians*, ed. Arthur Hertzberg and Leon A. Feldman (Philadelphia: Jewish Publication Society of America, 1964), 276–321.

93. Adolph Goldschmidt, review of *Die Haggadah von Sarajevo*, by Heinrich Müller and Julius v. Schlosser, *Repertorium für Kunstwissenschaft* 23 (1900): 337.

94. On Goldschmidt's training and method, see Brush, *The Shaping of Art History*, 19–53.

2. THE NATION WITH ART?

1. Janitschek, *Geschichte der deutschen Malerei*, 4.

2. On modern aniconic Jewish intellectuals, see Bland, *The Artless Jew*, 13–58, and chapter 3 of the present book.

3. Exodus 31:3. Bezalel is identified as the actual maker of the ark in 37:1–38:22.

4. Medieval sources are more interested in the Golden Calf than in Bezalel. See Bland, *The Artless Jew*, 116–29.

5. Henrietta Szold, "Bezalel," typescript, box 100, Jerusalem City Archives, Jerusalem, n.p. On early Bezalel in relation to Zionist imagery, see Michael Berkowitz, *Zionist Culture and West European Jewry* (Cambridge: Cambridge University Press, 1993), 140–43.

6. Boris Schatz, "Bezalel School of Handicrafts of Jerusalem," *Bezalel: Exhibition of Jewish Arts Worked in Bezalel School of Handicrafts of Jerusalem*, Exhibition Catalog (New York, 12–18 January 1914), n.p.

7. "Contrary to most art, Israeli art – the art created in modern Israel – had a clear-cut debut. It dates back to 1906, when the Bezalel School of Arts and Crafts was founded in Jerusalem." Gideon Ofrat, *One Hundred Years of Art in Israel*, trans. Peretz Kidron (Boulder CO: Westview, 1998), 7.

8. For general accounts of Israeli art in English, see Susan Tumarkin Goodman, *Artists of Israel: 1920–1980* (New York: Jewish Museum, 1981); Eugen Kolb, "Art in Israel," in *Jewish Art*, ed. Cecil Roth (New York: McGraw-Hill, 1961), 903–50; Ofrat, *One Hundred Years of Art in Israel*; and Benjamin Tammunz and Max Wykes, *Art in Israel* (London: W. H. Allen, 1966).

9. I write "turned out to be" to avoid the suggestion of inevitable progression to statehood. For a discussion of challenges to classic Zionist narratives, see Silberstein, *Postzionism Debates*.

10. Universal Exposition, St. Louis, 1904, *Official Illustrations of Selected Works in the Various National Sections of the Department of Art* (St. Louis, 1904), 368–69. Schatz was represented in the illustrated catalog with a sculpture of a Russian soldier holding a child. He received a silver medal.

11. Boris Schatz, "The Bezalel Institute," in *Zionist Work in Palestine*, ed. Israel Cohen (Leipzig: T. Fischer Unwin, 1911), 60.

12. Leo Kenig (Koenig), "Jewish Art," in *The Way We Think: A Collection of Essays from the Yiddish*, ed. and trans. Joseph Leftwich (South Brunswick NJ: Thomas Yoseloff, 1969), 720. Ilya Gintsburg founded the school for which Antokolsky called in Vilna. Mirjam Rajner, "The Awakening of Jewish National Art in Russia," *Jewish Art* 16–17 (1990–91): 119–20.

13. Gideon Ofrat-Friedlander, "The Periods of Bezalel," in *Bezalel 1906–*

1929, ed. Nurit Shilo-Cohen (Jerusalem: Israel Museum, 1983), 33–34. Bulgarian sources report that he came to Bulgaria after meeting Bulgarian students in Paris. Lazar Marinski, *Natzionalna khudozhestvena galeriia: Bulgarska skulptura 1878–1974* (A catalog of Bulgarian sculpture (1878–1974) in the National Gallery of Art) (Sofia: Bulgarski khudozhnik, 1975), 28.

14. Ofrat-Friedlander, "The Periods of Bezalel," 33; Theodor Herzl, *Briefe und Tagebücher*, ed. Alex Bein et al. (Berlin: Ullstein, 1983–96), 2:416–17.

15. Atanas Bozhkov, *Bulgarskata khudozhestvena akademiia* (The Bulgarian Academy of Fine Arts) (Sofia: Bulgarski khudozhnik, 1962), 20–21.

16. Ivan D. Shishmanov, "Znachenieto i zadachite na nashata etnografiia" (The Importance and Objectives of Ethnography in Bulgaria) (1889), in *Izbrani suchineniia* (Selected works) (Sofia: Bulgarska akademiia na naukite, 1966), 2:53–55.

17. Ivan Vazov, "Natsionalizmut v nashiia teatur i izkustvo" (The national in Bulgarian theater and art) (1910), in *Subrani suchineniia* (Collected works) (Sofia: Bulgarski pisatel, 1979), 20:253.

18. "Un cadre en style vieux bulgare," *La Bulgarie a l'exposition universelle internationale de 1900 a Paris: Catalogue spécial du Pavillon Bulgare et de la section Bulgare au palais des beaux-arts* (Paris: Imprimerie et librairie centrales de chemins de fer, 1900), 58.

19. Quoted in Bozhkov, *Bulgarskata khudozhestvena akademiia*, 31.

20. Quoted in Bozhkov, *Bulgarskata khudozhestvena akademiia*, 31.

21. I have been unable to confirm this often mentioned aspect of Schatz's activities. See J. Thon, "Bezalel," *Ost und West* 5 (1905): 625. The report of the Bulgarian Ministry of Commerce and Agriculture for 1907 says little about government efforts to revive handicrafts but ties the significance of the textile industry to its beginnings in an internationally esteemed house industry that included carpets. *Bulgaria of Today*, Balkan States Exhibition, Earl's Court (London: Bulgarian Ministry of Commerce and Agriculture, 1907), 172–77; Alexander Gerschenkron, *Economic Backwardness in Historical Perspective: A Book of Essays* (Cambridge MA: Belknap, 1962), esp. 223–24.

22. Kokesh and Herzl to Schatz (29 January 1902) acknowledge the receipt of Schatz's first proposal but request details before advising him to come to Vienna to present the plan. Herzl, *Briefe und Tagebücher*, 417–18. Schatz represented Bulgaria in the expositions in Paris, 1900, and St. Louis, 1904, but received few public commissions. He may have had difficulties as a Russian, a Jew, a conservative artist, or all of the above. Andrei Protich, spokesman of the Society of Contemporary Art, criticized Schatz's statues in an official venue in 1907 as "devoid of artistic merit" and added that they "have exercised no

influence on Bulgarian sculpture." Andrey Protitch, *Fine Art in Bulgaria*, supp. to *Bulgaria of Today*, 9. On Bulgarian modernist movements, see S. A. Mansbach, "An Introduction to the Classical Modern Art of Bulgaria," *Art Bulletin* 81 (1999): 149–62.

23. Ofrat-Friedlander, "The Periods of Bezalel," 37.

24. Derek J. Penslar, *Zionism and Technocracy: The Engineering of Jewish Settlement in Palestine, 1870–1918* (Bloomington: Indiana University Press, 1991), 73–74.

25. Boris Schatz, "The Bezalel," *The New York Zionist Annual* (1905): 21.

26. Nurit Shilo-Cohen, "Introduction," in *Bezalel 1906–1929*, ed. Shilo-Cohen, 19; Ilona Oltuski, *Kunst und Ideologie des Bezalels in Jerusalem: ein Versuch zur judischen Identitatsfindung* (Frankfurt am Main: Kunstgeschichtliches Institut der Johann Wolfgang Goethe-Universität, 1988), 129.

27. Schatz to Harry Friedenwald, 15 September 1930, cited in Richard I. Cohen, *Jewish Icons*, 215. See also Kolb, "Art In Israel"; and Berkowitz, *Zionist Culture and West European Jewry*.

28. Oskar Bie, in *Berliner Börsencourier*, reprinted in "Jüdische Kunst: Ueber Lesser Ury," *Die Welt* 5 (15 September 1901): 10.

29. See also Yigal Zalmona and Tamar Manor-Friedman, *To the East: Orientalism in the Arts in Israel* (Jerusalem: Israel Museum, 1998), 97–99.

30. Schatz, "The Bezalel Institute," 22.

31. This title is used in Max Blanckenhorn, *Naturwissenschaftliche Studien am Toten Meer und im Jordantal: Bericht über eine im Jahre 1908 (im Auftrage S.M. des Sultans der Türkei Abdul Hamid II. und mit Unterstützung der Berliner Jagor-Stiftung) unternommene Forschungsreise in Palästina* (Berlin: R. Friedländer and Sohn, 1912), 17–18:395.

32. Nurit Shilo-Cohen and Yigal Zalmona, "The Style and Iconography of Bezalel Objects," in *Bezalel 1906–1929*, ed. Shilo-Cohen, 216; Ofrat, "The Utopian Art of Bezalel," *Ariel* 61 (1982): 57; Mordechai Narkiss, "Boris Schatz and His Vision, Bezalel," *Onamuth* 3, no. 1 (1942): 9. The zoological collection went to Hebrew University in 1925.

33. Hermann Struck, "Einige Worte ueber den "Bezalel," *Ost und West* 7 (1907): 23–24.

34. Nurit Shilo-Cohen and Daphna Freudenthal-Lapidot, "Appendices," in *Bezalel 1906–1929*, ed. Shilo-Cohen, 367. On Eliezer Ben-Yehuda, see Shlomo Avineri, *The Making of Modern Zionism: The Intellectual Origins of the Jewish State* (New York: Basic Books, 1981), 83–87.

35. According to oral communication by the artist Jacob Pins and others, students were summoned to Hebrew-speaking meals at the Ben-Yehuda

household. In 1932, Hemda Ben-Yehuda wrote Schatz's obituary in *Doar Hayom.* Nurit Shilo-Cohen, "Boris Schatz," in *Bezalel 1906–1929,* ed. Shilo-Cohen, 146, and 149 n.14.

36. Boris Schatz, "Work Possibilities in Eretz Israel," a series published in *Doar Hayom,* 1921, listed in the bibliography in Oltuski, *Kunst und Ideologie des Bezalels,* 224.

37. After 1909, the Hebrew teacher was Kadish Yehuda Silman. Shilo-Cohen and Freudenthal-Lapidot, "Appendices," 377.

38. Rajner, "The Awakening of Jewish National Art in Russia," 110–12; Yigal Zalmona, "Hirszenberg, Lilien and Pann – Painters at Bezalel," in *Bezalel 1906–1929,* ed. Shilo-Cohen, 202–4; Zalmona and Manor-Friedman, *To the East,* 96–98. On the reception of Assyrian art in the nineteenth century, see Frederick N. Bohrer, "Inventing Assyria: Exoticism and Reception in 19th Century England and France," *Art Bulletin* 80 (June 1998): 336–56. On indigenous techniques, see Shilo-Cohen and Zalmona, "The Style and Iconography of Bezalel Objects," 232.

39. See William Morris, "The Gothic Revival," pts. 1 and 2, *The Unpublished Lectures of William Morris,* ed. Eugene D. Lemire (Detroit MI: Wayne State University Press, 1969), 54–93.

40. Schatz, "The Bezalel Institute," 62.

41. Shilo-Cohen, "Boris Schatz," 148; and Schatz, *Jerusalem Rebuilt,* typescript.

42. Schatz, "Bezalel School of Handicrafts of Jerusalem," n.p.

43. Shilo-Cohen and Zalmona, "The Style and Iconography of Bezalel Objects," 215.

44. "Opening Remarks," *Bezalel* 2 (1963), n.p.; and Norm Gutharz, "Home at Last," an interview with Ran Shechori, director of Bezalel Academy from 1978. "Bezalel Academy 80th anniversary 1906–1986," *Jerusalem Post,* supp., 11 May 1986, sec. 3. One source refers to the building as a former orphanage. Ofrat-Friedlander, "The Periods of Bezalel," 44.

45. Oskar Marmorek, "Baugedanken für Palästina 1. Der Tempel (1897)," in Markus Kristan, *Oskar Marmorek: Architekt und Zionist, 1863–1909* (Vienna: Böhlau, 1996), 138. I owe this reference to Géza Hajós.

46. On the staging of ethnicity, see Barbara Kirshenblatt-Gimblett, *Destination Culture: Tourism, Museums, and Heritage* (Berkeley: University of California Press, 1998).

47. Herzl, *Briefe und Tagebücher,* 2:594.

48. Herzl, *Altneuland,* 2d ed. (Leipzig: Hermann Seemann Nachfolger, n.d.), 282; Perrot and Chipiez, *Le Temple de Jérusalem.* Some of the illustrations were

reproduced in D. Joseph, "Stiftshuette, Tempel- und Synagogenbauten," *Ost Und West* 1 (1901): 593–608.

49. Schatz, *Jerusalem Rebuilt*, typescript, 6–7.

50. Schatz, "Bezalel School of Handicrafts of Jerusalem."

51. Ofrat, "The Utopian Art of Bezalel," 62.

52. Similar issues come up in music. See Philip V. Bohlman, "Afterward: Shireh 'Am, Shireh Medinah (Folk Song, National Song)," in *Israeli Folk Music: Songs of the Early Pioneers*, ed. Hans Nathan (Madison WI: A-R Editions, 1994), 39–55.

53. Kirshenblatt-Gimblett, *Destination Culture*, 118–20.

54. An advertisement for membership on the basis of such "prizes" could still be found in the *Palestine Weekly* after the school had closed. "The Jewish Room," *Palestine Weekly*, 1 August 1930, 11. A Megilla (plural, Megillot) is a scroll containing the biblical story of Esther, which is read on the Jewish holiday of Purim.

55. Boris Schatz, "After the Bezalel Exhibition in America," in Schatz, *Bezalel: Its Aim and Purpose* (New York: Friends of Professor Boris Schatz, 1926), 52.

56. Numbers 13:23.

57. Thanks to Steven Fine for iconographical help.

58. Schatz, "The Bezalel Institute," 22.

59. For example, Thon, "Bezalel," 641, writes of the benefits of aesthetic education to the "Schmutz verkommenen Bevölkerung."

60. See chapter 3 for a discussion of such thinkers.

61. Rav A. Y. Kook, *Selected Letters*, trans. Tzvi Feldman (Ma'aleh Adumim: Ma'aliot Publications of Yeshiva Birkat Moshe, 1986), 194–95. I am indebted to Hillel Braude for this reference. On Rabbi Kook, see Avineri, *The Making of Modern Zionism*, 187–197; and Bland, *The Artless Jew*, 33–35.

62. Kook, *Selected Letters*, 196.

63. Kook, *Selected Letters*, 196–97.

64. Oltuski, *Kunst und Ideologie des Bezalels*, 163 n.4.

65. A Shabbas Goy is a non-Jewish person engaged to perform tasks forbidden to Jews on the Sabbath.

66. Elliot B. Lefkovitz, *A Passion for Life: The Story of Herman and Maurice Spertus* (Chicago: Spertus Institute for Judaica, 1994), 37. Information about gifts from the Spertus family to the Spertus Museum can be found in the Chicago Jewish Archives, Spertus Institute of Jewish Studies, collection no. 96, Spertus Family Papers.

67. A letter signed by Mrs. Eli Daiches, director, Friends of Bezalel, Chicago, May 1932, quotes an undated statement by Einstein in support of Bezalel. Box 222, file 145, Jerusalem City Archives.

68. Ofrat-Friedlander, "The Periods of Bezalel," 63, 90–99.

69. Boris Schatz, "What Professor Schatz Has to Say," in Schatz, *Bezalel: Its Aim and Purpose*, 11.

70. C. R. Ashbee, *A Palestine Notebook, 1918–1923* (Garden City NY: Doubleday, Page, 1923), 245–49. See also Alan Crawford, *C. R. Ashbee: Architect, Designer and Romantic Socialist* (New Haven CT: Yale University Press, 1985), 191 and 444 n.74. On the Guild of Handicraft, see Fiona MacCarthy, *The Simple Life: C. R. Ashbee in the Cotswolds* (London: Lund Humphries, 1981).

71. Gideon Ofrat-Friedlander attributes Bezalel's downfall to its financial dependence on local bodies. Ofrat-Friedlander, "The Periods of Bezalel," 99. The Bauhaus experience is relevant to this aspect of Bezalel's finances.

72. Israel Abrahams gives an account of a lecture in Hebrew by Schatz in Cambridge University in *The New Palestine*, 27 March 1925. Schatz is also on the schedule (17 September 1931) of a Yiddish-speaking "Kultur Club" in Chicago, where he mounted an exhibit. Philip L. Seman, *Community Culture in an Era of Depression* (Chicago: Jewish People's Institute, 1932), 42, 56–57.

73. On the waves of immigration, see Walter Lacquer, *A History of Zionism* (New York: Schocken Books, 1976), 270–337.

74. The museum remained in the home of Meir Dizengoff, the first mayor of Tel Aviv, until 1971.

75. The word "New" was added to the name of the school, it is alleged, to distinguish it from artisans who were still using the name Bezalel as a trademark. Letter, possibly from Arthur Ruppin, to W. H. Tates, Esq., Alston MA, c. 1936. Box 222, folder 132, Jerusalem City Archives.

76. Michele Vishny, *Mordechai Ardon* (New York: Harry N. Abrams, 1973), 23.

77. Josef Budko, minutes of meeting with [Ze'ev] Raban and Gur Aryeh on 19 February 1934, enclosed in draft of letter, possibly from Arthur Ruppin, to W. A. Stewart, esq. Jerusalem, 10 January 1936. Box 222, folder 143, Jerusalem City Archives.

78. Gideon Ofrat, *Bezalel HaChadash* (Hebrew) (Jerusalem: Bezalel Academy of Art and Design, 1987), 30.

79. *Doar Hayom* 21 Kislev 5696 (17 December 1935), quoted in Ofrat, *Bezalel HaChadash*, 30.

80. Exodus 1:8. The entire sentence reads "And a new king arose who knew not Joseph." S. Schwarz, "Let Us Prevent Deeds of Injustice," trans. Mark Wegner, *Doar Hayom* (Hebrew), 12 December 1935.

81. Ofrat mentions Klausner's presence at the meeting with Herzl in "The Utopian Art of Bezalel," 63. On Klausner, see David N. Myers, *Re-Inventing the Jewish Past: European Jewish Intellectuals and the Zionist Return to History* (New York: Oxford University Press, 1995), 94–98.

82. Klausner's objections to New Bezalel, its name, and its brief against the memory of Boris Schatz are quoted in an inquiry from the Philadelphia Chapter of the Friends of Bezalel. J. Rabinovitz to Mordechai Narkiss, 12 March 1936. L42/124, Central Zionist Archives, Jerusalem.

83. On Jabotinsky, see Lacquer, *A History of Zionism*, 338–83; and Avineri, *The Making of Modern Zionism*, 159–86.

84. In 1949, the Revisionists proposed Klausner as their candidate for the first president of Israel in opposition to Chaim Weizmann.

85. Ofrat-Friedlander, "The Periods of Bezalel," 99; Ofrat-Friedlander, "The Bezalel Museum," in *Bezalel 1906–1929*, ed. Shilo-Cohen, 353.

86. Wischnitzer, "From My Archives," *Journal of Jewish Art* 6 (1979): 7.

87. Karl Schwarz, *Jewish Artists of the 19th and 20th Centuries* (New York: Philosophical Library, 1949), 117. Schwarz, the first director of the Tel Aviv Museum, softened his rhetoric in 1961. Karl Schwarz, "Jewish Sculptors," in *Jewish Art*, ed. Roth, 865.

88. Alfred Werner, "Boris Schatz, Father of an Israeli Art," *Herzl Year Book* 7 (1971): 395–410.

89. Josef Klausner, "Prof. B. Schatz," in *Boris Schatz: 31 Oil Paintings* (Jerusalem: s.n., 1929), 2–3.

90. Karl Schwarz, *Jewish Artists*, 117. On the term "Galut," see Silberstein, *Postzionism Debates*, 21–30.

91. Olin, *Forms of Representation*, 24–30.

92. M. Narkiss, "Fifty Years: Israel's National Museum," *Jewish Quarterly* 4 (1956–57): 24.

93. Bezalel Narkiss acknowledges he was one of about a dozen such Bezalels by command born in the 1920s. Calev Ben-David, "An Artful Life," *Jerusalem Post Magazine*, 30 April 1999, 19.

94. For example, see Mordechai Narkiss to J. Rabinovitz, 12 May 1936. L42/124, Central Zionist Archives, Jerusalem.

95. *Omanuth* 2, no. 2–3 (June 1941): 30; portion of a letter of January 1935, signed by A. Ruppin, chair, W.D. Senator, treasurer, Anna Ticho, Dr. A. Granowski, Dr. G. Landauer, Dr. J. Lurie, Prof. L. A. Mayer, Erich Mendelsohn, Salman Schocken, and Hermann Struck. Box 216, folder 9, Jerusalem City Archives; and Ofrat, *Bezalel HaChadash*, 28.

96. Mordechai Ardon in 1949, quoted in Vishny, *Mordechai Ardon*, 28.

97. Mordechai Narkiss, "The 'Bezalel' National Museum (Its Value, Development and Needs)," *Palestine Weekly*, 1 August 1930; Mordechai Narkiss to Rudolf Bermann, 15 June 1932. L42/224, Central Zionist Archives, Jerusalem. See also H. Cramer, in *Omanuth* 2, no. 2–3 (June 1941): 49.

98. Mordechai Narkiss to Bermann, 15 June 1932. L42/227, Central Zionist Archives, Jerusalem.

99. Mordechai Narkiss to Bermann, 12 February 1932, L42/227, Central Zionist Archives, Jerusalem. The reference is to the illustrations by Uriel Birnbaum to a German edition of Louis Carroll's *Alice im Wunderland*, which appeared in 1923. On Birnbaum, see Georg Schirmers, ed., *Uriel Birnbaum, 1894–1956: Dichter und Maler* (Hagen: Fernuniversität-Gesamthochschule- in Hagen, Universitätsbibliothek, 1990).

100. *Omanuth* 2 (1941): 30.

101. M. Narkiss in "Jerusalem and Art" (1954). Quoted in Oltuski, *Kunst und Ideologie des Bezalels*, 48.

102. M. Narkiss, "Fifty Years," 25.

103. F. Schiff to Chief Rabbi Dr. Melchior, 28 December 1949. L42/222, Central Zionist Archives, Jerusalem. The correspondent was probably Marcus Melchior (1897–1969), chief rabbi of Denmark after 1947.

104. See, for example, the heartrending letter from one Chaim H. Fluss, in Berlin, 22 July 1938, urgently requesting immediate admission and consequently emigration for his apparently underage son. Box 222, folder 145, Bezalel Archives, Jerusalem City Archives. See also a letter containing bad news about visas from the commissioner for migration and statistics, Jerusalem. Edwin Sammuel to Dr. Budko, 3 July 1939, box 222, folder 156, Bezalel Archives, Jerusalem City Archives.

105. Mordechai Narkiss sought to funnel money to Ardon by hiring him as a restorer, enabling him to teach less and paint more without appearing to accept help. Mordechai Narkiss to Hans Moller, Vienna, 19 January 1937. L42/126, Central Zionist Archives, Jerusalem.

106. *Omanuth* 2, no. 2–3 (June 1941): 47.

107. On the later history of the school, see "Bezalel Academy 80th anniversary 1906–1986," *Jerusalem Post*, supp., 11 May 1986. As of summer 1999, according to the school's then Web site, *www.bezalel.ac.il*, the "historic building" was home to a postgraduate, joint Israeli-Palestinian seminar.

108. Tali Tamir, "The New Bezalel: The Universalist Trend," *Israel Museum Journal* 9 (1990): 43–50.

109. Ben-David, "An Artful Life," 19.

110. For example, Sarit Shapira, ed., *Routes of Wandering: Nomadism, Voyages and Transitions in Contemporary Israeli Art* (Jerusalem: Israel Museum, 1991). See also Ofrat, *One Hundred Years of Art in Israel*; and Susan Tumarkin Goodman, ed., *After Rabin: New Art from Israel* (New York: Jewish Museum, 1998).

111. Silberstein, *Postzionism Debates*, 236 n.51. The reference is to Said, *Orientalism*.

112. The catalog also expresses regret for the omission of the Arab Israeli voice. Zalmona and Manor-Friedman, *To the East,* vii.

113. Other such "centers" were planned, most prominently the Central Archives of Jewish Art at Oxford University. See Bernhard Blumenkranz, "The Case for a Central Archives of Jewish Art: An Introduction to the Discussion on the Possibility of Establishing a Central Photographic Archives of Jewish Ceremonial Art," in *The Visual Dimension: Aspects of Jewish Art,* ed. Clare Moore (Boulder CO: Westview, 1993), 121–28.

114. Bezalel Narkiss, *Shoshanim Le David Synagogue Ritual Objects* (Jerusalem: Center for Jewish Art, Index of Jewish Art, 1981), n.p.

115. Mordechai Narkiss, *One Nation out of Many Peoples* (Jerusalem: National Museum Bezalel, 1953), 1.

116. M. Narkiss, *One Nation out of Many Peoples,* 1.

117. See Cohen, "Collecting and Preserving the Jewish Past: Judaica in the Israel Museum," *Israel Museum Journal* 9 (1990): 54.

118. See Bezalel Narkiss, "Introduction," *Journal of Jewish Art* 1 (1974): 5; and Aliza Cohen-Mushlin, "Editor's Note," *Jewish Art* 16–17 (1990–91): 3. The latter issue, sixteen years into the *Journal,* contains articles on Giorgione's *Trial of Moses* and on the Jewish identity of Anton Raphael Mengs.

119. Bezalel Narkiss and Gabrielle Sed-Rajna, *Index of Jewish Art: Iconographical Index of Hebrew Illuminated Manuscripts* (Jerusalem: Israel Academy of Sciences and Humanities, 1978), 7.

120. B. Narkiss, *Shoshanim Le David Synagogue Ritual Objects,* n.p.

121. Ariella Amar and Ruth Jacoby, *Ingathering of the Nations: Treasures of Jewish Art: Documenting an Endangered Legacy* (Jerusalem: Center for Jewish Art, 1998).

122. An exception is Heinrich Strauss, *Die Kunst der Juden im Wandel der Zeit und Umwelt: Das Judenproblem im Spiegel der Kunst* (Tübingen: Verlag Ernst Wasmuth, 1972), 124.

123. For example, by Gabrielle Sed-Rajna, "Défense et illustration de l'art juif," in Sed Rajna et al., *L'art Juif* (Paris: Éditions Citadelles & Mazenod, 1995), n.p. This is also the tact taken by Helen Rosenau (not an Israeli), who writes that "positively, [architecture] is able to express in an abstract and non-representational manner the Jewish ideals of the unity and the holiness of God." Rosenau, *A Short History of Jewish Art* (London: James Clarke, 1948), 14.

124. This concept has been discussed in studies of anti-Semitism, most recently in Saul Friedländer, *Nazi Germany and the Jews,* vol. 1, *The Years of Persecution, 1933–1939* (New York: Harper Collins, 1997), 85. The implications of these and other forms of nationalism for Jewish politics are detailed in

Ezra Mendelsohn, *On Modern Jewish Politics* (New York: Oxford University Press, 1993).

125. On paradigms of ending in Israel in modern literature, see Sidra DeKoven Ezrahi, *Booking Passage: Exile and Homecoming in the Modern Jewish Imagination* (Berkeley: University of California Press, 2000).

3. DAVID KAUFMANN'S STUDIES IN JEWISH ART

1. Georg Hermann, "Max Liebermann," in *Jüdische Künstler*, ed. Martin Buber (Berlin: Jüdischer Verlag, 1903), 115.

2. Ludwig Geiger, *Das Studium der hebraeischen Sprache in Deutschland vom Ende des XV. bis zur Mitte des XVI. Jahrhunderts* (Breslau: Schletter, 1870); *Cambridge History of the Bible*, vol 3, *The West from the Reformation to the Present Day*, ed. S. L. Greenslade (Cambridge: Cambridge University Press, 1963), 48–55; *Theologische Realenzyklopaedie*, s.v. "Hebraeisch,"; *Jüdisches Lexikon*, s.v. "Hebraisten, christliche"; and *Encyclopedia Judaica*, s.v. "Hebraists, Christian." I am indebted to Erika Rummel for guidance.

3. On Gesenius, see *Theologische Realenzykolpedie*, s.v. "Gesenius, Wilhelm (1786–1842)."

4. Yosef Hayim Yerushalmi, *Zakhor: Jewish History and Jewish Memory*, 2d ed. (New York: Schocken Books, 1989), 81–103; Leon Wieseltier, "Etwas über die jüdische Historik: Leopold Zunz and the Inception of Modern Jewish Historiography," *History and Theory* 20 (1981): 135–49; Ismar Schorsch, *From Text to Context: The Turn to History in Modern Judaism* (Hanover MA: Brandeis University Press, 1994), 266–302; Gershom Scholem, *The Messianic Idea in Judaism and Other Essays in Jewish Spirituality* (New York: Schocken, 1971), 304–13; and Michael A. Meyer, *Deutsch-jüdische Geschichte in der Neuzeit* (Munich: C. H. Beck, 1996), 2:343–48.

5. On the accommodation of Jewish religious practices to Christian sensibilities, see Michael A. Meyer, *Response to Modernity: A History of the Reform Movement in Judaism* (Oxford: Oxford University Press, 1988; reprint, Detroit MI: Wayne State University Press, 1995), 48, 64, 124–25. I have drawn from Meyer's account of the development of Reform Judaism for this chapter.

6. David Jan Sorkin, *The Transformation of German Jewry, 1780–1840* (New York: Oxford University Press, 1987).

7. Meyer, *Response to Modernity*, 49, 170; Bland, *The Artless Jew.*

8. Meyer, *Response to Modernity*, 28.

9. For example, Richard Krautheimer, *Mittelalterliche Synagogen* (Berlin: Frankfurter Verlags-Antstalt, 1927), 12.

10. See Meyer, *Response to Modernity*, esp. 74.

11. Review of Moses Hess, *Rom und Jerusalem, Die Allgemeine Zeitung des Judenthums.* Quoted in Isaiah Berlin, *The Life and Opinions of Moses Hess* (Cambridge: W. Heffer and Sons, 1959), 42. Thanks to Paul Ritterband and Allen Glicksman for this citation, via H-Judaic. See also Shlomo Avineri, *Moses Hess: Prophet of Communism and Zionism* (New York: New York University Press, 1985).

12. As in the assembly convened by Napoleon in Paris in 1806. Meyer, *Response to Modernity,* 27–28.

13. An exponent of this position was Hermann Cohen, *Religion of Reason out of the Sources of Judaism,* trans. Simon Kaplan (1919; reprint, Atlanta: Scholars Press, 1995).

14. Solomon Formstecher, for example, emphasized the developing nature of Jewish theology. Meyer, *Response to Modernity,* 67–74.

15. On the term "Wissenschaft" and related moral attitudes toward scholarship, see Ringer, *The Decline of the German Mandarins,* 102–13.

16. Leopold Zunz, "Etwas über die rabbinische Literatur" (1818), in *Gesammelte Schriften* (Hildesheim: Georg Olms, 1976), 30–31.

17. "Das erste war der Nachweis der Verkettung der allgemeinen Cultur mit der jüdischen, sonach der allgemeinen Literatur mit der jüdischen unerschütterlich zu erhärten, das zweite war, in Form und Schreibweise, d.h. im Aeußeren auf derselben Stufe zu stehen, die die Wissenschaft anderer Gebiete einnahm." Ignaz Ziegler, "Prof. Dr. David Kaufmann: Ein Lebensbild," in *Brandeis' illustrierten israel. Volkskalender* (Prague: Richard Brandeis, 1900), 9.

18. Samuel Holdheim, quoted in Meyer, *Response to Modernity,* 131.

19. On German historicism and "Aufklärung," see Peter Hanns Reill, *The German Enlightenment and the Rise of Historicism* (Berkeley: University of California Press, 1975). On the national idea in German historicism, see Georg Iggers, *The German Conception of History: The National Tradition of Historical Thought from Herder to the Present* (Middletown CT: Wesleyan University Press, 1968), 29–43. In the present context, the term "historicism" denotes the practice of history in Germany in the nineteenth century, represented, for example, by Leopold von Ranke.

20. Yerushalmi, *Zakhor,* 88; Meyer, *Response to Modernity,* 75–77.

21. Meyer, *Response to Modernity,* 76. In their neutral stance they resembled other German historians. Ringer, *Decline of the German Mandarins,* 113–27.

22. Schorsch, *From Text to Context,* 51–70.

23. Michael A. Meyer, "Jewish Scholarship and Jewish Identity: Their Historical Relationship in Modern Germany," *Studies in Contemporary Jewry* 8 (1992): 187–88.

24. Yerushalmi, *Zakhor*, 81. But Jewish studies were instituted on a university level in Germany in the 1920s. Alfred Jospe, "The Study of Judaism in German Universities before 1933," *Leo Baeck Institute Year Book* 27 (1982): 163–64; Schorsch, *From Text to Context*, 68–69 n.75.

25. Marchand, *Down from Olympus*, 50.

26. A possible example of an art history professor of Jewish heritage who converted to Christianity was Moriz Thausing (1838–84), professor in Vienna from 1873 to his death in 1884. Thausing is identified as Jewish, as far as I know, only in Hans Tietze, *Juden in Wien: Geschichte – Wirtschaft – Kultur* (1933; reprint, Vienna: Wiener Journal Zeitschriftenverlag, 1987), 232. On Thausing, see Julius von Schlosser, *Die Wiener Schule der Kunstgeschichte: Rückblick auf ein Säkulum deutscher Gelehrtenarbeit in Österreich, Mitteilungen des Österreichischen Instituts für Geschichtsforschung*, supp. 13 (Innsbruck: Universitäts-Verlag Wagner, 1934), 159–60; and Anton Springer, "Moriz Thausing," *Repertorium für Kunstwissenschaft* 8 (1885): 142–47.

27. Among the few early exceptions are Zofja Ameisenowa, "The Tree of Life in Jewish Iconography," *Journal of the Warburg Institute* 2 (1938): 326–45; and Helen Rosenau, "The Synagogue and Protestant Church Architecture," *Journal of the Warburg Institute* 4 (1940–41): 80–84.

28. Berenson entertained Meyer Schapiro at Villa I Tatti. Their mutual responses are recorded in Ernest Samuels, *Bernard Berenson: The Making of a Legend* (Cambridge MA: Belknap, 1987), 353–54. See Margaret Olin, "Violating the Second Commandment's Taboo: Why Art Historian Meyer Schapiro Took on Bernard Berenson" (Review of *Theory and Philosophy of Art: Style, Artist, and Society*, by Meyer Schapiro), *Forward*, 4 November 1994, 23.

29. Scholem, *The Messianic Idea in Judaism*, 304–13.

30. "Sogar über *Malerei* und *Stickerei*, wenigstens aus neuerer Zeit, könnte ein Liebhaber etwas zusammenbringen." Zunz, "Etwas über die rabbinische Literatur," 15 n.2.

31. Wieseltier, "Etwas über die jüdische Historik," 136.

32. Bland, *The Artless Jew*, esp. 20–23.

33. Moritz Güdemann, "Das Judenthum und die bildenden Künste," in *Gesellschaft für Sammlung und Conservirung von Kunst- und historischen Denkmäler des Judenthums, Zweiter Jahresbericht 1897* (Vienna, 1898), 61.

34. "Man könnte das ehemalige Palästina für ein orientalisches Deutschland halten." Güdemann attributes the passage to Heine's *Englische Fragmenten*. "Das Judenthum und die bildenden Künste," 56–57.

35. Heinrich Graetz, *The Structure of Jewish History and Other Essays*, trans. and ed. Ismar Schorsh (New York: Jewish Theological Seminary of America, 1975), 68–69. I owe this reference to Kalman Bland.

36. Hermann Cohen, *Aesthetik des Reinen Gefühls* (Berlin: B. Cassirer, 1912), 1:186–87. See also H. Cohen, *Religion of Reason out of the Sources of Judaism*, 50–58.

37. K(aufmann Kohler), "Art, Attitude of Judaism Toward," *The Jewish Encyclopedia* (New York: Funk and Wagnalls, 1902), 142.

38. Güdemann, "Das Judenthum und die bildenden Künste," 65.

39. On the role of collections of Jewish artifacts in the development of European Jewish identity, see R. Cohen, *Jewish Icons*, 186–219.

40. The society's support was acknowledged in the forward. Müller and Schlosser, *Die Haggadah von Sarajevo*.

41. On Frankel, see Schorsch, *From Text to Context*, 255–65.

42. Religious conservatism may not have been the only reason for Kaufmann's failure to win the post in Berlin. Zunz, to whom the sermons in Berlin were dedicated, suggested that they were "vielleicht zu hoch für ein Synagogen-Publikum" (perhaps pitched too high for a synagogue audience). Zunz to Kaufmann, 19 June 1877, in Marcus Brann, "Mittheilungen aus dem Briefwechsel zwischen Zunz und Kaufmann," *Jahrbuch für jüdische Geschichte und Literatur* 5 (1902): 185.

43. Ziegler, "Prof. Dr. David Kaufmann," 14. Tefillin are small boxes with leather straps containing passages from the Bible. According to ritual, Jewish men bind them around their arms and heads during daily prayers.

44. See listings for the relevant years in the annual publication *Jahresbericht der Landes-Rabbinerschule in Budapest* (Budapest: Kön. Ung. Universitäts-Buchdruckerei).

45. Marcus Brann, "Verzeichniss der Schriften und Abhandlungen David Kaufmann's," in *Gedenkbuch zur Erinnerung an David Kaufmann*, ed. Marcus Brann and Ferdinand Rosenthal (Breslau: Schles. Verlags-Anstalt v. S. Schottländer, 1900), lvii–lxxxvii.

46. Among the essays on non-Jewish topics republished in his collected essays are ones on literature and on the use of the phonograph for the blind. David Kaufmann, *Gesammelte Schriften* (Frankfurt am Main: Kommissionsverlag von J. Kauffmann, 1908), 1:352–62, 203–6.

47. "So wenig man Tertullian und Eusebius wegen ihrer tiefgewurzelten Ablehnung aller Kunst unter die Barbaren wird werfen wollen, darf man aber auch einzelne rabbinische Äußerungen über die Entfernung aller Abbilder aus den Gotteshäusern als Beweise dieses angeblich jüdischen Hasses gegen die Welt des Schönen in Anspruch nehmen." Kaufmann, *Gesammelte Schriften*, 1:87.

48. David Kaufmann, "Art in the Synagogue," *Jewish Quarterly Review* 9 (1897): 263–65.

49. Kaufmann, "Art in the Synagogue," 254.

50. Kaufmann, "Art in the Synagogue," 259.

51. Kaufmann, *Gesammelte Schriften,* 1:96–103.

52. Kaufmann, *Gesammelte Schriften,* 1:169–73.

53. The illustrated Bible turned up after the Second World War in Poland. Until recently it was in the Jewish Historical Institute, Warsaw. Moses dal Castellazzo, *Bilder-Pentateuch von Moses dal Castellazzo, Venedig 1521: vollstandige Faksimile-Ausgabe im Originalformat des Codex 1164 aus dem Besitz des Judischen Historischen Instituts Warscha,* ed. Kurt Schubert (Vienna: Bernthaler & Windischgraetz, 1983–86).

54. "Tier- wie Pflanzenornamente zeugen von einer Meisterhand und besonders in ihrer Zusammenstellung von hoher Originalität." Kaufmann, *Gesammelte Schriften,* 3:201.

55. "Keineswegs mehr von der Darstellung so harmloser Vorwürfe wie Tier- und Vogelgestalten befriedigt, sah man bald keine Schranke mehr, vor der man Halt machen müßte und erlustigte sich in übermütigen Drachenkämpfen und ausgelaßenen Teufelsfratzen mit der kühnsten Gothik um die Wette." Kaufmann, *Gesammelte Schriften,* 3:186.

56. Olin, *Forms of Representation,* 3–16.

57. "Die in Pesaro 1481 vollendeten Illustrationen meiner zweibändigen Machsorhandschrift in Oktav atmen eine so intime Kenntnis des synagogalen Zeremoniells, dessen einzelne Momente sie wiedergeben, daß der jüdische Ursprung dieses Meisterwerkes der Kleinmalerei schon dadurch gesichert erscheint." Kaufmann, *Gesammelte Schriften,* 3:218.

58. See chapter 2.

59. Kaufmann, *Gesammelte Schriften,* 3:213–15.

60. Kaufmann, *Gesammelte Schriften,* 3:187.

61. Kaufmann, *Gesammelte Schriften,* 3:213.

62. Kaufmann, "Sens et origine des symboles tumulaires de l'Ancien-Testament dans l'art Chrétien primitif," *Revue des Études Juives* 14 (1887): 33–48, 217–53.

63. Kaufmann, "Sens et origine des symboles tumulaires," 252–53.

64. Kaufmann, *Gesammelte Schriften,* 3:197. For a similar motif, see Olin, *Forms of Representation,* 14–15.

65. My account diverges from Kalman Bland's summation of the discourse around Jewish art as "the dispute between 'some sort of art' and 'no such thing as Jewish art.' " Bland, *The Artless Jew,* 13. This distinction may do for theology, but, partly due to the ambiguity of the phrase "no such thing as Jewish art," an understanding of discourses within the world of art or art historical scholarship demands more complex discriminations.

66. Kaufmann, *Gesammelte Schriften*, 1:1–38.

67. Adolf Brüll, "David Kaufmann," *Allgemeine deutsche Biographie* 51 (1906): 83. See also Stern, *The Politics of Cultural Despair*, 3–94. Kaufmann's pamphlet "Paul de Lagarde's jüdische Gelehrsamkeit" (1887) is reprinted in Kaufmann, *Gesammelte Schriften*, 1:207–57.

68. Kaufmann, *Gesammelte Schriften*, 3:521–36.

69. "Die tiefsten Denker des Mittelalters bei den Juden, Jude Halewi und Musa Mamuni, haben Christentum und Islam als Hilfsarbeiter am messianischen Werke mit Offenheit anerkannt," Kaufmann, *Gesammelte Schriften*, 3:525.

70. On Stöcker, see Pulzer, *The Rise of Political Anti-Semitism in Germany and Austria*, 83–97.

71. David Kaufmann, *Geschichte der Attributenlehre in der jüdischen Religions-Philosophie des Mittelalters von Saadia bis Maimuni* (Gotha: F.A. Perthes, 1877).

72. David Kaufmann, "Die Sinne: Beiträge zur Geschichte der Physiologie und Psychologie im Mittelalter," in *Jahresbericht der Landes-Rabbinerschule in Budapest* (Budapest: Kön. Ung. Universitäts-Buchdruckerei, 1884), 8. See also Bland, *The Artless Jew*, 71–74.

73. Kaufmann, "Die Sinne," 85–86.

74. Brann, "Mittheilungen aus dem Briefwechsel zwischen Zunz und Kaufmann," 160–61.

75. David Kaufmann, *George Eliot and Judaism: An Attempt to Appreciate "Daniel Deronda,"* trans. J. W. Ferrier, 2d ed. (1877; reprint, New York: Haskell House, 1970), 87.

76. Kaufmann, *George Eliot and Judaism*, 94.

77. Theodor Herzl, "Solution of the Jewish Question," *Jewish Chronicle* (London), 17 January 1896. Kaufmann's translation was to appear in Joseph Samuel Bloch's *Österreichische Wochenschrift*. Bloch did not publish it, supposedly because Kaufmann's translation was inadequate. Herzl, however, believed that Bloch had simply let him down. Herzl, *Briefe und Tagebücher*, 2:296, 298, and 831 nn. 315 and 316.

78. Kaufmann to Güdemann, 22 April 1897. Leo Baeck Institute, New York, Güdemann Collection, AR 7067.

79. Kaufmann was responding to Moritz Güdemann, *Nationaljudenthum* (Vienna: M. Breitenstein's Verlags-Buchhandlung, 1997). Güdemann locates the task of the Diaspora in its negation of nationalism and its transformation of a nation into a religion.

80. In 1948, the Institutum Judaicum Delitzschianum was reestablished at the Evangelisch-Theologischen Facultät, University of Münster. Its Web site does not profess a missionary aim: *www.uni-muenster.de/Judaicum/english.html*.

81. Kaufmann, *Gesammelte Schriften*, 1:290–306.

82. Friedrich Delitzsch, *Bibel und Babel* (Leipzig: J. C. Hinrichs, 1902); Friedrich Delitzsch, *Die grosse Täuschung* (Stuttgart: Deutsche Verlagsanstalt, 1920). On *Bibel und Babel*, see Marchand, *Down from Olympus*, 223–27.

83. Samuel Krauß, *David Kaufmann: Eine Biographie* (Berlin: S. Calvary, 1901), 16. Kaufmann published extensively in Hungarian and in many other languages. See Brann, "Verzeichniss der Schriften und Abhandlungen David Kaufmann's."

84. Kaufmann, *Gesammelte Schriften*, 1:360.

85. This claim is revealed as in part a product of nostalgic hindsight by Steven Beller, "Patriotism and the National Identity of Habsburg Jewry, 1860–1914," *Leo Baeck Institute Yearbook* 41 (1996): 215–38. On multiculturalism in the empire, see Olin, "Alois Riegl: The Late Roman Empire," and other essays in the same volume. Marsha L. Rozenblit, "The Dilemma of Identity: The Impact of the First World War on Habsburg Jewry," in *The Habsburg Legacy: National Identity in Historical Perspective*, ed. Robertson and Timms, 144–57, emphasizes the loyalty of Habsburg Jewry to the empire.

86. On the position of assimilation in the Jewish political spectrum, and the pressures on it, see Mendelsohn, *On Modern Jewish Politics*.

87. Kaufmann to Zunz, 17 September 1878, in Brann, "Mittheilungen aus dem Briefwechsel zwischen Zunz und Kaufmann," 121.

88. Kaufmann to Zunz, 17 September 1878, in Brann, "Mittheilungen aus dem Briefwechsel zwischen Zunz und Kaufmann," 122; and Zunz to Kaufmann, 30 September 1878, in Brann, "Mittheilungen aus dem Briefwechsel zwischen Zunz und Kaufmann," 123. Renan wrote to that effect in his "History of the People of Israel" (1855), in Renan, *Oeuvres Complètes*, 7:88.

89. David Kaufmann, "Aus der Pariser Weltausstellung," *Israelitischen Wochenschrift* 9 (September/October 1878). See also Cohen, *Jewish Icons*, 155, 187, 196.

90. Kaufmann, *Gesammelte Schriften*, 3:151.

91. Kaufmann, *Gesammelte Schriften*, 3:153.

92. Kaufmann, "Aus der Pariser Weltausstellung," 349.

93. Narkiss and Sed-Rajna, *Index of Jewish Art*, vol. 4, *Illuminated Manuscripts of the Kaufmann Collection at the Library of the Hungarian Academy of Sciences* (1988).

94. He is said to have refused at least one offer to return to Breslau. George Alexander Kohut, *David Kaufmann: An Appreciation* (n.p., 1900), 20.

95. Krauß, *David Kaufmann*, 48.

96. See the publication of a seminar on Jewish art preceding the establish-

ment of this master's degree. Vivian B. Mann and Gordon Tucker, *The Seminar on Jewish Art: January-September 1984* (New York: Jewish Theological Seminary of America and the Jewish Museum, 1985). See also chapter 2.

97. Franz Landsberger, *Einführung in die Jüdische Kunst* (Berlin: Philo Verlag, 1935). See Joseph Gutmann, "Franz Landsberger, 1883–1964," *Studies in Bibliography and Booklore* 8 (spring 1966): 3–9.

98. Franz Landsberger, *A History of Jewish Art* (Cincinnati: Union of American Hebrew Congregations, 1946). Meyer Schapiro called this edition the standard work in a 1976 letter to Albert Boime, whom I thank for sharing this correspondence.

99. The quotation is from Joseph Gutmann, "Introduction," to *Beauty in Holiness*, xi. But see also his essay "The 'Second Commandment' and the Image in Judaism," in Gutmann, *Beauty in Holiness*, 1–14.

100. Joseph Gutmann, *No Graven Images: Studies in Art and the Hebrew Bible* (New York: Ktav Publishing House, 1971); Gutmann, "The 'Second Commandment' and the Image in Judaism."

101. Meyer, "Jewish Scholarship and Jewish Identity," 185. "We are still unable to say how much of the text of the Commandment in its present form belongs to the original formulation and how much of it is a later Deuteronomic addition." Gutmann, *No Graven Images*, xv. See also Gutmann, *Beauty in Holiness*, 8.

102. Joseph Gutmann, *Hebrew Manuscript Painting* (New York: George Braziller, 1978), 8–9.

103. Gutmann, "Jewish Art: Fact or Fiction?" *Central Conference American Rabbis Journal* (April 1964): 53.

104. See also Roth, introduction to Roth, *Jewish Art*, 18–26.

105. Gutmann, *Hebrew Manuscript Painting*, 9.

106. Gutmann, *No Graven Images*, xv–xvi.

107. Per telephone conversation with the author, 12 June 1997. I thank Professor Gutmann for sharing this information with me.

108. Gutmann, "Jewish Art and Jewish Studies," 195.

109. Suzanne Marchand showed how the growth of Assyriology lessened the importance of Judaism as a source for Christianity. Marchand, *Down from Olympus*, 220–27. This began at a moment when the impact on present-day culture of newly emancipated Jews was becoming noticeable. A similar process obviated the need for a Jewish section in art historical surveys.

110. Carol Krinsky, *Synagogues of Europe* (New York: Architectural History Foundation; Cambridge: MIT Press, 1985), 1.

4. MARTIN BUBER

1. This speech, under the title "Von jüdischer Kunst," was excerpted in *Die Welt* and reprinted in Buber, *Die jüdische Bewegung: Gesammelte Aufsätze und Ansprachen*, 2d ed. (Berlin: Jüdischer Verlag, 1920), 1:57–66.

2. Hans Kohn, *Martin Buber: Sein Werk und seine Zeit: Ein Beitrag zur Geistesgeschichte Mitteleuropas 1880–1930*, 3rd ed. (Cologne: Joseph Melzer, 1961), 38.

3. Buber, *Jüdische Künstler*; Buber, "Die Entdeckung von Palaestina," *Ost und West* 2 (1905): 127–28; Buber, "Lesser Ury," *Ost und West* 1, heft 2 (1901): 114–25.

4. On Buber's discovery of Hasidism, see, for example, Kohn, *Martin Buber*, 68–74.

5. Theoretical, Hegelian concerns pervade his medieval scholarship in other fields, however. See Bland, *The Artless Jew*, 71–75.

6. My information about Buber's coursework in Vienna comes from the *Nationalen*, Universitätsarchiv, Vienna.

7. Some of this information, and the account of Buber's coursework in Leipzig, is collected, among other sources, in Gilya Gerda Schmidt, *Martin Buber's Formative Years: From German Culture to Jewish Renewal, 1897–1900* (Tuscaloosa: University of Alabama Press, 1995), 127–30. Documentation concerning those courses in Vienna that Schmidt did not find in Buber's archives is in the *Nationalen*, Universitätsarchiv, Vienna.

8. On the importance of Lamprecht for art historians, see Brush, *The Shaping of Art History*, 35–45.

9. Hans Kohn cites Buber's *rigorosen* with Riegl and Wickhoff, although he was apparently unaware of the second exam, or Reisch's participation in it. Kohn, *Martin Buber*, 301.

10. Archives of the University of Vienna, *Rigorosen*. Buber's effort to write a *Habilitation* is mentioned in Martin Buber, *Briefwechsel aus sieben Jahrzehnten*, ed. Grete Schaeder (Heidelberg: Lambert Schneider, 1972–75), 2:187 n.6. The placement of this note, not among the numerous letters from Florence but in a 1924 letter from Hans Kohn, reminding Buber that he was once an art historian, is symptomatic of the lack of attention devoted to Buber's art historical studies. I have been unable to obtain information about the proposed topic of the *Habilitation*, or Buber's reasons for abandoning it, although Buber's granddaughter recalls that her grandparents enjoyed remembering the year in Florence and often perused fondly the photographs of North Italian churches that they brought back from it. Personal communication from Professor Judith Buber-Agassi. See also Grete Schaeder, "Martin Buber: Ein biographischer Abriß," in *Martin Buber: Briefwechsel aus sieben Jahrzehnten* (Heidelberg: Lambert Schneider, 1972) 1:41.

11. The lack of attention that Buber's art historical aspirations have had may in part be due to Buber's own comments about his university experiences. In his autobiographical work *Meetings*, Buber downplayed the subjects of the courses he took in Vienna, commenting only on the dialogue he admired in the seminars "into which I had prematurely flung myself." Martin Buber, *Meetings* (La Salle IL: Open Court, 1973), 31. Only a few authors have tried to address Buber's interest in art as a tool for Jewish regeneration and for Zionism. Paul Mendes-Flohr, *From Mysticism to Dialogue: Martin Buber's Transformation of German Social Thought* (Detroit: Wayne State University Press, 1989), 83–92; Michael Berkowitz, "Art in Zionist Popular Culture and Jewish National Self-Consciousness," *Studies in Contemporary Jewry* 6 (1990): 9–42; Schmidt, *Martin Buber's Formative Years*, 72–79.

12. On Buber's early Viennese experiences, see Schmidt, *Martin Buber's Formative Years*; Laurence J. Silberstein, *Martin Buber's Social and Religious Thought: Alienation and the Quest for Meaning* (New York: New York University Press, 1989), 18–42; and Kohn, *Martin Buber*, 13–55. For accounts of Jung Wien and the culture that nurtured it, see Carl Schorske, *Fin de Siècle Vienna: Politics and Culture* (New York: Knopf, 1980); and William M. Johnston, *The Austrian Mind: An Intellectual and Social History, 1848–1938* (Berkeley: University of California Press, 1972).

13. Buber, "On Viennese Literature," trans. Robert A. Rothstein, in William M. Johnston, "Martin Buber's Literary Debut: 'On Viennese Literature'" (1897), *German Quarterly* 47 (1974): 559–66.

14. Martin Buber, "Zu Schopenhauers Lehre vom Erhabenen," unpublished ms. Ms. Var. 350 B/7a, Martin Buber Archives, National Library, Jerusalem. See Schmidt, *Martin Buber's Formative Years*, 23–33.

15. Ernst Mach, *The Analysis of Sensations and the Relation of the Physical to the Psychical* (1885), trans. C. M. Williams, rev. Sydney Waterlow (New York: Dover, 1959). See Olin, *Forms of Representation*, 106–7.

16. Martin Buber, "Über Jakob Boehme," *Wiener Rundschau* 12 (15 June 1901): 252–53.

17. Martin Buber, "Zur Geschichte des Individuationsproblems (Nicholaus von Cues und Jakob Böhme)," unpublished ms. Ms. Var. 350 A/2, Martin Buber Archives, National Library, Jerusalem.

18. Buber's compilation *Ecstatic Confessions* begins with a section on Indian mysticism. Martin Buber, *Ecstatic Confessions*, ed. Paul Mendes-Flohr, trans. Esther Cameron (1909; reprint, San Francisco: Harper and Row, 1985), 12–30. An interest in Chinese mysticism later bore fruit in, for example, Martin Buber, ed., *Reden und Gleichnisse des Tschuang-Tse* (Leipzig: Insel-Verlag, 1910).

19. The other author, Hermann Bahr, was treated least sympathetically by Buber, who criticized his superficiality. Buber, "On Viennese Literature," 559–61.

20. He seems to have taken a year, probably from August 1902 to August 1903, to prepare for these examinations. Berthold Feiwel to Martin Buber, 28.7.1902, in Buber, *Briefwechsel*, 1:175–76 and 175 n.1.

21. Martin Buber, *Die Geschichten des Rabbi Nachman* (Frankfurt am Main: Rütten und Loening, 1906).

22. Mosse, *Toward the Final Solution*, 96–97.

23. Report of discussion with Max Liebermann, Buber to Herzl, 24 July 1902. Buber, *Briefwechsel*, 1:174. Tzitzis are fringes worn by men under their outer garments, as prescribed by ritual law.

24. Aubrey Beardsley was probably the main aesthetic influence on Lilien's art. See Milly Heyd, "Lilien and Beardsley: To the Pure All Things Are Pure," *Journal of Jewish Art* 7 (1980): 58–69.

25. Paul Mendes-Flohr, "*Fin-de-Siècle* Orientalism, the *Ostjuden* and the Aesthetics of Jewish Self-Affirmation," *Studies in Contemporary Jewry* 1 (1984): 96–139.

26. Güdemann, "Das Judenthum und die bildenden Künste," 65. See chapter 3.

27. Buber, *Die Geschichten des Rabbi Nachman*, dedication page. See Sorkin, *The Transformation of German Jewry*, 41–78.

28. Buber's granddaughter attests that, while she knows of no objections to Buber's study of art, his father expressed his dislike for Buber's studies of Jewish mysticism. Personal communication.

29. Gershom Scholem, *On Jews and Judaism in Crisis: Selected Essays* (New York: Schocken, 1976), 126–71.

30. Martin Buber, *Die Legende des Baalschem* (1908; reprint, Berlin: Schocken Verlag, 1932), 11: "Es gibt in unseren Tagen noch Hunderttausende von Hasidim; der Hasidismus ist verdorben." See also page 7. Jiri Langer (1894–1943), a friend of Kafka, became, for a time, a follower of a Hasidic Rabbi in Poland. Mordechai Georgo (Jiri) Langer, *Nine Gates to the Hasidic Mysteries*, trans. Stephen Jolly (New York: Behrman House, 1961). Joseph Roth (1894–1939) traveled east to report journalistically on present-day Hasidism. Joseph Roth, *Juden auf Wanderschaft* (1927; reprint, Amsterdam: Allert de Lange, 1976), 22–38. On Buber's neo-Romantic view of Hasidism and its appeal to secular German Jews, see Steven E. Aschheim, *Brothers and Strangers: The East European Jew in German and German Jewish Consciousness, 1800–1923* (Madison: University of Wisconsin Press, 1982), 121–38.

31. His granddaughter, Judith Buber-Agassi, speculated that the collection of photographs of churches from Buber's Italian sojurn might relate to the topic of his intended *Habilitation*. Personal communication.

32. Adolph Goldschmidt only received his first professorship, in Halle, in 1904. See chapter 5.

33. Buber, *Die jüdische Bewegung*, 1:8, 15.

34. Martin Buber, "Kultur und Zivilization: Einige Gedanken zu diesem Theme," *Kunstwart* 14, no. 15 (1 May 1901): 81. See also Mosse, *Germans and Jews*, 85–94; Manuel Duarte de Oliviera, "Passion for Land and Volk: Martin Buber and Neo-Romanticism," *Leo Baeck Institute Yearbook* 41 (1996): 239–60. On the terms "culture" and "civilization," see Raymond Williams, "Culture and Civilization," in *Encyclopedia of Philosophy*, s.v.; and Geoffrey H. Hartman, *The Fateful Question Of Culture* (New York: Columbia University Press, 1997).

35. Quoted in Mendes-Flohr, *From Mysticism to Dialogue*, 71.

36. Buber, *Die jüdische Bewegung*, 1:62.

37. Buber, preface, *Jüdische Künstler*, n.p. Buber published essentially the same essay, retitled "Kunst und Judentum," as an appendix to the second edition of *Die jüdische Bewegung*, 1:245–52. The only substantial change is the omission, in the later publication, of the reference to Wagner quoted in the epigram to this chapter. The essay is dated 1902. Further page references will be to the essay as published in *Die jüdische Bewegung*. Some of the essays in *Jüdische Künstler* also mouthed antiartistic stereotypes of Jews. Georg Hermann's essay on Max Liebermann, for example, cites the foreign builders of Solomon's temple as proof that most of the best qualities in the art of Jews comes from their host countries. Hermann, "Max Liebermann," in *Jüdische Künstler*, ed. Martin Buber, 115.

38. "The racial identity of the Volk was symbolized by the nature within which it lived. Thus, every race had its landscape: the Aryans were set in the German forest, and the Jews in the desert, which expressed their rootlessness and the barrenness of their souls." George Mosse attributes these sentiments to Julius Langbehn but does not cite a source. Mosse, *Toward the Final Solution*, 97.

39. Buber, *Die jüdische Bewegung*, 1:247.

40. Buber, *Die jüdische Bewegung*, 1:247.

41. Buber, *Die jüdische Bewegung*, 1:247.

42. Buber, *Die jüdische Bewegung*, 1:250. Later in his career he addressed the topic of the Second Commandment directly, explicitly disassociating from Moses the notion that it forbade art. Buber, *Moses* (Oxford: East and West Library, 1946), 127.

43. Buber, *Die jüdische Bewegung*, 1:250–51.

44. Buber, *Die jüdische Bewegung*, 1:252.

45. "An der Schwelle einer Epoche, deren Wesen es zu sein scheint, über all die Substanzen in Beziehung aufzulösen und in Seelenwerte umzusetzen." Buber, *Die jüdische Bewegung*, 1:252.

46. According to Scholem's critique of Buber's studies of Hasidism, Buber's reliance on legend and story in his interpretation of the Hasidim adds to its anachronism. Scholem, *The Messianic Idea in Judaism*, 228–51. For a critical treatment of the Nachman legend, see Arthur Green, *Tormented Master: A Life of Rabbi Nahman of Bratslav* (New York: Schocken Books, 1981).

47. Buber, *Die Geschichten des Rabbi Nachman*, 1.

48. Martin Buber to Gustav Landauer, 9 November 1905, Buber, *Briefwechsel*, 1:233. On the Donnerstagtisch, see Schaeder, "Martin Buber," 52. The same year in which Buber published *Die Geschichten des Rabbi Nachman*, he began publication with the same press of a series of monographs on sociology. These were decorated in a similar style by Peter Behrens and Hermann Kirchmayr. Mendes-Flohr, *From Mysticism to Dialogue*, 83–84. According to Mendes-Flohr, the decorations of the tales of Rabbi Nachman were by Emil Rudolf Weiss. Mendes-Flohr, "Editor's Introduction," in Buber, *Ecstatic Confessions*, xxv n.6.

49. Buber first published "The Rabbi and His Son" in *Ost und West* in 1905. All citations will refer to the book.

50. For a line-by-line comparison between Nachman's tale and Buber's retelling of it, see Hans Hermann Blettgen, "Der Rabbi und sein Sohn: Martin Bubers Verarbeitung einer Geschichte des Rabbi Nachman von Bratzlaw," in *Beter und Rebellen: Aus 1000 Jahren Judentum in Polen*, ed. Michael Brocke (Frankfurt am Main: Deutscher Koordinierungsrat der Gesellschaften für Christlich-Jüdische Zusammenarbeit, 1983), 107–29.

51. Buber, *Die Geschichten des Rabbi Nachman*, 57.

52. Buber, *Die Geschichten des Rabbi Nachman*, 59.

53. See Steven Kepnes, *The Text as Thou: Martin Buber's Dialogical Hermeneutics and Narrative Theology* (Bloomington: Indiana University Press, 1992), 13–16.

54. Buber, *Die Geschichten des Rabbi Nachman*, 55.

55. See chapter 1.

56. One of the few authors who mentions Buber's studies with Riegl (or any other art historian) is Avram Kampf, "Krakauer in Vienna, 1990–1924," in *Leopold Krakauer, Painter and Architect*, ed. Meira Perry-Lehmann and Michael Levin (Jerusalem: Israel Museum, 1996), 29.

57. See Olin, *Forms of Representation*, esp. 129–53.

58. Alois Riegl, *Spätrömische Kunstindustrie* (1901; reprint, Darmstadt: Wissenschaftliche Buchgesellschaft, 1973), 403.

59. Buber, *Die jüdische Bewegung*, 1:152. For the German, see note 45 above.

60. See Olin, *Forms of Representation*, 175–80, also 119–27.

61. Buber, "Lesser Ury," in *Jüdische Künstler*, ed. Buber, 45.

62. Martin Buber, "Lesser Ury," in *Die Welt* (3 April 1901): 12.

63. Martin Buber, "Lesser Ury," in *Die Welt* (3 April 1901): 12.

64. Alois Riegl, notes for the course "Holländische Malerei" (1896–1897), Riegl *Nachlaß*, carton 6, folder 1, archives of the Institut für Kunstgeschichte, Vienna. Some of the notes for the course are found in carton 6, folder 2, with the notes for a later course on Dutch art of the seventeenth century. See also Olin, *Forms of Representation*, 167.

65. Olin, *Forms of Representation*, 108–11.

66. Olin, *Forms of Representation*, 93–103.

67. Olin, *Forms of Representation*, 155–69.

68. Archives of the University of Vienna, *Nationalen, Rigorosen*. Buber studied "German-Dutch Art and Cultural History in the Age of the Renaissance" with August Schmarsow in Leipzig in 1898–99. Schmidt, *Martin Buber's Formative Years*, 128.

69. For example, by Mendes-Flohr, *From Mysticism to Dialogue*, 31–47; also Silberstein, *Martin Buber's Social and Religious Thought*, 86 and 290 n.44.

70. Georg Simmel, *Soziologie: Untersuchungen über die Formen der Vergesellschaftung* (Leipzig: Duncker & Humblot, 1908), 646–51.

71. Riegl, *Holländische Malerei*, 19, 87, Riegl *Nachlaß*. He made a similar argument in his course in Flemish art, in 1896. Olin, *Forms of Representation*, 123.

72. Riegl, *Holländische Malerei*, 247, in Riegl *Nachlaß*, quoted in Olin, *Forms of Representation*, 225, n. 17.

73. "Ruisdael spricht zu uns namentlich durch seinen Bäumen, die uns wie Individuen begrüssen." Riegl, *Holländische Malerei*, 150, in Riegl *Nachlaß*.

74. "Man gewahrt fast nichts als Bäume, aber jeder derselben tritt uns als ein Individuum entgegen." Riegl, *Gesammelte Aufsätze*, 140.

75. Riegl, *Gesammelte Aufsätze*, 141.

76. "Die Seele des Baumes ist die unaufhörliche Umwandlung des Baumes. Buber, "Lesser Ury," in *Jüdische Künstler*, 46.

77. Buber, "Lesser Ury," in *Jüdische Künstler*, 70.

78. "Nicht Natur schlechthin, natura naturans ist überall, in mir, in Dir, von mir zu Dir, von Dir zu mir." Buber, "Lesser Ury," in *Jüdische Künstler*, 71.

79. Riegl, *Gesammelte Aufsätze*, 28–39.

80. Olin, *Forms of Representation*, 122–27.

81. On the concept of *Stimmung*, see also Leo Spitzer, *Classical and Christian Ideas of World Harmony: Prolegomena to an Interpretation of the Word "Stimmung"* (Baltimore: Johns Hopkins University Press, 1963).

82. Buber, "Die Entdeckung von Palaestina," 127. I have been unable to locate Herzl's essay cited by Buber.

83. See particularly Buber, *Die Geschichte von Rabbi Nachman*, 6–7; and Buber, "Das Leben der Hasidim," in *Die Legende des Baalschem*, 15–54.

84. The essays on historical preservation, 1903–5, are the main ones to take this approach, discussed in Olin, *Forms of Representation*, 175–80.

85. Gustav Landauer, *Skepsis und Mystik: Versuche im Anschluß an Mauthners Sprachkritik* (Berlin: Egon Sleischel, 1903), 150–53.

86. Wolfgang Riedel, *"Homo Natura": Literarische Anthropologie um 1900* (Berlin: Walter de Gruyter, 1996), 19. On this conception of mysticism, see Mendes-Flohr, "Editor's Introduction."

87. Hugo von Hofmannsthal, *Gesammelte Werke* (Berlin: S. Fischer, 1924), 2:184.

88. Hofmannsthal, *Gesammelte Werke*, 2:214. On the relation of Hofmannsthal's preoccupation with vision as a means of redemption to Riegl's art historical theories, see also Olin, *Forms of Representation*, 185.

89. Hofmannsthal, *Gesammelte Werke*, 2:175.

90. Buber, *Briefwechsel*, 1:235–38.

91. Graetz, *The Structure of Jewish History*, 68.

92. On Schnaase's use of this concept, see chapter 1.

93. Buber, *Die Geschichten des Rabbi Nachman*, 6–7.

94. Martin Buber, "The Spirit of the Orient and Judaism" (1916), in *On Judiasm*, ed. Norman Glatzer (New York: Schocken, 1967), 64.

95. Buber, "The Spirit of the Orient and Judaism," 58.

96. Martin Buber, *Ich und Du* (1923), reprinted in Martin Buber, *Das dialogische Prinzip* (Darmstadt: Wissenschaftliche Buchgesellschaft, 1984), 12.

97. Buber, *The Knowledge of Man: A Philosophy of the Interhuman*, ed. Maurice Friedman (New York: Harper Torch Books, 1965), 66.

98. Martin Buber, *Der Mensch und Sein Gebild* (Heidelberg: Lambert Schneider, 1955), 46; translated and abridged as "Man and His Image-Work," trans. Maurice Friedmann, *Portfolio* 7 (1963): 88–89. The translation here is my own.

99. Buber, *Der Mensch und Sein Gebild*, 49–50. My translation is a slightly revised version of Friedman's: Buber, "Man and His Image-Work," 98.

100. Buber, "Ein Beispiel: Zu den Landschaften Leopold Krakauers," *Merkur* 139 (1959): 840–42. Buber published two abridged, but illustrated, versions of

the same essay: "Die Landschaft Jerusalems – Naturbegegnungen des Zeichners Leopold Krakauers," *Die Kunst und das schöne Heim*, 3/62 (December 1963): 114–15; and "The Anguish of Solitude – The Art of Leopold Krakauer," *Ariel* (winter 1964/65): 5–6.

101. Buber, "Ein Beispiel," 840.

102. Buber, "Ein Beispiel," 840.

5. "JEWISH CHRISTIANS"

1. On Goldschmidt, see Brush, *The Shaping of Art History*; Carl Georg Heise, ed., *Adolph Goldschmidt zum Gedächtnis, 1863–1944* (Hamburg: Kommissionsverlag Dr. Ernst Hauswedell, 1963); and Kurt Weitzmann, *Adolph Goldschmidt und die Berliner Kunstgeschichte* (Berlin: Kunsthistorisches Institut, Fachbereich Geschichtswissenschaften der Freien Universität Berlin, 1985).

2. Another early example was Karl Neumann. On Neumann, see *Metzler Kunsthistoriker Lexikon*, s.v. Neumann.

3. A major venue was the journal *Kritische Berichte zur kunstgeschichtlichen Literatur*, which published between 1927 and 1937. Jewish scholars like Panofsky and Edgar Wind participated in this methodological controversy, together with Christians, such as Hans Sedlmayr. See Heinrich Dilly, *Deutsche Kunsthistoriker, 1933–1945* (Munich: Deutscher Kunstverlag, 1988), 11–22.

4. See chapter 3.

5. Erwin Panofsky, "Rembrandt und das Judentum," *Jahrbuch der Hamburger Kunstsammlungen* 18 (1973): 75–108; Meyer Schapiro, *Late Antique, Early Christian and Medieval Art: Selected Papers* (New York: G. Braziller, 1979), 20–33, 380–86. On Schapiro's Jewish identity, see Olin, "Violating the Second Commandment's Taboo"; Linda Seidel, " 'Shalom Yehudin!': Meyer Schapiro's Early Years in Art History," *Journal of Medieval and Early Modern Studies* 27 (1997): 559–94; and Donald Kuspit, "Meyer Schapiro's Jewish Unconscious," in *Jewish Identity in Modern Art History*, ed. Soussloff, 200–217. On Panofsky's relation to Judaism, see Michael Zell, "Eduard Kolloff and the Historiographic Romance of Rembrandt and the Jews," *Semiolus*, forthcoming.

6. Helen Rosenau, who emigrated after the race laws prevented her *Habilitation*, wrote a Ph.D. thesis, "The Architectural Development of the Synagogue," and other works, including the book *A Short History of Jewish Art*. On Rosenau and other émigrés, see the many entries in Ulrike Wendland, *Verfolgung und Vertreibung deutschsprachiger Kunsthistoriker im Nationalsozialismus: Ein biographisches Handbuch* (Munich: K. G. Saur-Verlag, 1998). Rachel Wischnitzer's Jewish publications began in 1912 with her work on the Russian edition of the *Jewish Encyclopedia*.

7. Wischnitzer-Bernstein, "Jüdische Kunstgeschichtsschreibung" (1930), in *Wissenschaft des Judentums im deutschen Sprachberieich*, ed. Kurt Wilhelm, Schriftenreihe Wissenschaftlicher Abhandlungen des Leo Baeck Instituts 16 (Tübingen: J.C.B. Mohr, 1967), 2:635–40.

8. Rudolf Hallo, *Schriften zur Kunstgeschichte in Kassel: Sammlungen Denkmäler Judaica*, ed. Gunter Schweikhart (Kassel: Gesamthochschulbibliothek, 1983).

9. Krautheimer, *Mittelalterliche Synagogen.*

10. Bruno Italiener et al., *Die Darmstädter Pessach-Haggadah Codex orientalis 8 der Landesbibliothek zu Darmstadt aus dem vierzehnten Jahrhundert* (Leipzig: K. W. Hiersemann, 1927).

11. Cohn-Wiener, *Die jüdische Kunst.*

12. For example, Karl Schwarz, *Die Juden in der Kunst* (Berlin: Welt-Verlag, 1928), half of which covers the modern era; Waldemar George, "Introduction," in *Jüdische Künstler unserer Zeit*, exhibition catalog (Zurich: Salon Henri Brendle, 1929).

13. The series was published by Le Triangle, Paris, and included a monograph by Waldemar George on Lipchitz. Romy Golan, *Modernity and Nostalgia: Art and Politics in France between the Wars* (New Haven CT: Yale University Press, 1995), 137–54.

14. In later years, Krautheimer called his book on synagogues "not a good book." Richard Krautheimer, "And Gladly Did He Learn and Gladly Teach," in Krautheimer and Leonard E. Doyle, *Rome: Tradition, Innovation and Renewal* (Victoria BC: Printing & Duplicating Services, University of Victoria Press, 1991), 97. In another version of the essay, Krautheimer recounts that his first attempt at a *Habilitation* ended when he refused the Ordinarius's demand that he convert although he was not a believing Jew. Krautheimer, *Ausgewählte Aufsätze zur europäischen Kunstgeschichte* (Cologne: Dumont, 1988), 11.

15. Julie Miller, "Planning the Jewish Museum, 1944–1947," *Conservative Judaism* 47 (fall 1994): 70.

16. E. L. Sukenik, "Discovery of an Ancient Synagogue," *Art and Archaeology* 33 (1932): 207–12.

17. Clark Hopkins, *The Discovery of Dura-Europos*, ed. Bernard Goldman (New Haven CT: Yale University Press, 1979), 131.

18. Hopkins, *The Discovery of Dura-Europos*, 177.

19. Ernst H. Gombrich, *The Story of Art*, 12th ed. (New York: Phaidon, 1972), 90.

20. H. W. Janson, *History of Art*, 5th ed., rev. Anthony F. Janson (New York: Harry N. Abrams, 1995), 210–11 (in a subsection on "Eastern Religions"); Fred-

erick Hartt, *Art: A History of Painting, Sculpture, Architecture*, 3rd ed. (Englewood Cliffs NJ: Prentice-Hall; New York: H. N. Abrams, 1989), 1:291–92 (the section is entitled "The Earliest Christian Art"); and Hugh Honour and John Fleming, *The Visual Arts: A History*, 3rd ed. (New York: Abrams, 1995), 267, 270 (the section is entitled "The Beginnings of Christian Art").

21. Thomas F. Mathews, *The Clash of Gods: A Reinterpretation of Early Christian Art* (Princeton NJ: Princeton University Press, 1993), 76. The index does not contain the term "Judaism."

22. Howarth, "Jewish Art and the Fear of the Image," 146.

23. Erwin Ramsdell Goodenough, *By Light, Light: The Mystic Gospel of Hellenistic Judaism* (New Haven CT: Yale University Press; London: H. Milford, Oxford University Press, 1935), 258–59.

24. Gombrich, *The Story of Art*, 89.

25. Wharton, *Refiguring the Post Classical City*, 39. The discussion is expanded from her earlier essay "Good and Bad Images from the Synagogue of Dura Europos: Contexts, Subtexts, Intertexts," *Art History* 17 (March 1994): 1–25.

26. Quoted in Marchand, *Down from Olympus*, 186.

27. See preface.

28. "Nach so vielen Beweisen ursprünglicher Zusammengehörigkeit aller dieser Stile und ihrer Uebereinstimmung mit der dekorativen altchristlichen Kunst darf wohl der Wahn, es habe eine urgermanische Ornamentik gegeben, für welche am entschiedensten Sophus Müller eingetreten ist, als beseitigt betrachtet werden. Es hat ja auch ebensowenig eine urgermanische Schrift existiert." Friedrich Portheim, *Über den dekorativen Stil in der altchristlichen Kunst* (Stuttgart: W. Spemann, 1886), 36–37.

29. Portheim complained that the Berlin professors had made Thausing a target of enmity. Portheim to Wickhoff, 22 January 1886. Wickhoff *Nachlaß*, carton 2, "Briefe von und zu Wickhoff," 4. Archives, Art Historical Institute, University of Vienna.

30. For example, he traces Rembrandt's achievement of his northern goals through the use of "romanische" paradigms. Alois Riegl, *Das holländische Gruppenporträt* (1902), ed. Karl M. Swoboda (Vienna: Verlag der Österreichischen Staatsdruckerei, 1931), 1:221; see also Olin, "Alois Riegl: The Late Roman Empire," 112; and Olin, *Forms of Representation*, 19 and 196 n.11.

31. Alois Riegl, "Neue Strömungen in der Denkmalpflege," *Mitteilungen der k.k. Zentralkommission für Erforschung und Erhaltung der Kunst- und historischen Denkmale*, 3rd ser. 4 (1905): 85–104. Riegl's cosmopolitanism earned him the posthumous displeasure of National Socialist authors, for example, Hans Gerhard Evers, *Tod, Macht und Raum als Bereiche der Architektur* (Munich: Neuer

Filser-Verlag, 1939), 283–303. See also Marion Wohlleben, "Vorwort," in Georg Dehio and Alois Riegl, *Konservieren, nicht restaurieren: Streitschriften zur Denkmalpflege um 1900* (Braunschweig, Wiesbaden: Friedr. Vieweg & Sohn, 1988), 7–33.

32. Olin, *Forms of Representation*, 18–19.

33. Josef Strzygowski, "A Henri Focillon," in *Correspondance*, vol. 4, *Civilizations: Orient-Occident, Génie du Nord-Latinité* (Paris: League of Nations, Society for International Cooperation, 1935), 75–127; and Henri Focillon, "A Josef Strzygowski," in *Correspondance*, 4:131–65.

34. *Entretiens sur Goethe a l'occaision du centenaire de sa mort* (Paris: League of Nations, Society for International Cooperation, 1932).

35. Strzygowski, "A Henri Focillon," 96. See Marchand, "The Rhetoric of Artifacts and the Decline of Classical Humanism."

36. Strzygowski, "A Henri Focillon," 86, 104.

37. Strzygowski, "A Henri Focillon," 103.

38. Strzygowski, "A Henri Focillon," 93–94.

39. Strzygowski, "A Henri Focillon," 99–100.

40. Strzygowski, "A Henri Focillon," 121.

41. Strzygowski, "A Henri Focillon," 103. See also Strzygowski, *Origin of Christian Church Art: New Facts and Principles of Research*, trans. O. M. Dalton and H. J. Braunholtz (Oxford: Clarendon, 1923), 103–4, 197.

42. Olin, *Forms of Representation*, 53–54.

43. Olin, *Forms of Representation*, 70–73.

44. Henri Focillon, *Témoignage pour la France* (New York: Brentano's, 1945).

45. "Qu'elle ait eu, chez les Barbares, un modèle de bois, on ne le conteste guère, et ce n'est pas là ce qu'il faut admirer, mais bien le souci mathématique qui en mesura et qui en distribua les parties." Focillon, "A Josef Strzygowski," 138.

46. Focillon, "A Josef Strzygowski," 159–60.

47. Focillon, "A Josef Strzygowski," 152.

48. Focillon, "A Josef Strzygowski," 153.

49. Focillon, "A Josef Strzygowski," 162.

50. Henri Focillon, *The Life of Forms in Art* (1934), 2d ed., trans. Charles B. Hogan and George Kubler (New York: Wittenborn, Schultz, 1948; reprint, New York: Zone Books, 1989).

51. Focillon, "A Josef Strzygowski," 163. The argument is as much as an answer to the determinist nationalism of the nineteenth-century French author Hippolyte Taine in its rejection of Taine's identification of "race, moment, and place," as to the racial interpretation of Strzygowski.

52. Others were Hermann Gundersheimer (1903-?), Guido Schönberger (1891–1974), and Irmgard Schüler. See Wendland, *Verfolfung und Vertreibung deutschsprachiger Kunsthistoriker im Nationalsozialismus*; Hermann Simon, *Das Berliner Jüdische Museum in der Oranienburger Straße: Geschichte einer zerstörten Kulturstätte* (Berlin: Union, 1988); and Felicitas Heimann-Jelinek, ed. *Was übrig blieb: das Museum Jüdischer Altertümer in Frankfurt, 1922–1938* (Frankfurt am Main: Jüdisches Museum, 1988).

53. Clark Hopkins, "Jewish Prototypes of Early Christian Art?" *Illustrated London News*, 29 July 1933.

54. Cumont to Lietzmann, 21 October 1932 and 12 May 1933, in Kurt Aland, ed., *Glanz und Niedergang der deutschen Universität: 50 Jahre deutscher Wissenschaftsgeschichte in Briefen an und von Hans Lietzmann (1892–1942)* (Berlin: Walter de Gruyter, 1979), 716–17, 735–36.

55. Kurt Weitzmann, *Sailing With Byzantium from Europe to America: The Memoirs of an Art Historian* (Munich: Editio Maris, 1994), 76.

56. Hermann Wolfgang Beyer and Hans Lietzmann, *Die jüdische Katakombe der Villa Torlonia in Rom*, Studien zur Spätantiken Kunstgeschichte, vol. 4 (Berlin: Walter de Gruyter, 1930), 15–27.

57. On the Mittwochs-Gesellschaft, see Klaus Scholder, ed., *Die Mittwochs-Gesellschaft: Protokolle aus dem geistigen Deutschland 1932–1944* (Berlin: Severin und Siedler, 1982). The group also included Theodor Wiegand (1864–1935), who supported Weitzmann's work and who, according to Weitzmann, "belonged to that group of intellectuals who felt that, by climbing on the Nazi bandwagon, they could work from the inside to avert some disasters." Weitzmann, *Sailing with Byzantium*, 71.

58. Other speakers discussed ethical liberalism in scholarship or the institution of freedom of thought in Germany (and its breakdown under National Socialism). But the circle also included Eugen Fischer, whose contributions usually consisted of National Socialist racial studies. Scholder, *Die Mittwochs-Gesellschaft*, 107, 125, 25–28, 169–70; Werner Weisbach, *Geist und Gewalt*, ed. Ludwig Schudt (Vienna: Anton Schroll, 1956), 348. See also W. H. C. Frend, "Foreword," in Hans Lietzmann, *A History of the Early Church*, trans. Bertram Lee Woolf (Cambridge, England: James Clarke, 1993), 1:i–ix. For evidence of Lietzmann's relations with Jewish scholars and his criticism of the regime, see the letters and the introduction to Aland, *Glanz und Niedergang der deutschen Universität*, esp. 125–47, in Aland's introduction.

59. Klaus Scholder, *The Churches and the Third Reich*, trans. John Bowden (Philadelphia: Fortress, 1988), 1:469 and 664 n.128.

60. Lietzmann, *A History of the Early Church*, 1:314–15, 411–12.

61. Hans Lietzmann, "Dura-Europos: Die neue ausgegrabene makedonisch-römische Garnisonstadt am Euphrat, "*Atlantis: Länder/Völker/Reisen* 9 (1937): 249. Lietzmann also reported on his trip to the Mittwochs-Gesellschaft, 3 February 1937. Scholder, *Die Mittwochs-Gesellschaft*, 362.

62. Hans Lietzmann, "Dura-Europos und seine Malereien" (review of M. Rostovtzeff, *Dura-Europos and Its Art*, and Comte Du Mesnil du Buisson, *Les Peintures de la Synagogue de Doura-Europos*), *Theologische Literaturzeitung* 65 (1940): 113–17.

63. Weitzmann, *Sailing with Byzantium*, 76; Kurt Weitzmann and Herbert L. Kessler, *The Frescoes of the Dura Synagogue and Christian Art* (Washington DC: Dumbarton Oaks Research Library and Collection, 1990), 3.

64. For a list of dissertations completed under Goldschmidt, see Adolph Goldschmidt, *Festschrift für Adolph Goldschmidt zum 60. Geburtstag am 15. Januar 1923* (Leipzig: E. A. Seemann, 1923), 143–48; and Goldschmidt, *Das siebente Jahrzehnt: Adolph Goldschmidt zu seinem siebenzigsten Geburtstag am 15. Januar 1933* (Berlin: Würfel Verlag, 1935), 173–74.

65. Weitzmann, *Sailing with Byzantium*, 77, 223. On the importance of party membership for academic employment, see Dilly, *Deutsche Kunsthistoriker*, 73.

66. Weitzmann, *Sailing with Byzantium*, 81.

67. Goldschmidt, *Das siebente Jahrzehnt*. This *Festschrift*, like the previous one, does not carry the name of an editor.

68. Weitzmann, "Preface," in Weitzmann and Kessler, *The Frescoes of the Dura Synagogue*, 3.

69. Note, for example, the title of Clark Hopkins's above-mentioned first publication of the paintings, in July 1933: "Jewish Prototypes of Early Christian Art?"

70. Kurt Weitzmann, *Byzantine Book Illumination and Ivories* (London: Variorum, 1980), 50–54; Weitzmann, "The Question of the Influence of Jewish Pictorial Sources on Old Testament Illustration," in *Studies in Classical and Byzantine Manusript Illumination*, ed. Herbert L. Kessler (Chicago: University of Chicago Press, 1971), 76–95; Weitzmann, *Sailing with Byzantium*, 541–42. On the arguments for and against the notion of the lost Jewish manuscripts, see Pierre Prigent, *Le Judaïsme et l'image* (Tübingen: J. C. B. Mohr (Paul Siebeck), 1990), 312–14.

71. On Weitzmann's methodology and its philological sources, see Mary-Lyon Dolezal, "Manuscript Studies in the Twentieth Century: Kurt Weitzmann Reconsidered, "*Byzantine and Modern Greek Studies* 22 (1998): 216–63. Dolezal, erroneously I believe, but in company with others, identifies Josepha Fiedler-Weitzmann, Kurt Weitzmann's wife, as Jewish: 230 n.45.

72. Kurt Weitzmann, "The Illustration of the Septuagint," in Weitzmann, *Studies in Classical and Byzantine Manusript Illumination*, 71–75. The essay was originally a lecture delivered in 1947.

73. Kurt Weitzmann, *Illustrations in Roll and Codex*, Studies in Manuscript Illumination, no. 2, ed. A. M. Friend (Princeton NJ: Princeton University Press, 1947), 7–9. But see "The Jewish Art Historian Defined" later in this chapter.

74. Weitzmann, *Illustrations in Roll and Codex*, 183.

75. Kurt Weitzmann, *Age of Spirituality: Late Antique and Early Christian Art, Third to Seventh Century* (New York: Metropolitan Museum of Art, 1977), xxi, xxvi.

76. Weitzmann and Kessler, *The Frescoes of the Dura Synagogue*, 146.

77. Weitzmann and Kessler, *The Frescoes of the Dura Synagogue*, 150, emphasis mine.

78. John North, "The Development of Religious Pluralism," *The Jews among Pagans and Christians in the Roman Empire*, ed. Judith Lieu, John North, and Tessa Rajak (London: Routledge, 1992), 174–93. This scholarship is not just another way to chronicle the supremacy of Christianity. It seeks to use new models that reject active/passive active/static readings of the relation of Christianity to paganism and to Judaism and instead treat changes in the religious climate of the period as a whole, recognizing that the history of any of these religions can only be understood with reference to their interactions with the others. See also Lieu, North, and Rajak, eds., *The Jews among Pagans and Christians in the Roman Empire*, 1–8. On the consequences of this model for art, particularly in Dura-Europos, see Jas Elsner, *Imperial Rome and Christian Triumph: The Art of the Roman Empire, AD 100–450* (Oxford: Oxford University Press, 1998), 212–19. Such works as Gager, *The Origins of Anti-Semitism*, are also indications of a move toward the emphasis on competitive dialogue between religions in antiquity, as is Mathews, *The Clash of Gods*. For writings on the subject emphasizing the Jewish side, see Steven Fine, ed., *Jews, Christians and Polytheists in the Ancient Synagogue: Cultural Interaction during the Greco-Roman Period* (London: Routledge, 1999), particularly, in that volume, Robin M. Jensen, "The Dura Europos Synagogue, Early-Christian Art, and Religious Life in Dura Europos," 174–89. For a model of interaction based on colonial theory, see Steven Fine, "Non-Jews in the Synagogues of Late-Antique Palestine: Rabbinic and Archaeological Evidence," in Fine, ed., *Jews, Christians and Polytheists in the Ancient Synagogue*, 224–42.

79. Kessler has pointed to the subversive intent behind Christian appropriation of Jewish images. Herbert L. Kessler, *Studies in Pictorial Narrative* (London: Pindar, 1994), 49–73, 74–96.

80. Weitzmann and Kessler, *The Frescoes of the Dura Synagogue*, 3, 146.

81. For a parallel relationship between a Jewish teacher, roughly contemporary to Goldschmidt, and his students, see Gelya Frank, "Jews, Multiculturalism, and Boasian Anthropology," *American Anthropologist* 99 (December 1997): 731–45.

82. Robert, Comte du Mesnil du Buisson, "Les peintures de la synagogue de Doura-Europos," *Revue Biblique* 43 (1934): 109; and Mesnil, "Les nouvelles découvertes de la Synagogue de Doura-Europos," *Revue Biblique* 43 (1934): 563.

83. Carl Kraeling, "The Synagogue. The Wall Decorations," in *The Excavations at Dura-Europos, Preliminary Report of the Sixth Season of Work*, ed. M. I. Rostovtzeff et al. (New Haven CT: Yale University Press, 1936), 380.

84. Robert, Comte du Mesnil du Buisson, *Les Peintures de la Synagogue de Doura-Europos 245–256 après J.-C.* (Rome: Pontificio Istituto Biblico, 1939), 2.

85. "Et ce monument précieux, unique, mérite de retenir l'attention de tous les hommes à la pensée haute qui regardent comme le bien suprême la dignité de la personne humaine et en trouvent la sauvegarde dans le respect d'une loi de justice." Gabriel Millet, "Introduction," in du Mesnil du Buisson, *Les Peintures de la Synagogue de Doura-Europos*, xxiv.

86. André Grabar, *L'art de la fin de l'antiquité et du moyen âge* (Paris: Collège de France, 1968), 2:687. The essay "Le thème religieux des fresques de la synagogue de doura (245–256 après J.-C)" first appeared in 1941.

87. Personal communication.

88. Ursula Schubert, *Spätantikes Judentum und frühchristliche Kunst*, Studia Judaica Austriaca, no. 2 (Vienna: Herold, 1974).

89. See, most recently, their contributions to a special issue on Jewish art, of the journal *Kunst und Kirche*. Kurt Schubert, "Jüdische Kultur als Bildkultur," *Kunst und Kirche* 4/96 (November 1996): 222–25; and Ursula Schubert, "Jüdische Bildkunst vom hohen Mittelalter bis zum Spätbarock," *Kunst und Kirche* 4/96 (November 1996): 226–30.

90. Weitzmann describes being impressed by Kurt Schubert's accounts of his efforts on behalf of Jews during World War II. Weitzmann, *Sailing with Byzantium*, 513–14.

91. Kurt Schubert and Ursula Schubert, *Jüdische Buchkunst* (Graz: Akademische Druck- u. Verlagsanstalt, 1983), 1:7.

92. Lesser Ury, "Gedanken über jüdische Kunst," *Ost und West* 1 (1901): 145–46.

93. E. M. Lilien, "Ein offener Brief (juedische Maecene und juedische Kunst)," *Ost und West* 2 (1902): 109–14.

94. Louis Felicien Joseph Caignart de Saulcy, *Histoire de l'art judaïque tirée des*

textes sacrés et profanes (Paris: Didier et cie, Libraires-Éditeurs, 1858). His (sometimes far-fetched) conclusions were not accepted. See the attack on them in Le Comte Melchior de Vogüé, *Le Temple de Jérusalem: Monographie du Haram-ech-Chérif* (Paris: Noblet & Baudry, 1864), vii.

95. See chapter 1.

96. Franz Delitzsch, *Iris: Farbenstudien und Blumenstücke* (Leipzig: Dörffling und Franke, 1888), 93–94. His defense was subtle. Immanuel Benzinger cited him in support of his own anti-Semitic position about the deficiency of the Jewish sense of color. Benzinger, "Art Among the Ancient Hebrews," 141. Israel Abrahams, while not accusing Delitzsch of anti-Semitism, at least thought that he assumed that primitive peoples had an undeveloped sense of color. Abrahams, *By-Paths in Hebraic Bookland*, 341.

97. "Sehr reich war sie [die Sammlung] an Vorbildern für den mohammedanischen und buddhistischen Cultus, obwohl weder Mohammedaner noch Buddhisten am Rheine wohnen." Heinrich Frauberger, "Zweck und Ziel der Gesellschaft zur Erforschung jüdischer Kunstdenkmäler zu Frankfurt a.M.," *Mitteilungen der Gesellschaft zur Erforschung jüdischer Kunstdenkmäler* 1 (October 1900): 3.

98. Richard Krautheimer thanked the Gesellschaft zur Erforschung jüdischer Kunstdenkmäler in the forward to his 1927 book on medieval synagogues. Krautheimer, *Mittelalterliche Synagogen*, 8.

99. *Encyclopedia Judaica*, CD-ROM version, 1.0, s.v. "Schubert, Kurt."

100. Personal communication.

101. Rachel Wischnitzer, *The Messianic Theme in the Paintings of the Dura Synagogue* (Chicago: University of Chicago Press, 1948).

102. Citing Martin Buber's lecture "Jüdische Religiosität," Krautheimer also tried to mitigate Jewish iconoclasm through the distinction between religion, a social phenomenon subject to rules (church building, or synagogue building, is a part of it), and religiosity, an individual affair. Truly religious individuals, as the Jews were from the fifth to the seventeenth centuries, are not against art; they are indifferent to it because their minds are on higher matters. As "religious people," he cited the Hasidic master, the Baal-schem, and some Christian examples: Francis of Assisi, Luther, and Bernard of Clairvaux. Krautheimer, *Mittelalterliche Synagogen*, 13–18. On the distinction in Buber, see Silberstein, *Martin Buber's Social and Religious Thought*, 80–91.

103. Cecil Roth, "Jewish Antecedents of Christian Art," *Journal of the Warburg and Courtauld Institutes* 16 (1953): 24. Fine points out that scholars of Islam and Christianity have also tended to blame iconoclasm respectively on Christians and Jews, or Jews and Moslems, as did iconophiles in the respective cultures. Fine, "Iconoclasm and the Art of Late Antique Palestinian Synagogues."

104. Roth, "Jewish Antecedents of Christian Art," 38.

105. Theodor Ehrenstein, *Über die Fresken der Synagoge von Dura Europos: Eine Studie* (Vienna: Kunstverlag Albert Konde, 1937), 3–4.

106. Ehrenstein, *Über die Fresken der Synagoge von Dura Europos*, 7.

107. "So wenig sich die Dura-Fresken an irgendwelche Werke der zeitgenössischen Kunst angelehnt haben, so wenig nahm sich der Miniator der Sarajevoer Haggadah irgendeine andere Handschrift in stilistischer Hinsicht zum Vorbild." Ehrenstein, *Über die Fresken der Synagoge von Dura Europos*, 15–16.

108. Kaufmann, review of *Iconographie der Taufe Christi* by Josef Strzygowski, *Archaeologiai Ertesito*, 2d ser., 6 (1886): 62–65. Martha Marton kindly translated this essay for me from Hungarian.

109. E. L. Sukenik, *Ancient Synagogues in Palestine and Greece* (London: Oxford University Press, 1934), 67.

110. Wischnitzer-Bernstein, "Jüdische Kunstgeschichtsschreibung," 2:635; Gutmann, *Hebrew Manuscript Painting*, 9; see also Gutmann, *No Graven Images*, xxxv; and Gutmann, "The Illustrated Jewish Manuscripts in Antiquity: The Present State of the Question," *Gesta* 5 (January 1966): 39–44.

111. Weitzmann, "The Question," 91–92; Weitzmann, *Sailing with Byzantium*, 39.

112. Strzygowski, *Nordischer Heilbringer und bildende Kunst*, 78.

113. Correspondence, 1964, Martin Buber Archives, National Library, Jerusalem.

114. Dilly, *Deutsche Kunsthistoriker*, 72.

115. Goldschmidt, *Adolph Goldschmidt 1863–1944: Lebenserinnerungen*, ed. Marie Roosen-Runge-Mollwo (Berlin: Deutscher Verlag für Kunstwissenschaft, 1989), 385.

116. It is possible that the synopsis omitted this troublesome aspect of the talk. "1. Hr. Goldschmidt sprach über 'Die deutsche Malerei und Plastik unter den sächsischen Kaisern,' " *Sitzungsberichte der Preußischen Akademie der Wissenschaften* (17 June 1937): 140. The other talk is probably the one on 31 March 1938, by Eduard Spranger, "Wie erkennt man einen Nationalcharakter?" The synopsis, in *Sitzungsberichte der Preußischen Akademie der Wissenschaften* (31 March 1938): 79, includes the remark that it would be published in full later. It did not, however, appear. Eduard Spranger (1882–1963) was later imprisoned by the Nazi regime for his suspected role in the failed assassination attempt against Hitler of 20 July 1944.

117. Since the published summary of Goldschmidt's last talk does not in the least correspond to the topic Weitzmann mentions, this talk was probably never given. It may, however, correspond to a manuscript that Weitzmann

could have seen. According to Goldschmidt, his talk for 1938 was complete and ready to deliver on his scheduled day a few weeks after his forced resignation. Goldschmidt, *Adolph Goldschmidt 1863–1944,* 395–96.

118. Weitzmann, *Adolph Goldschmidt und die Berliner Kunstgeschichte,* 29.

119. Goldschmidt, "English Influence on Medieval Art of the Continent," in *Medieval Studies in Memory of A. Kingsley Porter,* ed. Wilhelm R. W. Koehler (Cambridge: Harvard University Press, 1939), 2:709–28.

120. Yet another myth about Goldschmidt's last session of the Prussian Academy is propounded by Erwin Panofsky, who identifies it as the setting for a poignant anecdote concerning Goldschmidt and another scholar. This anecdote is at least partly inaccurate, since the other scholar did not belong to the academy. Panofsky, "Goldschmidt's Humor," in Heise, ed., *Adolph Goldschmidt zum Gedächtnis,* 31–32.

121. The phrase is a slightly reworded version of the famous cry of French students on the barricades in Paris, in May 1968: "We are all German Jews."

6. C[LEMENT] HARDESH (GREENBERG)

1. Raymond Escholier, quoted in Michéle C. Cone, "French Art of the Present in Hitler's Berlin," *Art Bulletin* 80 (September 1998): 564.

2. Waldemar George, "Introduction," 8.

3. Waldemar George, "Introduction," 9.

4. Waldemar George, *Gromaire* (Paris: Grande Librairie Universelle, 1928), xiv–xvi; and Matthew Affron, "Waldemar George: A Parisian Art Critic on Modernism and Fascism," in *Fascist Visions: Art and Ideology in France and Italy,* ed. Matthew Affron and Mark Antliff (Princeton NJ: Princeton University Press, 1997), 179.

5. Affron, "Waldemar George," 186.

6. Waldemar George, "The School of Paris," in *Jewish Art: An Illustrated History,* ed. C. Roth, 641.

7. Harold Rosenberg, *Discovering the Present: Three Decades in Art, Culture and Politics* (Chicago: University of Chicago Press, 1973), 228. See also Bland, *The Artless Jew,* 39–40.

8. Rosenberg, *Discovering the Present,* 231.

9. Rosenberg, *Discovering the Present,* 221–87.

10. Rosenberg, *Discovering the Present,* 238–41.

11. Matthew Baigell, "Barnett Newman's Stripe Paintings and Kabbalah: A Jewish Take," *American Art* 8 (1994): 40.

12. Harold Rosenberg, *Barnett Newman* (New York: Harry Abrams, 1978), 27, 79.

13. Clement Greenberg, *The Collected Essays and Criticism* (Chicago: University of Chicago Press, 1986–93), 2:216.

14. Greenberg, *The Collected Essays,* 2:216.

15. Greenberg, *The Collected Essays,* 3:20. The Jewish context of the latter remark (Friedman's memorial exhibit at the Jewish Museum) perhaps explains it. In a talk commemorating the same exhibition, he called Friedman the best Jewish artist in America. Box 26, folder 13, Clement Greenberg Archives, Getty Research Institute, Los Angeles.

16. Jean-Paul Sartre, *Anti-Semite and Jew,* trans. George J. Becker (1948; reprint, New York: Grove, 1962).

17. Olin, *Forms of Representation,* xvii–xxii.

18. See Michael Fried's evocation of "grace" in his 1967 essay "Art and Objecthood," in *Minimal Art: A Critical Anthology,* ed. Gregory Battcock (New York: E. P. Dutton, 1968), 147.

19. Greenberg, *The Collected Essays,* 2:216.

20. Greenberg, *The Collected Essays,* 2:216. On Ardon's Jewish themes, see Vishny, *Mordecai Ardon,* 28–60. See also chapter 2.

21. Greenberg, *The Collected Essays,* 2:85.

22. Greenberg, *The Collected Essays,* 1:165.

23. See also Greenberg, *The Collected Essays,* 2:304–5. On Chagall see Harshav, "The Role of Language in Modern Art: On Texts and Subtexts in Chagall's Paintings," *Modernism/Modernity* 1, no. 2 (1994): 51–85. On references to the Holocaust in the *Yellow Crucifixion,* see Zira Amishai-Maisels, *Depiction and Interpretation: The Influence of the Holocaust on the Visual Arts* (New York: Pergamon, 1992), 27, 184.

24. Greenberg, *The Collected Essays,* 1:164.

25. Greenberg, *Art and Culture: Critical Essays* (Boston: Beacon, 1961), 171–74; Greenberg, *The Collected Essays,* 2:271–75.

26. Olin, *Forms of Representation,* 132–37.

27. Cheetham, in his trenchant case for the relationship between purity in modern art theory and in Nazism, does not, however, attribute such power to formalist rhetoric. Mark Cheetham, *The Rhetoric of Purity and the Advent of Abstract Painting* (New York: Cambridge University Press, 1991), 135–38.

28. Rudolf Arnheim, "The Gestalt Theory of Expression," *Psychological Review* 56 (1949): 158 n.1.

29. Arnheim, "The Gestalt Theory of Expression," 159.

30. Arnheim, "The Gestalt Theory of Expression," 169; David Efron, *Gesture and Environment* (New York: King's Crown, 1941). Arnheim may have been personally acquainted with Efron, who taught at Sarah Lawrence from 1936 to at least 1941.

31. Bernard Berenson, *Aesthetics and History in the Visual Arts* (New York: Pantheon, 1948), 152. Although published in 1948, the book was completed by 1941, and the passages quoted here may have been written in 1938.

32. Berenson, *Aesthetics and History*, 167.

33. For example, George, "The School of Paris," 641; Ernest Namenyi, *The Essence of Jewish Art*, trans. Edouard Roditi (New York: Thomas Yoseloff, 1960), x–xi; and Bland, *The Artless Jew*, 40.

34. Berenson, *Aesthetics and History*, 162–63.

35. Nicholas Mirzoeff, "Pissarro's Passage: The Sensation of Caribbean Jewishness in Diaspora," in *Diaspora and Visual Culture: Representing Africans and Jews*, ed. Nicholas Mirzoeff (London: Routledge, 2000), 57–75. See also Linda Nochlin, "Degas and the Dreyfus Affair: Portrait of the Artist as an Anti-Semite," in *The Dreyfus Affair: Art, Truth and Justice*, ed. Norman L. Kleeblatt (Berkeley: University of California Press, 1987), 96–116; Richard I. Cohen, "The Visual Dreyfus Affair: A New Text?" *Studies in Contemporary Jewry* 6 (1990): 72–73.

36. Berenson, *Aesthetics and History*, 164. Greenberg reviewed this book tepidly for its theoretical statements, without mentioning the anti-Semitic remarks in it. Kenneth Clark mentions Berenson's hatred of Strzygowski. Clark, *Moments of Vision and Other Essays* (New York: Harper and Row, 1981), 127–28.

37. Cheetham, *The Rhetoric of Purity*, 121–29. The discussion is with reference to Mondrian.

38. Ernst E. Herzfeld, *Archaeological History of Iran* (London: British Academy, 1935), 51–52. Berenson, *Aesthetics and History*, 159, quotes this passage with approval.

39. Bhabha, *The Location of Culture*, 171–97; Stuart Hall, "Cultural Identity and Diaspora," in *Identity, Community, Culture, Difference*, ed. Jonathan Rutherford (London: Thames and Hudson, 1989), 19–49; Robert Venturi, *Complexity and Contradiction in Architecture* (New York: Museum of Modern Art, 1966).

40. The hybrid was also a concern in the first *Laocoön*, with respect to genre/gender. W. J. T. Mitchell, *Iconology: Image, Text, Ideology* (Chicago: University of Chicago Press, 1986), 109–11.

41. Greenberg, *The Collected Essays*, 1:24.

42. Greenberg, *The Collected Essays*, 2:8, 32.

43. See Mach, *The Analysis of Sensations*; and Donald B. Kuspit, *Clement Greenberg, Art Critic* (Madison: University of Wisconsin Press, 1979), 51–54.

44. Kuspit, *Clement Greenberg*, 30–56, has made a good case for the complexity Greenberg was willing to accept in art.

45. Greenberg, *The Collected Essays*, 2:195.

46. Peter Novick, *The Holocaust in American Life* (Boston: Houghton Mifflin, 1999), esp. 103–23.

47. Greenberg, *Art and Culture*, 111.

48. Greenberg, *The Collected Essays and Criticism*, 2:4, 216. Although Greenberg did say about Kandinsky that "his parti-colored expressionist landscapes are better than we, who have been brought up in the School of Paris, may rightly realize." Ibid., 2:16.

49. Greenberg, *Art and Culture*, 273.

50. Rosenberg, *Discovering the Present*, 259–69.

51. On the role of language in Jewish identity and anti-Semitism, see Gilman, *Jewish Self-Hatred*. Greenberg may really have been ignorant of Hebrew. His appreciative review of a Yiddish book of Jewish jokes printed in Roman letters suggests that his knowledge of Yiddish may have been limited to speaking, that he might possibly not have known the Hebrew letters in which it was written. Greenberg, *The Collected Essays*, 2:182–87.

52. Greenberg, *The Collected Essays*, 3:45.

53. Robert Storr, "No Joy in Mudville: Greenberg's Modernism Then and Now," in *Modern Art and Popular Culture: Readings in High and Low*, ed. Kirk Varnedoe and Adam Gopnik (New York: Museum of Modern Art and Hary N. Abrams, 1990), 174-76, also relates Greenberg's formalism to assimilation.

54. These statements of 1945 apply, respectively, to paintings by Hans Hofmann, who, however, perhaps "surrenders himself too unreservedly to the medium" (2:18), and Arshile Gorky, with whose latest works Greenberg expressed disappointment.

55. Kuspit, *Clement Greenberg*, 42.

56. See, in particular, Greenberg's answer to the literary symposium "Under Forty" (1944). Greenberg, *The Collected Essays*, 1:176–79.

57. The sincerity of Greenberg's commitment has been questioned. See Storr, "No Joy in Mudville," 166.

58. Margaret Olin, " 'It is Not Going to Be Easy to Look into Their Eyes': Privilege of Perception in *Let Us Now Praise Famous Men*," *Art History* 14 (March 1991): 92–115. Meyer Schapiro, who wrote eloquently against the notion of national character in the arts and sought to attribute styles to economic and social forces instead, might contrast interestingly with Greenberg in this respect. Meyer Schapiro, "Race, Nationality and Art," *Art Front* (March 1936): 10–12.

59. Platt takes Greenberg's analysis of Judaism as authoritative. "Carefully dissected, the conservatism of his criticism – in the original sense of that term – becomes evident. It was the result of his Jewish heritage, described

by Greenberg himself as emphasizing logic, abstraction, and the belief in an absolute." Susan Noyes Platt, "Clement Greenberg in the 1930s: A New Perspective on His Criticism," *Art Criticism* 5, no. 3 (1989): 59. In fact, it is Greenberg's description of that heritage that is relevant to his criticism, not the heritage itself, which can be described differently. For as nostalgic as he may have been for the spiritual life of the Ghetto, his traditional Judaism, like his view of art, was his own invention.

60. Greenberg, *The Collected Essays*, 2:183–84.

61. Two other writers have begun to consider seriously the relationship between Greenberg's formalism and his Jewish identity. Thierry de Duve reads between the lines when his instinct, like mine, connects Greenberg's attitude toward Jewish identity with his attitude toward artistic identity, in an sense much more explicitly than Greenberg would ever have authorized. Thierry de Duve, *Clement Greenberg between the Lines*, trans. Brian Holmes (Cambridge: MIT Press, 1996), 67. David Carrier notes that Greenberg's notion of Judaism questions the issue of the impossibility of a (universal) objective aesthetic judgment, since qualities that he otherwise does not value gain value as an expression of Jewishness. Greenberg avoids such reasoning in his criticism of the painting of such Jewish artists as Chagall and Soutine. Just by bringing up the ethnic, he problematizes the universal. Greenberg's judgment, according to Carrier, I think correctly, anticipates multicultural notions of pluralistic value, that is, the abandonment of objective aesthetic judgments. David Carrier, *High Art: Charles Baudelaire and the Origins of Modernist Painting* (University Park: Pennsylvania State University Press, 1996), 155–57 (and an explanatory note from the author).

7. GRAVEN IMAGES ON VIDEO?

1. The English translation from the Hebrew is the one that Akerman reads on the soundtrack of the installation. *Bordering on Fiction: Chantal Akerman's "D'est,"* exhibition, Walker Art Center, Minneapolis, 1995.

2. Marsha Kinder, "The Meetings of Anna," *Film Quarterly* 33 (1979): 40–46.

3. Ivone Margulies, *Nothing Happens: Chantal Akerman's Hyperrealist Everyday* (Durham NC: Duke University Press, 1996), 242 n.4. This book also has a filmography and useful bibliography. It is worth noting that even the eponymous heroine of *Jeanne Diehlman* has a Jewish name.

4. The melody is the same one used by Max Bruch in his 1880 adaptation for cello and orchestra, probably the reason it is played by the cello here.

5. I am told that no such transcript accompanied the installation as it was presented at the Walker Art Center. This information was kindly supplied to me by Peter Murphy, who installed the exhibit in Minneapolis.

6. The film is *Lettre d'un Cinéaste* (The filmmaker's letter; 16mm, 8 min. 1984). Margulies discusses its thematization of the contest between word and image, bringing out the layers of meaning in the word "lettre." Margulies, *Nothing Happens*, 166–70.

7. The words "thou shalt have no other gods before me" precede the commandment; it is followed by "thou shall not bow down to and worship such images." My interpretation of idolatry owes much to Moshe Halbertal and Avishai Margalit, *Idolatry*, trans. Naomi Goldblum (Cambridge: Harvard University Press, 1992), but also to Boaz Cohen, "Art in Jewish Law," and Bland, *The Artless Jew*, which explain the interpretations historically.

8. Emanuel Levinas (1906–1997), philosopher and Talmudist, espoused an influential philosophy based on the analysis of the relationship of self and Other. Levinas, *Totality and Infinity: An Essay on Exteriority*, trans. Alphonso Lingis (Pittsburgh: Duquesne University Press, 1969).

9. Stephane Bouquet, "Chantal Akerman: ce qui revient et ce qui arrive," *Cahiers du Cinema* 497 (December 1995): 44.

10. Margaret Olin, "The Gaze," in *Critical Terms in Art History*, ed. Nelson and Shiff, 208–19.

11. For an example of Levinas's influence on feminist theory, see Luce Irigaray, "The Fecundity of the Caress: A Reading of Levinas, *Totality and Infinity* section IV, B, 'The Phenomenology of Eros,' " in *Face to Face with Levinas*, ed. Richard A. Cohen (Albany: State University of New York Press, 1986), 231–56; and Bracha Lichtenberg, *The Matrixial Gaze* (Leeds: University of Leeds, Feminist Arts and Histories Network, 1995). Irigaray is not uncritical of Levinas, however.

12. Halbertal and Margalit, *Idolatry*, 9–36. Another important recent work on idolatry is Lionel Kochan, *Beyond the Graven Image* (New York: New York University Press, 1997).

13. See Halbertal and Margalit, *Idolatry*, 30–35.

14. As in Buber, *Ich und Du*. But for a critique of Buber's notion of a universal "I," see Emanuel Levinas, *The Levinas Reader*, ed. Sean Hand (Cambridge, England: Blackwell, 1989), 59–74. The interpretation of idolatry argued by Habertal and Margalit is also compatible with an interpretation that sees the prohibition as linked to the prohibition against incest. Jean-Joseph Goux, *Les iconoclastes* (Paris: Seuil, 1978), cited in Rebecca Comay, "Materialist Mutations of the *Bilderverbot*," *Public* 15 (1997): 82 n.7.

15. Bouquet, "Chantal Akerman," 44.

16. Akerman, *Bordering on Fiction*, soundtrack, third room. The versification comes from the transcript, n.p., original emphasis. For a different version,

see Michael Tarantino, "It's Not Just an Image: A Conversation with Chantal Akerman," *Parkett* 45 (1995): 166.

17. Tarantino, "It's Not Just an Image," 166, original ellipses.

18. Halbertal and Margalit, *Idolatry*, 37–66, 108–36.

19. Halbertal and Margalit, *Idolatry*, 42.

20. Sigmund Freud, "Fetishism," in *The Standard Edition of the Complete Psychological Works of Sigmund Freud*, trans. James Strachey (London: Hogarth, 1964), 21:152–57.

21. Saul Friedländer, *Reflections of Nazism: An Essay on Kitsch and Death*, trans. Thomas Weyr (Bloomington: Indiana University Press, 1984), 44.

22. Geoffrey H. Hartman, *The Longest Shadow: In the Aftermath of the Holocaust* (Bloomington: Indiana University Press, 1996), 129. The problem of limits has been explored most importantly by the authors in Saul Friedländer, ed., *Probing the Limits of Representation: Nazism and the Final Solution* (Cambridge: Harvard University Press, 1992); and Sidra DeKoven Ezrahi, *By Words Alone: The Holocaust in Literature* (Chicago: University of Chicago Press, 1980).

23. For example, Jacques Lacan, *The Four Fundamental Concepts of Psycho-Analysis*, ed. Jacques-Alain Miller, trans. Alan Sheridan (New York: W. W. Norton, 1977), 67–119.

24. Adorno's reference was not to visual depiction but to Schoenberg's piece "Survivor from Warsaw," which he felt risked exploitation. Theodor Adorno, *Notes to Literature* (1965), ed. Rolf Tiedemann, trans. Shierry Weber Nicholsen (New York: Columbia University Press, 1991–92), 2:88.

25. Theodor Adorno, "Cultural Criticism and Society," *Prisms*, trans. Samuel and Shierry Weber (Cambridge: MIT Press, 1981), 34.

26. Theodor Adorno, *Negative Dialectic*, trans. E. B. Ashton (1966; reprint, New York: Continuum, 1997), 204–7.

27. Friedländer introduces his important volume on the representation of the Holocaust with a reference to Adorno, *Probing the Limits*, 2, and Adorno is referenced repeatedly in that volume, as well as in Geoffrey H. Hartman, ed., *Holocaust Remembrance: Shapes of Remembrance* (Oxford: Blackwell, 1994). See also Ezrahi, *By Words Alone*, 6–7; and Shoshana Felman and Dori Lau MD, *Testimony: Crises of Witnessing in Literature, Psychoanalysis, and History* (New York: Routledge, 1992), 33–35.

28. For a discussion, with relevant bibliography, see Margaret Olin, "Lanzmann's *Shoah* and the Topography of the Holocaust Film," *Representations* 57 (winter 1997): 1–23.

29. Claude Lanzmann, "Holocauste, la représentation impossible," *Le Monde* (3 March 1994).

30. Lanzmann, "Holocauste, la représentation impossible"; Lanzmann, "De l'holocauste a *Holocauste* ou comment s'en débarrasser," in *Au Sujet de Shoah: Le Film de Claude Lanzmann*, ed. Michel Deguy (Paris: Belin, 1990), 309–10.

31. Lanzmann, "De l'holocauste a *Holocauste*," 310. This notion of the uniqueness of the Holocaust has been attacked repeatedly, most recently and persuasively in Novick, *The Holocaust in American Life*, 195–99.

32. Lanzmann, "Holocauste, la représentation impossible." See also Lanzmann, "Seminar with Claude Lanzmann, 11 April 1990," *Yale French Studies* 79 (1991): 99.

33. Lanzmann, "Holocauste, la représentation impossible."

34. Lanzmann, "Holocauste, la représentation impossible."

35. Julia Kristeva, *The Kristeva Reader*, ed. Toril Moi (New York: Columbia University Press, 1986), 145–56.

36. Gertrud Koch, "Mimesis and Bildverbot," *Screen* 34 (autumn 1993): 218. Koch's source on Gnosticism is Malka Rosenthal, "'Mach dir kein Bildnis' (Ex.20,4) und 'Im Ebenbild erschaffen' (Gen. 1,26f): Ein Beitrag zur Erforschung der jüdischen Ikonophobie im Mittelalter," in *Wenn der Messias kommt: Das jüdisch-christliche Verhältnis im Spiegel mittelalterlicher Kunst*, ed. Lieselotte Kötzsche-Breitenbruch and Peter von der Osten-Sacken (Berlin: Institut Kirche und Judentum, 1984), 92. For a different interpretation of abstraction in Holocaust art, see Amishai-Maisels, *Depiction and Interpretation*, 243–87.

37. Miriam Bratu Hansen, "*Schindler's List* Is Not *Shoah*: The Second Commandment, Popular Modernism, and Public Memory," *Critical Inquiry* 22 (winter 1996): 302. A similarly elaborated use of Koch's interpretation characterizes Salzman's analysis of Adorno's legacy for postmodernism. Salzman is wisely reluctant to take the argument to the same lengths to which Koch does, that is, to draw the conclusion of modern critical theory's "fundamental Jewishness." Lisa Salzman, "To Figure, or Not to Figure: The Iconoclastic Proscription and Its Theoretical Legacy," in *Jewish Identity in Modern Art History*, ed. Soussloff, 68.

38. See also Jay, *Downcast Eyes*, esp. 548–86.

39. For example, Clark Dougan and Stephen Weiss et al., eds., *The American Experience in Vietnam* (New York: W. W. Norton and Company, 1988), 167, where one can see a photograph of the bodies of women and children killed in the Mi Lai massacre.

40. Richard Whelan, *Robert Capa: A Biography* (New York: Alfred A. Knopf, 1985; reprint, Lincoln: University of Nebraska Press, 1994), 95–100. After sev-

eral pages on this issue, he concludes that the controversy is "morbid and trivializing" since the photograph's importance is "in its symbolic implications."

41. Bill Nichols has written that "tact matters less for lives that matter little." Nichols, *Ideology and the Image* (Bloomington: Indiana University Press, 1981), 187.

42. See Martha Rosler, *Three Works* (Halifax: The Press of the Nova Scotia College of Art and Design, 1981), 59–86.

43. Although the report by the Brookings Institution and the World Peace Foundation on the media's role in dealing with atrocity and genocide contains considerable discussion of the power of the media, its only reference to privacy is in a brief mention of the privacy act. Fred H. Cate, "Communications, Policy-Making, and Humanitarian Crises," in *From Massacres to Genocide: The Media, Public Policy, and Humanitarian Crises*, ed. Robert I. Rotbert and Thomas G. Weiss (Cambridge MA: World Peace Foundation, 1996), 39–40.

44. John Shattuck, "Human Rights and Humanitarian Crises," in *From Massacres to Genocide*, ed. Rotbert and Weiss, 174. "Compassion fatigue," as understood by Shattuck, differs from the limits on empathy postulated by Hartman, since it does not raise the issue of the audience's fantasies. See also Susan D. Moeller, *Compassion Fatigue: How the Media Sell Disease, Famine, War and Death* (New York: Routledge, 1999).

45. Late medieval Jews used this argument against Christian idolatry. See Bland, *The Artless Jew*, 142–43.

46. Rosenberg, *Discovering the Present*, 238–41.

47. Again, the earlier religious basis, or rather lack thereof, is the subject of Bland, *The Artless Jew*.

48. Clark, *Moments of Vision*, 32–33.

49. Steven Schwarzschild, *The Pursuit of the Ideal: Jewish Writings of Steven Schwarzschild*, ed. Manachem Kellner (Albany: State University of New York Press, 1990), 116. On the subject of this and the following paragraph, see also Bland, *The Artless Jew*, 37–58.

50. Stephen S. Kayser, "Our Opening Exhibit," in *Inaugural Exhibition: The Giving of the Law and the Ten Commandments, Jewish Art of Late Antiquity, Works of Contemporary Artists, the Torah in Synagogue Art* (New York: Jewish Museum, 1944), n.p.

51. Mann and Tucker, *The Seminar on Jewish Art*, 29. The work alluded to is Rybach and Aronson, "Die Vegen fun der Yiddischer Malerei," in *Oifgang* (Kiev: Kulturlige, 1919), translated in part in Ruth Apter-Gabriel, ed., *Tradition and Revolution: The Jewish Renaissance in Russian Avant-Garde Art, 1912–1928* (Jerusalem: Israel Museum, 1987), 229.

52. Rosenberg, *Discovering the Present,* 230.

53. Rosenberg, *Discovering the Present,* 230, original emphasis.

54. According to an interview with the artist.

55. Eduardo Kac, *Storms* (1993), interactive Web site, formerly at *http//:www.ekac.org.storms.sea.* On *http://www.ekac.org,* an active site at this writing, it is possible to find a description under "multimedia." One may also see reproductions of other explicitly Jewish works, such as the Holopoem *Sh'ma.* (As of 1 September 2000, the work can be downloaded in Macintosh format from *www.ekac.org/multimedia.html.*)

56. See chapter 2.

57. On this phenomenon, see Sander L. Gilman, *Smart Jews: The Construction of the Image of Jewish Superior Intelligence* (Lincoln: University of Nebraska Press, 1996), esp. 28–29.

58. See, for example, Luce Irigaray, *This Sex Which Is Not One,* or Hélène Cixous, "The Laugh of the Medusa," in *New French Feminisms: An Anthology,* ed. Elaine Marks and Isabelle de Courtivron (New York: Schocken Books, 1981), 245–64.

59. Susan A. Handelman, *The Slayers of Moses: The Emergence of Rabbinic Interpretation in Modern Literary Theory* (Albany: State University of New York Press, 1982).

60. Pier Marton, "Speakeasy: Singing at the Ghetto's Gate," *New Art Examiner* 24 (June 1997): 11. On the pernicious results that can come from the Holocaust turned into kitsch, see Avishai Margalit, "The Kitsch of Israel," *New York Review of Books* (24 November 1988), 20–24.

61. In one of Buber's legends of the Baal Shem, a Jewish boy who has been raised by non-Jews returns to the synagogue "at the hour in which the Kol Nidre is spoken, the prayer of salvation and holy freedom." Buber, *Die Legende des Baalschem,* 110. A famous nonfictional example is the important Jewish thinker Franz Rosenzweig. Nahum N. Glatzer, *Franz Rosenzweig: His Life and Thought,* 3rd ed. (Indianapolis: Hackett, 1998), 25.

62. This is the explanation given, for example, in *Encyclopedia Judaica,* CD-ROM version, 1.0, s.v. "kol nidre"; also A. Z. Idelsohn, *Jewish Music in Its Historical Development* (1932; reprint, New York: Dover, 1995), 159.

63. Rabbi Jules Harlow, ed., *Mahzor for Rosh Hashana and Yom Kippur: A Prayer Book for the Days of Awe* (New York: Rabbinical Assembly, 1978), 325.

64. Harlow, ed., *Mahzor for Rosh Hashana and Yom Kippur,* 353.

65. Johann Andreas Eisenmenger, *Entdecktes Judenthum . . . .,* ed. and trans. Franz Xaver Schieferl (Dresden: Otto Brandner, 1893), 408–9.

66. Herman Kieval, "The Curious Case of Kol Nidre," *Commentary* 46 (October 1968): 55.

67. Stuart Weinberg Gershon, *Kol Nidrei: Its Origin, Development, and Significance* (Northvale NJ: Jason Aronson, 1994), 107–8, 113–14; Meyer, *Response to Modernity*, 49–50.

68. Schlomo Deshen, "The *Kol Nidre* Enigma: An Anthropological View of the Day of Atonement Liturgy," *Ethnology* 18 (April 1979): 123.

69. Kieval, "The Curious Case of *Kol Nidre*," 56–57.

70. Joseph S. Bloch, *Kol Nidre und seine Entstehungsgeschichte* (Vienna: K. Löwith, 1917), thought the tradition began to deal with forced conversions by the Visigoths in the seventh century. On the Kol Nidre, see also Theodor Reik, "*Kol Nidre*," in *Ritual: Psychoanalytic Studies*, ed. Theodor Reik (London: Hogarth, 1931), 167–219. Ismar Elbogen, *Der jüdische Gottesdienst in seiner geschichtlichen Entwicklung*, 4th ed. (Hildesheim: Georg Olms, 1962), 153–54, does not make this point.

71. A. Z. Idelsohn, *Jewish Liturgy and Its Development* (New York: Henry Holt, 1932; reprint, New York: Dover, 1995), 228.

72. Chaim Stern, ed., *Gates of Repentance: The New Union Prayerbook for the Days of Awe* (New York: Central Conference of American Rabbis, 1984), 250–52.

73. Schoenberg, *Kol Nidre*, Opus 39 (1938; reprint, Los Angeles: Belmont Music Publisher, 1973), 20–21. The work is for speaker, chorus, and orchestra, with text by Schoenberg and Jacob Sonderling.

74. Amishai-Maisels, *Depiction and Interpretation*, 34–37.

75. For a discussion of this issue, see Olin, "Lanzmann's *Shoah* and the Topography of the Holocaust Film." On counternarratives, see Ezrahi, *Booking Passage*.

76. On the relationship between the secular and the sacred in Friedrich's altarpiece, see Joseph Leo Koerner, *Caspar David Friedrich and the Subject of Landscape* (London: Reaktion Books, 1990), 29–148; also Isaiah Berlin, *Roots of Romanticism* (Princeton NJ: Princeton University Press, 1999).

77. On neutral spaces, see Moshe Halbertal, "Coexisting with the Enemy: Jews and Pagans in the Mishnah," in *Tolerance and Intolerance in Early Judaism and Christianity*, ed. Graham N. Stanton and Guy G. Stroumsa (Cambridge: Cambridge University Press, 1998), 159–72.

78. As in Greenberg, *The Collected Essays*, 2:304–5.

79. See the epigrams for part 1, part 3, and chapter 6.

80. Without feeling the need to emphasize the Jewish context, the Irish author Fintan O'Toole could cite the quotation from *Ulysses* that serves as the epigraph to part 1 of this book to stress the need in Ireland for a new, flexible sense of what a nation is. Fintan O'Toole, "Letter from Northern Ireland: The Meanings of Union: Taking the Trouble out of the Troubles," *New Yorker* 74 (27 April and 4 May 1998), 56.

81. On the connection between linear time and the geographical space of the nation state, see Smadar Lavie and Ted Swedenburg, eds., *Displacement, Diaspora and Geographies of Identity* (Durham NC: Duke University Press, 1996), 2. For a discussion of competing views of time, see John Davis, "History and the People without Europe," in *Other Histories*, ed. Kirsten Hastrup (London: Routledge, 1992), 14–27. His "people without Europe," the Uduk, could be compared with the Jews in that both live in the pendulum swing between prosperity and annhilation (21). On Kugler, see chapter 1, and Nelson, "Living on the Byzantine Borders of Western Art," 6–7.

82. See Margaret Olin, "Validation by Touch in Kandinsky's Early Abstract Art," *Critical Inquiry* 16 (autumn 1989): 144–72. The notion of the unitary subject has recently fallen into disfavor. See Steve Pile and Nigel Thrift, eds., *Mapping the Subject: Geographies of Cultural Transformation* (London: Routledge, 1995).

83. The draft for this response contains several more protestations of Greenberg's offended Jewish identity. Clement Greenberg Archives, Getty Research Institute, Los Angeles.

84. Ernst H. Gombrich, *The Visual Arts in Vienna Circa 1900, and Reflections on the Jewish Catastrophe* (London: Austrian Cultural Institute, 1997), 5, 28. Malachi Haim Hacohen, "Dilemmas of Cosmopolitanism: Karl Popper, Jewish Identity, and 'Central European Culture,'" *Journal of Modern History* 71 (1999): 105–49, analyzes the case of Karl Popper, whom Gombrich cites.

85. Although he mentions Jewish art, Schapiro's real target is the segregation of African American culture, in "Race, Nationality and Art," 10; Edmund Jabès, in an interview with Bracha Lichtenberg, in *Routes of Wandering*, ed. Shapira, 253.

86. Landsberger, *A History of Jewish Art*, 8–9.

87. Landsberger, *A History of Jewish Art*, 13.

88. For example, the Francocentric element of Focillon's reply to Strzygowski (see chapter 5); see also Michael Baxandall, *Patterns of Intention: On the Historical Explanation of Pictures* (New Haven CT: Yale University Press, 1985), 58–62; and Harold Bloom, *Anxiety of Influence: A Theory of Poetry* (London: Oxford University Press, 1973).

89. The importance of marginality mirrors the importance of hybridity in postcolonial theory. See Bhabha, *The Location of Culture*, 139–70.

90. For example, the discussion of Benjamin Franklin in Anderson, *Imagined Communities*, 62. On the inadequacies of the paradigm of print culture, see, for example, Prasenjit Duara, "Bifurcating Linear History: Nation and Histories in China and India," *Positions* 1:3 (winter 1993), 780–84.

Index

In the *Texts and Contexts* series

Affective Genealogies
Psychoanalysis, Postmodernism, and the "Jewish Question" after Auschwitz
By Elizabeth J. Bellamy

Sojourners
The Return of German Jews and the Question of Identity
By John Borneman and Jeffrey M. Peck

Serenity in Crisis
A Preface to Paul de Man, 1939–1960
By Ortwin de Graef

Titanic Light
Paul de Man's Post-Romanticism, 1960–1969
By Ortwin de Graef

The Future of a Negation
Reflections on the Question of Genocide
By Alain Finkielkraut
Translated by Mary Byrd Kelly

The Imaginary Jew
By Alain Finkielkraut
Translated by Kevin O'Neill and David Suchoff

The Wisdom of Love
By Alain Finkielkraut
Translated by Kevin O'Neill and David Suchoff

The House of Joshua
Meditations on Family and Place
By Mindy Thompson Fullilove

Inscribing the Other
By Sander L. Gilman

Antisemitism, Misogyny, and the Logic of Cultural Difference
Cesare Lombroso and Matilde Serao
By Nancy A. Harrowitz

Opera
Desire, Disease, Death
By Linda Hutcheon and Michael Hutcheon

Man of Ashes
By Salomon Isacovici and Juan Manuel Rodríguez
Translated by Dick Gerdes

Between Redemption and Doom
The Strains of German-Jewish Modernism
By Noah Isenberg

Poetic Process
By W. G. Kudszus

Keepers of the Motherland
German Texts by Jewish Women Writers
By Dagmar C. G. Lorenz

Madness and Art
The Life and Works of Adolf Wölfli
By Walter Morgenthaler
Translated and with an introduction by Aaron H. Esman in collaboration with Elka Spoerri

The Nation without Art
Examining Modern Discourses on Jewish Art
By Margaret Olin

Organic Memory
History and the Body in the Late Nineteenth and Early Twentieth Centuries
By Laura Otis

Crack Wars
Literature, Addiction, Mania
By Avital Ronell

Finitude's Score
Essays for the End of the Millennium
By Avital Ronell

Herbarium/Verbarium
The Discourse of Flowers
By Claudette Sartiliot

Atlas of a Tropical Germany
Essays on Politics and Culture, 1990–1998
By Zafer Şenocak
Translated and with an introduction by Leslie A. Adelson

The Inveterate Dreamer
Essays and Conversations on Jewish Culture
By Ilan Stavans

Budapest Diary
In Search of the Motherbook
By Susan Rubin Suleiman

Rahel Levin Varnhagen
The Life and Work of a German Jewish Intellectual
By Heidi Thomann Tewarson

The Jews and Germany
From the "Judeo-German Symbiosis" to the Memory of Auschwitz
By Enzo Traverso
Translated by Daniel Weissbort

Richard Wagner and the Anti-Semitic Imagination
By Marc A. Weiner

Undertones of Insurrection
Music, Politics, and the Social Sphere in the Modern German Narrative
By Marc A. Weiner

The Mirror and the Word
Modernism, Literary Theory, and Georg Trakl
By Eric B. Williams